STREET DEMOCRACY

THE MEXICAN EXPERIENCE
William H. Beezley, series editor

STREET
DEMOCRACY

VENDORS, VIOLENCE, AND PUBLIC SPACE
IN LATE TWENTIETH-CENTURY MEXICO

Sandra C. Mendiola García

UNIVERSITY OF NEBRASKA PRESS | LINCOLN AND LONDON

Library of Congress Cataloging-in-Publication Data
Names: Mendiola García, Sandra C., author.
Title: Street democracy: vendors, violence,
and public space in late twentieth-century
Mexico / Sandra C. Mendiola García.
Description: Lincoln: University of Nebraska
Press, [2017] | Series: The Mexican experience |
Includes bibliographical references and index.
Identifiers: LCCN 2016042875
ISBN 9780803275034 (cloth: alk. paper)
ISBN 9780803269712 (pbk.: alk. paper)
ISBN 9781496200013 (epub)
ISBN 9781496200020 (mobi)
ISBN 9781496200037 (pdf)
Subjects: LCSH: Street vendors—Political activity—
Mexico. | Informal sector (Economics)—Political
aspects—Mexico. | Government, Resistance to—
Mexico. | Vending stands—Political aspects—Mexico.
Classification: LCC HF5459.M58 M45
2017 | DDC 381/.180972—dc23
LC record available at https://
lccn.loc.gov/2016042875

Set in Garamond Premier by John Klopping.
Designed by N. Putens.

Para mis padres Celia García y Serafín Mendiola

To Chad and Lucia Pearson

CONTENTS

ILLUSTRATIONS

ACKNOWLEDGMENTS

Many people helped me research, write, and publish this book. Jeffrey Bortz introduced me to the archives in Puebla, my hometown, in Veracruz, and in Mexico City. He also encouraged me to come to the United States to study history, which changed my life. Mariano Torres enriched his classes with dry humor and introduced me to the first street vendor I interviewed, Doña Rosa, who later introduced me to her stepson, who gave me the phone number of a man nicknamed "El Huaraches," a former student who began working with street vendors in the 1970s. Putting aside my shyness, I called El Huaraches, who was one of the kindest people I met during the several years I spent researching this independent vendor organization. Indeed José Luis Díaz introduced me to at least two dozens vendors and former students who founded the organization that I explore in these pages. At Puebla's municipal archives I had the fortune to meet wonderful women who were tremendously helpful and patient as I requested boxes related to markets and street vendors. Many thanks to all of them, especially Aurelia Hernández Yahuitl and Rocío (Chío) del Carmen Gómez and to the two friends I met there, Rosa María García Juárez and Janette Gayoso del Valle. Their knowledge and friendship over the years have meant a lot to me. I would like to thank Pilar Pacheco Zamudio, now directing the Archivo Histórico Universitario de la Benemérita Universidad de Puebla, for her help and kindness throughout the years.

In New Jersey life was good thanks to the friendship and support of fellow historians Jennifer Miller, Laurie Marhoefer, Gregory Swedberg, Robert Alegre, Iben Trino-Molenkamp, and Stephen Allen, who since then have listened to me, responded to my questions, and read drafts of whatever I sent them. At Rutgers I had the best advisor, Mark Wasserman, who always believed in and supported my research. Rutgers also became a special intellectual home where I learned much from tremendously smart and caring historians: Temma Kaplan, Gail Triner, Bonnie Smith, Camilla Townsend, Kim Butler, Paul Clemens, Aldo Lauria-Santiago, and Rudy Bell. They are an endless source of inspiration.

I have been very lucky to have great colleagues and friends at two institutions. At the University of Alabama in Huntsville, where I taught for four years, I would like to thank Molly Johnson, Stephen Waring, Andrew Dunar, Christine Sears, Randall Dills, and Evan Ragland. They supported every decision I took and introduced me to their families, who became my own. Special thanks go to Ingrid Reck and Beverly Gentry, who lovingly took care of my family and me. I'd also like to thank my wonderful and accomplished colleagues in the History Department at the University of North Texas, especially Jennifer Wallach, Clark Pomerleau, Michael Wise, Robert Citino, Todd Moye, Marilyn Morris, Rachel Moran, Nancy Stockdale, Richard McCaslin, Alexander Mendoza, and Roberto Calderón. They have patiently listened to me, mentored me, and some read several drafts of my work. Thank you all for your unconditional support, warmth, and good humor. Many thanks to the women of La Colectiva at UNT for offering their friendship and for sharing their intellectual pursuits. Special thanks and *mucho cariño* go to Laila Amine, Priscilla Ybarra, and Valerie Martínez-Ebers for reading sections of this book and for their all-encompassing support. Thanks to my students who provided much enthusiasm and insightful comments: Michelle Findlater, Richard Velázquez, Hugo Martínez, Mario Ovalle, Vogel Castillo, Christopher Menking, and Miriam Calixto.

Scholars close and far have provided much wisdom. Thanks to Alicia Re Cruz, Mariela Nuñez-Janes, Gabriela Soto Laveaga, Andrew Paxman, Robert Weis, Jaime Pensado, Elaine Carey, Christina Jiménez, Ingrid Bleynat, Jocelynn Olcott, Nara Milanich, Elizabeth Hutchison, Gregory Crider, Christopher Boyer, Susan Gauss, Meredith Abarca, Julie Livingston, Jeffrey Pilcher, Monica Rankin, Gareth Jones, Alexander Aviña, and Heather Ann Thompson. Some of them commented on my work in conferences, others read parts of this book and offered very helpful suggestions. Jezy Gray, Amanda Sewell, and Lyndsay Knecht have helped me improve my grammar. Bridget Barry and her amazing team at the University of Nebraska Press have kindly and professionally guided me through the process of publishing this book. Many thanks to Judith Hoover for her thorough copyediting work. I also appreciate the valuable feedback and suggestions I received from the blind readers.

With true generosity several friends have supported me throughout the years, feeding my family, donating airline miles to commute during a very difficult year, and taking care of Lucia when we have needed it the most: Holger Bretz, Angélica Villasana, Paula Gaetano, Michael Thompson, Meredith Buie, Justin Lemons, Deborah Armintor, and Jodi Ismert. I can't thank them enough for providing peace of mind.

Nothing, absolutely nothing would have educated me and given me the opportunities I've had without the endless love, economic aid, and patience from my now deceased father, Serafín Mendiola Corro, my very alive mother, Celia García Gallardo, and my brother, Juan Manuel Mendiola García. My father began working at the age of four and finished elementary school only at the age of seventeen. That was the end of his formal education. He worked every day of his life and taught himself several subjects until just before he died in March 2006. He would have been very proud of this book. Since my mother doesn't read English, this is for her: *Mami, muchas gracias por todo tu amor y por todo lo que has hecho por mí y mi hija. Eres la fuente de todo lo que soy. Como verás, este libro también va dedicado a tí.* Thanks to my brother, Juan Manuel, and his family for making me smile and laugh no matter what. Thanks too to my aunt Patricia Quiroga for her fabulous meals and advice. I always appreciate the intellectual discussions with my uncle Juan De la Cruz Gallardo, who also patiently listens to all of my ideas and encourages me to pursue them.

Many thanks to my husband and fellow historian, Chad Pearson. His love, constant encouragement, weekly chocolates, and daily jokes have kept me happy all these years. I look forward to many more. Finally, thank you, Lucia, *mi niña de amor*, for your understanding when Mommy has to work, for cooperating with me, for all your kisses and love.

ABBREVIATIONS

CAPU   Central de Autobuses de Puebla (Puebla's bus station)

CCE   Consejo Coordinador Empresarial
(Business Coordinating Council)

CCI   Central Campesina Independiente
(Independent Peasant Organization)

CCI   Coordinadora de Colonias Independientes
(Association of Independent Neighborhoods)

CFE   Comisión Federal de Electricidad
(Federal Electricity Commission)

CGC   Consejo General Campesino (General Peasant Council)

CGOM   Confederación General de Obreros y
Campesinos de México (General Confederation
of Mexican Workers and Peasants)

CGT   Confederación General de Trabajadores
(General Confederation of Workers)

CLETA   Centro Libre de Experimentación Teatral y Artística
(Free Center of Theater and Artistic Experimentation)

CNC   Confederación Nacional Campesina
(National Peasant Confederation)

CNOP   Confederación Nacional de Organizaciones Populares
(National Confederation of Popular Organizations)

CROC   Confederación Revolucionaria de Obreros y Campesinos
(Revolutionary Confederation of Workers and Peasants)

CROM   Confederación Regional Obrera Mexicana
(Regional Confederation of Mexican Workers)

CTM   Confederación de Trabajadores de México
(Confederation of Mexican Workers)

DFS   Dirección Federal de Seguridad
(Federal Security Directorate)

DGIPS   Dirección General de Investigaciones Políticas y Sociales
(General Directorate of Political and Social Investigations)

FROC   Federación Regional de Obreros y Campesinos
(Regional Federation of Workers and Peasants)

FUA   Frente Universitario Anti-comunista
(Anticommunist University Front)

INAH   Instituto Nacional de Antropología e Historia
(National Institute of Anthropology and History)

IPN   Instituto Politécnico Nacional
(National Polytechnic Institute)

ISI   Industrialización por substitución de importaciones
(Import Substitution Industrialization)

MSJF   Mary Street Jenkins Foundation
(Fundación Mary Street Jenkins)

PAN   Partido Acción Nacional (National Action Party)

PCM   Partido Comunista Mexicano (Mexican Communist Party)

PRD   Partido de la Revolución Democrática
(Party of the Democratic Revolution)

PRI   Partido Revolucionario Institucional
(Institutional Revolutionary Party)

TENAZ   Teatro Nacional de Aztlán (National Theater of Aztlán)

UAP   Universidad Autónoma de Puebla
(Autonomous University of Puebla)

UNAM   Universidad Nacional Autónoma de México
(National Autonomous University of Mexico)

UNESCO   United Nations Educational, Scientific
and Cultural Organization

UOI   Unión Obrera Independiente
(Independent Workers Union)

UPVA   Unión Popular de Vendedores Ambulantes
(Popular Union of Street Vendors)

STREET DEMOCRACY

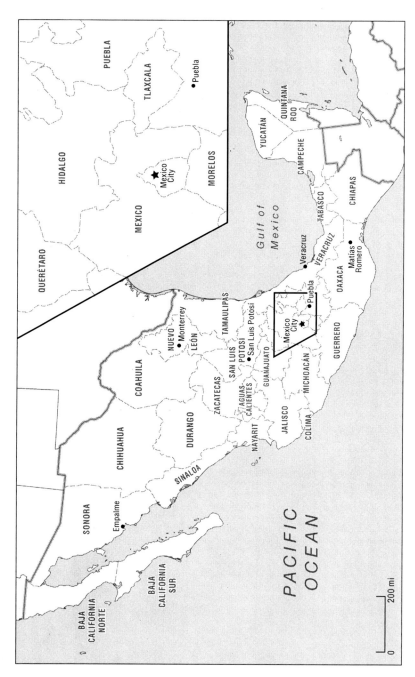

MAP I. Mexico. Courtesy of Robert Alegre.

INTRODUCTION

In the early 1970s, a few years after Yolanda Bejarano began selling fruit in Puebla's downtown streets, she met "El Botas," a student at the state university who was helping vendors organize. They began dating and fell in love. The young couple had a baby, but soon after, El Botas disengaged from his parental responsibilities. Bejarano became a single mother, selling wares with her son by her side. To this day she keeps photographs of the boy playing on top of the wooden cart she used to transport and display her merchandise. When the police arrived and tried to prevent vendors from selling in public spaces, Bejarano, like many peddlers, could quickly pull the cart, loaded with fruit and her child, and flee. Tired of evading the police and losing merchandise, she became a leading union organizer among her fellow vendors. In the fall of 1973 Bejarano and approximately four hundred others formed the Unión Popular de Vendedores Ambu-lantes (Popular Union of Street Vendors, UPVA). Unlike most Mexican unions the UPVA was independent from the ruling Partido Revolucionario Institucional (Institutional Revolutionary Party, PRI). During the union's height in the mid-1980s it had some ten thousand members, making the UPVA the largest organization of its kind in Mexico's province.[1]

Like their friend Bejarano, Adolfo Corona and his wife, Paula Javier, were politically active vendors. In 1974 they participated in the UPVA's cultural commission, a group that used art to publicize vendors' strug-gles. Corona and Javier wanted to demonstrate how local police officers repressed vendors, so Corona performed the role of a police officer in a play the sellers entitled *Street Vendors*. They believed their play was an effective political strategy to express the troubles peddlers met on a daily basis. Ideologically the couple was inspired by their close connection to young leftist students and by some of their own reading. For years Corona and Javier received the *Pekín Informa* (*Peking Review*), the Maoist weekly magazine published in China and circulated in Mexico in Spanish.[2] Although Javier was illiterate, she enjoyed listening to her husband read aloud. Corona liked the magazine because it was attuned to his own political ideas and to poor people's struggle for dignity.

The lives of these three individuals exemplify a slice of the complex economic and political conditions that thousands of street vendors in Puebla, Mexico's fourth-largest city, experienced during the last three decades of the twentieth century. *Street Democracy* tells the story of ordinary men and women—people like Bejarano, Corona, and Javier—who fought against social, economic, and political oppression during the waning of the Mexican Miracle and the rise of the neoliberal turn. From the 1940s to the 1970s the country witnessed a sustained economic growth—the Mexican Miracle—in which the GDP grew 6.2 percent annually.[3] After the 1982 debt crisis, the political elite began implementing neoliberal reforms in which the state significantly reduced its expenditure in key areas of the economy, promoted market-oriented reforms, sold or closed state-owned industries, and drastically modified government policies toward labor.[4]

By bringing together street vendors' economic and political histories, this book explains how vendors made a living during these turbulent years and how they organized politically against the backdrop of increasing state authoritarianism. Focusing on the UPVA offers an opportunity to understand an independent union of actors in the informal economy that has maintained a grassroots resistance to the PRI state for over four decades. In a city known for its political and social conservatism, vendors found allies among left-wing students. This alliance helped vendors create a militant and democratic union. Vendors borrowed from the student movement several political strategies they put into practice to defend their right to make a living in public spaces. Studying this regional case also allows us to expand our understanding of left-wing militant and working-class students. These students did not take up arms and join guerrillas, did not become proletarian in an effort to educate workers in factories, and did not succumb to co-optation by the PRI. Instead they continued their activism among actors in the informal economy. In short, a group of militant Poblano students took an alternative path of resistance by helping vendors organize a PRI-independent and militant union. The vendor-student alliance also illustrates the role each played in building the New Left in the city of Puebla, including their "transnational dimension of social and cultural protest" and their "non-armed aspects of radical challenges to political and social norms."[5]

The union that vendors formed in 1973 allowed the illiterate, the urban poor, and recent migrants to take part in the political life of their city and country. For vendors democracy meant the right to make a living in public spaces such as sidewalks, streets, and markets; the right to organize independently from the PRI and to publicly dissent from authorities. Democracy also meant the right to elect their union leaders, participate in daily union activities, learn skills, be elected to union positions, and create alternative narratives. In short, organized vendors exercised forms of direct democracy and challenged state authoritarianism and its control over Mexico's unions.[6] *Street Democracy* is the first book to discuss the role of informal workers in a broader wave of independent labor insurgency that reached its height in the 1970s and continues to exist.[7]

As historians have demonstrated, beginning in the 1940s the PRI state faced great resistance from groups of rural and urban Mexicans of diverse class backgrounds and numerous locations across the country.[8] Puebla's organized street vendors belong to this history of resistance that demystifies the Pax Priísta, the belief that Mexico enjoyed political stability thanks to the PRI-led government. The UPVA case demonstrates that the PRI could not co-opt all unions or avoid cross-sectoral alliances. But like many other Mexicans across the country, independently organized vendors also paid for their defiance. Agents of the state relied on a combination of strategies, including negotiation, collaboration, and most often illegal procedures and violence, to try to end dissent; local, state, and federal officials also carried out these tactics against vendors and their leaders. [9]

Through their independent union vendors ultimately were able to sell their wares on prime downtown streets and make a living for thirteen years, from 1973 to 1986. After 1986, when the local government forced them to relocate, vendors secured stalls at newly built municipal markets. Securing these spots on the streets and at markets allowed them to work and make a living during the most acute economic crises of late twentieth-century Mexico—no minor victory.

OFFICIAL AND INDEPENDENT UNIONS

In order to control organized labor and to build a base of support among the working class, the ruling party co-opted, or at least tried to co-opt most unions into its ranks. The co-optation of unions and the often artificial base of support that the regime created was part of the corporatist structure of the ruling party. [10] Strong efforts to consolidate this corporatism happened during the administration of President Lázaro Cárdenas (1934–40). In 1938 Cárdenas transformed the Partido Nacional Revolucionario (National Revolutionary Party) into the Partido de la Revolución Mexicana (Party of the Mexican Revolution)—the predecessors of the PRI—and reorganized it to incorporate unions of peasants, industrial workers, and the military into the party's sectors. These sectors were mainly represented by large confederations: the Confederación Nacional Campesina (National Peasant Confederation), the Confederación de Trabajadores de México (Confederation of Mexican Workers, CTM), and, after its creation in 1943, the Confederación Nacional de Organizaciones Populares (National Confederation of Popular Organizations), which also included the organizations of the so-called popular classes and the middle class. The military's official participation in its own confederation was relatively brief, from 1938 to 1941. [11]

The street vendors' unions were among those that the state incorporated into the Confederación Nacional de Organizaciones Populares, a confederation that included a motley crew of teachers, public-sector employees, intellectuals, women's associations, lawyers, manufacturers, small and medium-size businesses, industrialists and landowners, as well as those the state did not recognize as workers and those who did not identify as such.[12] It also included individual military men who became involved in official politics after President Manuel Ávila Camacho dissolved the military sector in 1941.[13] Once incorporated into the PRI—the name of the Partido de la Revolución Mexicana since 1946—the party rewarded union loyalty with political and economic benefits for union leaders and some benefits for the membership.[14] In the case of vendors' unions, the party traded their votes and support to PRI politicians for temporary spaces in commercially attractive locations and offered some political posts for vendors' leaders.[15] The co-opted vendors' unions became, at least in theory, one of the pillars of the party's corporatist structure.

The unions that the ruling party incorporated and co-opted became the official unions.[16] After 1948 they were also known as *charro* unions because the party often selected leaders called *charros* (cowboys).[17] For the most part, charros placated the rank-and-file and guaranteed the unions' loyalty to the PRI, to state policies, and to employers.[18] Among other requirements, affiliation to the party meant that union members had to vote for official candidates at the local, state, and federal levels. In theory, by inserting these groups into the party's ranks and allegedly neutralizing them, the PRI helped facilitate Mexico's economic growth by allowing employers to keep wages low and subdue potential strikes.

Not all workers allowed the party machine to control the political life of their organizations. Workers in a variety of industries and in the countryside sought to democratize their charro unions from within or formed independent unions that refused to be incorporated into the PRI.[19] By doing so they challenged the party corporatist structure. Generally speaking, independent unions had democratic characteristics and were committed to fight for the interests of their members.[20] Members usually had the freedom and the mechanisms to elect their own leaders, who were known individuals within the group. To avoid a monopoly of power by one or more individuals, leaders were not supposed to hold positions for extended periods of time. Instead elections happened on a regular basis. The independent leadership did not force their members to vote for the PRI and tended to be more militant. At least in theory, members of the independent unions actively and voluntarily participated in their organizations. They attended meetings and carried out protests and strikes. Rank-and-file members also had a say in the union's decision-making process. This participation allowed people to have a more thorough knowledge of their unions. In contrast, workers in official and "white unions"—the equivalent of "company unions" in the United States—sometimes did not even know to which union they belonged, what the purpose of the union was, or even who their leaders were.[21]

Union independence in Mexico has a long and rich history that, although not always completely successful, goes back to the revolutionary period. Since the 1920s the Confederación Regional Obrera Mexicana (Regional Confederation of Mexican Workers, CROM) had a near monopoly on organized labor. The first attempts to organize autonomously occurred when unions sought to disengage from the CROM during the 1920s and 1930s. In 1921 some unions, influenced by anarchosyndicalist groups, joined the Confederación General de Trabajadores (General Confederation of Workers), which was committed to maintaining its autonomy from the CROM and from President Álvaro Obregón's presidency.[22] In 1933 different labor and peasant unions formed the Confederación General de Obreros y Campesinos de México (General Confederation of Workers and Peasants of Mexico, CGOCM), which promoted state independence and union democracy. Three years later a broad range of organizations—including the CGOCM—merged to become the Confederación de Trabajadores Mexicanos, which, during its early years, tried to form broad coalitions of industrial and agricultural laborers. Many unions in the CTM became disillusioned when President Cárdenas incorporated the CTM into the ruling party in 1938.[23] In Puebla, for instance, after the 1940 presidential elections the Federación Regional de Obreros y Campesinos (Regional Federation of Workers and Peasants, FROC) severed its ties with the CTM, remaining "one of the more militant mainstream labor federations into the mid-1940s."[24] At the national level large industrial unions in the railroad, oil, and mining and metalworker industries left the CTM and supported the leftist Popular Party in 1948. As a result the state countered union dissidence by replacing militant leaders with charros.[25] Workers, however, continued fighting, so even if charro leaders dominated organized labor for decades, they faced much rank-and-file resistance. Some charros, however, secured benefits for workers; as a result these workers viewed the charros as legitimate leaders.[26]

Yet in the mid-1960s and especially in the early 1970s Mexico's organized labor witnessed the increasing and rapid emergence of a wave of independent unionism that scholars have identified as the "new labor insurgency," whose novelty stemmed from the unions' rupture with the PRI.[27] More important, at its core the "labor insurgency was mainly a democratizing movement."[28] By the end of the 1970s workers in different industries had created approximately one hundred independent unions.[29] These included unions in the auto, food processing, and garment industries, as well as among university faculty and staff.[30] Some of these independent unions joined umbrella organizations such as the Frente Auténtico del Trabajo (Authentic Labor Front), the Unidad Obrera Independiente (Independent Workers Union), and the Central Campesina Independiente (Independent Peasant Organization).[31]

The new labor insurgency was fueled by President Luis Echeverría's democratic opening (1970–76), in which he tried, for political reasons, to distance his administration from the CTM.[32] But the rise of independent unions did not necessarily emerge from top-down policies, as some scholars have suggested.[33] While Echeverría's democratic opening facilitated the conditions for independent unions to multiply, it cannot fully explain why workers chose these kinds of organizations. As Michael Snodgrass has noted, changes in industrial relations resulted in new production methods that negatively affected workers. In turn, they resisted their bosses by organizing independent unions or by working to form democratic currents within official unions.[34]

Street Democracy demonstrates that militant and democratic unions originated not only on shop floors and in the fields but also on the streets. The UPVA's case shows that the labor insurgency of the 1970s emerged from the bottom up and included members of the informal sector. Street vendors did not have employers who pressured them to increase production while keeping wages low. Their independent unionism developed out of a new sociopolitical context on the streets of Puebla. The harsh conditions that vendors experienced and the support of militant left-wing students at Puebla's Autonomous State University fueled the organization of the UPVA. The emergence of the vendors' union also occurred as Puebla's political elite, the *avilacamachistas*, faced a rupture with the federal government.[35] By the early 1970s the political context in the streets of Puebla was ripe for vendors to organize an independent union.

CHALLENGES TO THE STATE

Independent unions presented several challenges to the state, to official union leaders, and to employers. By striking and demanding higher wages and better working and housing conditions, independent unions posed an economic threat to the state. Since UPVA members did not have employers and could not strike, their main challenge occurred in the political sphere. Vendors used public spaces to march, protest, perform theater, read, and discuss ideas, offering alternatives to more traditional forms of political action. For instance, when vendors took to the streets to protest, they were making themselves visible and were publicly drawing attention to their problems.[36] This represented a challenge for the PRI state, which claimed to support the interests of ordinary people.

Vendors also publicly protested the clientelistic structure of the state. In the past, as the political sociologist Leonardo Avritzer points out, "material improvements for ordinary citizens represent[ed] favors to be delivered by elite political mediators."[37] Indeed from the moment vendors formed unions, members relied on the will of official leaders to achieve their demands. In the case of the UPVA, its independence allowed vendors to negotiate directly with authorities. They did so by organizing in political commissions, marching on the most important avenues, occupying the streets surrounding the municipal palace, and entering in direct dialogue with municipal and state authorities. Vendors did not need official union leaders to achieve their goals in exchange for their political support of the ruling party. In this way vendors' use of public space forced authorities to engage in a political dialogue with them.

Since the UPVA did not make their members vote for ruling party politicians, the PRI faced the possibility that organized vendors might support oppositional parties such as the Partido Acción Nacional (National Action Party, PAN) or, later, the Partido de la Revolución Democrática (Party of the Democratic Revolution). The PRI also lost its ability to use independent union members as *acarreados*, people dragged to rallies, auditoriums, and stadiums during campaigns to give the impression that PRI politicians enjoyed broad popular support.[38] Last, the party could not use independent unionists, like UPVA vendors, to attack political enemies. For instance, when a PAN mayor won Puebla city's elections in 1996, the PRI governor at the time sent PRI-affiliated street vendors to set up their stalls in downtown streets to create an image of disorder that the PAN mayor was allegedly unable to resolve.[39] In this situation official union members acted as pawns of the state governor; UPVA members did not.

Moreover Puebla's independently organized vendors created alliances with different groups in society, an act that defied one of the supposed tenets of corporatism: maintaining the different sectors of the PRI within the party but apart from each other.[40] Thus the PRI tried to avoid cross-sectoral alliances. But as historians have demonstrated, workers, peasants, students, and middle-class groups formed alliances with one another that showed the limitations of the party.[41] By not affiliating with the PRI, the UPVA was also free to create cross-sectoral alliances. These relationships led to the creation of fronts, which had the potential of promoting political change in Mexico. Over the decades vendors joined some of these organizations. In the early 1970s, for instance, they participated in the Frente de Activistas Emiliano Zapata (Emiliano Zapata Activists Front) with students and in the Frente de Autodefensa del Pueblo (People's Self-Defense Front), which included tenants, peasants, vendors, and students.[42]

LOSSES

Choosing union independence was a bold move for street vendors in the authoritarian regime of the Mexican state. Independence resulted in several political and material losses to the unions. Not surprisingly the ruling party gave more material and political concessions and rewards to official unions than to independent organizations. For instance, independent unions did not receive money or subsidies from the state for daily operations.[43] Under these circumstances the UPVA leadership had to rely exclusively on member fees for all expenses. A more dangerous consequence for independent leaders and members was their vulnerability to repression by local, state, and federal authorities. Therefore a second theme of *Street Democracy* is state repression. Although the state's tolerance of independent unions was an important characteristic of President Echeverría's democratic opening, if these organizations became too militant the state crushed them with the same violence that had characterized previous administrations. In fact all forms of state violence became a large component of the street vendor experience. Even before vendors organized their union in the fall of 1973, police beat vendors, seizing their merchandise and destroying their stalls, and detaining them for hours or even days. Worse still, police sometimes jailed men and women together with their young children.

Once vendors organized the UPVA, they went from being a local problem to a concern of the state and federal governments. It was then that local, state, and federal authorities struck back. The federals spied on the organization, while local and state governments employed legal and illegal mechanisms to incarcerate their leaders, torturing some of them in order to neutralize the power of the union. In Puebla the state used violence alongside the rhetoric of historical heritage preservation, which provided an effective strategy to mask its authoritarianism during the neoliberal turn. Referring to neoliberal cities around the world, the urban geographer David Harvey correctly asserts that "violence is required to build the new urban world on the wreckage of the old."[44] This book shows that such violence and intimidation have not ceased.

NEOLIBERALISM

By the mid-1980s, as Mexico entered its neoliberal phase, the state used new strategies, in addition to physical violence, to destroy activists and their independent or militant organizations, while at the same time trying not to appear authoritarian. A third theme in *Street Democracy* is Mexico's engagement with neoliberal policies, specifically the redefinition of the use of public space and the fierce fight against unions. The state presented itself as a defender of urban order and capitalist modernization and violently punished those who, like street vendors, appeared to disrupt it. As a supporter of modernization the state selectively encouraged the efforts of some social groups to move forward economically. Following a centuries-long tradition, local and state authorities regulated what they considered the appropriate use of public space and, with the neoliberal turn, fully privileged the projects of the upper and middle classes over those of the urban poor and the working class. I trace the transformation of public space from a relatively community-oriented and working-class space to a neoliberal space where large capital dominated. With the aid of business leaders, local and state governments devised a more effective strategy that could finally solve the problem of street vending—and eliminate the UPVA in the process—all while authorities appeared to defend and protect Puebla's historical heritage. In the mid-1980s several state agencies petitioned the United Nations Educational, Scientific and Cultural Organization (UNESCO) to include Puebla's downtown on the World Heritage Site list.[45] As part of this petition, these groups committed to "rescue" and "dignify" the downtown area before and after Puebla's inclusion.[46]

In 1986 municipal authorities supported by business groups began to remove street vendors from the so-called historic downtown to the new markets in the outskirts of the city. In connivance with state authorities, economic elites closed La Victoria market and, years later, transformed it into a shopping mall that housed, among others, two Walmart-owned retailers. Once more Harvey is correct: "The right to the city, as it is now constituted, is too narrowly confined, restricted in most cases to a small political and economic elite who are in a position to shape cities more and more after their own desires."[47] In this context it is not surprising that vendors of fruits and knickknacks like Bejarano, Javier, and Corona practically disappeared from the streets at the heart of the neoliberal city.

During Mexico's neoliberal phase, while factory workers lost their jobs because state-led enterprises closed down or decreased the labor force, local authorities prevented vendors from selling in the streets and privileged the interests of large capitalists. Vendors, regardless of their political affiliation, lost their workplace in prime commercial areas and found themselves trying to make a living on the margins of the city and the economy. Puebla and the UPVA case also demonstrate that during the neoliberal turn, both official and independent unions faced the increasing authoritarianism of the Mexican state. President Carlos Salinas de Gortari (1988–94) unleashed a ferocious attack against powerful charro and independent leaders and their organizations. The closure of La Victoria market and the removal of vendors from the surrounding streets also represented a blow to democracy: ordinary people lost their political stage and local authorities undermined democratic practices. After all, the marketplace is one of those places that "can be nexuses that open up the possibility of interaction between diverse groups."[48] Afterward, vendors had a harder time holding meetings, marches, and protests in downtown spaces.

LABOR

One of the goals of *Street Democracy* is to expand and rethink understandings of *work* and *workers*. The vendors who organized the UPVA saw themselves as workers; this was partly a political tactic to continue demanding their right to work on the streets to make a living.[49] Their refusal to see themselves as business people or entrepreneurs also represented an ideological decision related to the left-wing origins of their union. By identifying themselves as workers, they pushed the idea that they had common interests with broader sectors of society, specifically with the working class. This identification allowed them to expand their political demands and practices. For example, when vendors participated in Labor Day parades, they publicly inserted themselves into the ranks of the working class and created links of solidarity with other independent organizations. By publicly identifying themselves as vendors and as workers, they contested the state's definition of *worker*. And they used alternative ways of organizing and protesting.

Recent scholarship has questioned the definition of *work* and *workers* and the different sites where work takes place.[50] The historian Michael Denning, for example, has written that, traditionally, writers are guilty of "normalizing" the worker as one who receives a wage. As part of the informal economy, street vendors in Puebla did not receive wages, did not collect benefits, and did not have employers. They had, as Denning put it, a "wageless life."[51] Harvey has concluded that "the concept of work has to shift from a narrow definition [attached] to industrial forms of labor to the far broader terrain of the work entailed in the production and reproduction of an increasingly urbanized daily life."[52] The political scientist Margaret Kohn writes, "The myths of the factory and the proletariat have obscured the transformative role played by other sites of resistance."[53] Indeed the everyday experiences of millions of urban residents in Mexico demonstrate the several kinds of labor that sellers carried out simultaneously in the streets. *Street Democracy* invites the reader to conceptualize late twentieth-century Mexican street vendors as informal workers carrying out productive, reproductive, and political labor on the streets. At the same time, the Poblano vendor decenters the factory as the main site of production and class conflict.

Irrespective of their gender or age, vendors did not simply buy and resell merchandise from wholesalers; they added work and value to their wares. Vendors of vegetables and fruits sorted the products, removed spoiled pieces, peeled onions, bunched herbs, removed thorns from *nopales* (cacti), and cut the tails off radishes and onions. They cut small cubes of carrots and zucchini, mixed them with peas, green beans, and corn kernels, and put the combination in small plastic bags, ready to be cooked. This work added monetary value to their merchandise. Similarly vendors of prepared food transformed raw produce and meat into snacks and entire meals for a mostly working-class clientele.[54] In fact street vendors offered a large selection of prepared food. Puebla is famous for its cuisine, and its vendors sold local specialties such as *mole, chalupas, cemitas, molotes, camotes, tacos árabes,* and *chanclas.*[55]

In terms of social reproductive labor, female and some male vendors and their older children fed, entertained, educated, trained, and took care of younger children—backbreaking and emotional labor that people usually carry out in their home but that vendors had to do on the streets. As one vendor put it, "When one didn't have anyone to take care of children at home, children grew up on the streets by one's side. I used to take five kids to the streets. . . . Even if they got all dirty and looked unkempt, I always kept an eye on them. Sometimes, in the high commercial season, we even slept on the streets. Their home was the street."[56] As children grew older they helped their parents take care of younger siblings, which allowed adults to participate in union activities.

Vendors' political work consisted of producing fliers and banners, organizing meetings and study groups, attending marches, and collecting fees for their union. If these vendors had been employees in supermarkets, restaurants, day care centers, or union halls, these activities would have been considered work, but on the streets their labor continues to be unacknowledged by customers, journalists, and scholars.

THE STREETS AS HYBRID PLACES

The different kinds of labor that vendors performed in the streets erased the boundaries between the workplace, the home, and the political arena. On the streets vendors simultaneously sold their merchandise, added value to it, and carried out social reproductive labor as well as union-related work, reconfiguring the streets as workplaces and homes to fulfill their commercial and familial needs. Some placed open burlap bags, pieces of cardboard, or sheets of plastic on the ground as mats to display their products; besides being cost effective, this allowed them to quickly pick up the merchandise and run from police raids. Others, like Bejarano, placed their products on carts or built tables using recycled materials such as empty wooden fruit boxes. Still other vendors had metal, semi-fixed stalls that provided a roof made of a sturdy fabric or plastic sheets to protect themselves, their children, and their merchandise from the elements. Vendors often kneeled on the ground or sat on stools while they sold their merchandise. Those with semi-fixed stalls stored merchandise in their stalls overnight and slept on the streets to guard it. Vendors placed their napping babies and toddlers in empty fruit boxes. Javier attached her child's walker to her stall with a cord so the child would not go too far.[57] Women sat behind their stall and breastfed their children while selling. Lack of bathrooms, electricity, and running water became a problem for all vendors. Most had to rely on enclosed public markets that had bathrooms and water. Those who needed electricity often accessed it illegally by connecting their own cables to electric posts. Vendors also dealt with a growing city and an increasing number of buses, cars, and trucks that passed inches away from them.

On heavy commercial days, such as during preparations for Day of the Dead, vendors placed their stalls in the middle of the street, converting them into pedestrian markets and preventing vehicles and buses from circulating through the area (see fig. 2). Because it was difficult for police cars to enter these areas, vendors could practice their political activities safely. As Kohn points out, "Oppositional movements need to control spaces in order to organize their activities without being subject to repression."[58] Streets thus served vendors as political places where they could perform as vendors, workers, parents, and active citizens who criticized authority and demanded their constitutional rights, especially their right to work in the profession of their choice.[59]

Just like factories, the streets and other public areas were not neutral; a power hierarchy existed in these spaces. As Harvey has pointed out, "the dynamics of class exploitation are not confined to the workplace."[60] Written and unwritten rules governed the streets where vendors worked, spent most of their day socializing, and engaged in politics. Though they did not have employers, they still had to face powerful people who did not always understand or defend their plight and who policed their commercial, social, and political activities. Members of the municipal government—the mayor, fee collectors, established business owners, upper-class neighbors, marketers, and the police—challenged vendors' ability to make a living by charging them multiple fees, demanding bribes, harassing the women, and threatening to remove them. After the neoliberal turn these and other challenges increased considerably.

For the upper classes the hybrid space of the vendor represented a cultural, economic, and political problem in their vision of the city. By using the streets as workplaces, homes, and political stages, organized vendors defied those who wanted to see the streets free of the urban poor. The UPVA challenged elites' monopoly on the use of prime public spaces. Puebla's elites were notorious for emphasizing the cultural, economic, and racial background that differentiated them from the urban poor and from rural populations. Their alleged European descent, their class and formal education, distinguished Poblano elites from vendors, especially those who were rural or descendants of indigenous people. Even during the Mexican Revolution, Puebla's urban dwellers disdained the rural mestizos and indigenous people who were followers of Pancho Villa and Emiliano Zapata and who supported traditional ways of life. Urban Poblanos supported Venustiano Carranza's projects, which emphasized modernization and the strength of capitalism.[61] This trend continued throughout the century to the point that in the late 1990s, when the geographers Gareth Jones and Ann Varley studied urban changes in downtown Puebla, they noted tacit ideas of race among middle-class people that explained their understanding of difference.[62] While references to race and ethnicity are absent in written archival documents of the modern period, in municipal archival photographs male and female vendors appear wearing *huaraches* (sandals), white cotton clothes, and small sombreros. Some are barefoot. Some women wear *rebozos* (traditional Mexican shawls) folded over their braided hair. Their clothing, illiteracy, and supposed "ignorance" bothered certain Poblanos who were proud of their alleged European ancestry and disdained indigenous people and practices.[63]

VENDORS

Throughout *Street Democracy* I refer to street vendors as the men, women, and children who sold their products inside covered markets or from mats, tables, carts, or semi-fixed structures on streets and sidewalks and in other public spaces.[64] Although the Spanish term *vendedores ambulantes* translates as "ambulatory vendors," they usually secured a fixed spot in a public area but did not own stalls inside markets.[65]

In the early 1970s, when this story begins, some street vendors came to the city from the impoverished countryside in Puebla and the neighboring states of Tlaxcala, Veracruz, Morelos, and Oaxaca. Street vendors belong to the history of migration from rural areas to the cities and of the rapid urbanization that occurred during the second half of the twentieth century.[66] State economic policies during the Import Substitution Industrialization (ISI) program, which took place from approximately the 1940s to the beginning of the 1980s, did not quite reach rural areas, except for financing agribusinesses targeting foreign markets.[67] ISI was a "type of forced industrialization aimed at replacing imports and characterized by the use of protection to encourage domestic production of manufactured goods."[68] In the meantime poverty in the countryside was rampant. Rural areas lacked basic services such as health clinics and education beyond elementary school. If lower-class people wanted to survive economically, or if the middle classes in small towns wanted their children to receive higher education, they had to move to urban areas like Puebla or Mexico City. Migrating to the United States was another alternative for some.[69]

From the late 1960s to the mid-1990s street vendors represented a rather eclectic group. Some were recent migrants from the countryside; some were born in Puebla; some commuted from small towns surrounding the city and went back to their community after selling their products. Some were the children of the urban poor, of other street vendors, and even of modest market sellers. Bejarano, for instance, was the child of a market seller at La Victoria, and Corona was the son of street vendors. About half of the street-vending population were women. A 1969 Labor Ministry census indicates that, of 228 street vendors listed in downtown, 51 percent were women.[70] Ten years later a study led by the municipal government concluded that fewer than 45 percent of vendors were women.[71] Visual evidence, particularly photographs of Puebla's streets taken by municipal employees and pictures published in the city's most widely circulated newspaper, *El Sol de Puebla*, show the ubiquity of female vendors and their children, suggesting that the 1969 census and the 1979 government study may have misrepresented or underreported the actual numbers.[72] The same census indicates that some children were in charge of stalls: 24 of 228 vendors (10.5 percent) were under the age of eighteen, and 15 of those 24 (62.5 percent) were female.[73]

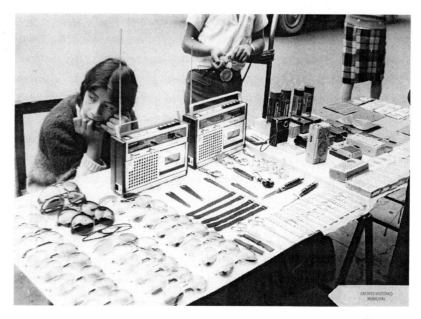

FIG. 1. A fayuca stall. Courtesy of Archivo General Municipal de Puebla, image 169, Administración Municipal, 1975–78.

The products that vendors sold were diverse and changed constantly. All year long they sold fruit, vegetables, flowers, clothes, notions, coal, toys, and live animals.[74] Vendors also sold seasonal products. During Day of the Dead, for instance, vendors offered all the items people needed to set up altars for their dead loved ones: sugarcane, oranges, marigolds (*cempasuchitl* flowers), skull-shaped sugar candy, incense, candles, and *pan de muerto* (sweet bread flavored with anise seeds and orange flower water and decorated with sesame seeds). For Christmas they sold peanuts, guavas, piñatas, fireworks, ceramic baby Jesus figurines, and all sorts of decorations for nativities.

Although some vendors never varied their merchandise, most were flexible and adapted their inventory to their location and economic circumstances. Teresa Rosales, a lifelong vendor, sold fruit on the streets around La Victoria in the late 1960s and 1970s. When she left the downtown streets in the mid-1980s, she did not acquire a stand in a market.

Instead she relocated a block away from the entrance to Puebla's newly built main bus station in the northern part of the city; there her clientele consisted of travelers and commuters, so she began selling tote bags, sunglasses, socks, caps, and traditional candy (*camotes*) that customers could bring home as souvenirs. In the winter she targeted unprepared travelers, offering scarves and gloves as the temperature dropped significantly in the morning and at night.[75] A small group of street vendors sold *fayuca*, smuggled goods that usually came from the United States when Mexico still promoted ISI policies. These products were mainly radios, televisions and other electronics. People also bought from these vendors, known as *fayuqueros*, "luxury" products at accessible prices that were unavailable in Mexico, like Dove soap, Revlon shampoo, and American toys. Vendors did not begin selling pirated goods, such as movies and music CDs, until the end of the twentieth century.[76]

PUEBLA

The city experienced a second wave of industrialization beginning in the 1960s with the arrival of heavy industries such as Hojalata y Lámina de México (Hylsa), a Mexican steelmaker; Volkswagen; Phelps-Dodge, producer of cables and electrical conductors; National Cash Register; Ciba-Geigy pharmaceuticals; Alumex, an aluminum manufacturer; and Cementos Atoyac, a cement maker.[77] These new industries boosted Puebla's economy. Volkswagen employed over 7,000 people, and in 1971 Hylsa employed 1,500.[78] In addition the textile industry, which had made Puebla one of Mexico's most important cities since the colonial era, continued to exist.[79] By the mid-1970s there were about 40 cotton textile industries in town.[80] In 1982 there were 495 small textile businesses registered in the Directorio Industrial del Estado de Puebla (Industrial Directory of Puebla), making the textile industry the most important in the city, employing approximately 21,000 people by 1985.[81]

The new wave of industrialization that began in the 1960s corresponds to what some scholars have identified as a second stage of ISI, when national and foreign companies produced capital goods.[82] For Poblanos this industrialization meant access to hundreds of jobs; blue-collar as well as white-collar employment opened up, especially for men. Some lower- and middle-class women took secretarial jobs in these new companies, but for the most part, Poblano women worked in areas that society considered extensions of the private and domestic sphere, such as teaching, nursing, cooking, and domestic service. Others worked in the informal economy. Working-class women held only 3 percent of jobs in the cotton-textile industry.[83] Union leaders justified this low percentage by claiming that the country's economic and social stability depended on women as efficient mothers and housewives.[84]

Along with Mexico City, Guadalajara, and Monterrey, Puebla was a city with a strong industrial sector that experienced fast urban growth after the 1960s.[85] In 1960 the city had 305,469 people, a number that almost doubled by 1970 and more than tripled by 1990, when the city had over a million inhabitants.[86] The city became physically larger as well, growing from 23 square kilometers in 1965 to 52 in 1974 and 140 in 1984.[87] The construction industry boomed along with this growth. In the mid-1960s and 1970s developers constructed thousands of homes and apartment buildings for the working and middle class (*unidades habitacionales*). Between 1973 and 1979, for example, about 8,701 families were moving to these new homes.[88] Working-class neighborhoods popped up in the northern parts of the city, close to the new factories and the new Mexico City–Veracruz highway, completed in 1962, which continued to favor Puebla as a convenient commercial center between these two cities.[89]

THE INFORMAL ECONOMY

Puebla's case shows that the rise of the informal economy occurred in tandem with large economic growth during the Mexican Miracle and continued to grow as the country embraced neoliberalism. Toward the end of the Miracle, Puebla was still a magnet for those seeking to make a living in the formal and informal sectors.[90] Parallel to the formal economic growth that the city experienced, the informal sector continued to expand; as Manuel Castells and Alejandro Portes, argue, "Far from being independent of each other, the formal and informal sectors are related to each other."[91] Street vendors were tapping into the economic opportunities that the formal sector put into motion. Blue-collar workers, service-sector employees, bureaucrats, and their families required prepared and raw food, clothes, toys, and a variety of seasonal products that vendors could offer all year long, at all hours, in different locations, and at affordable prices. As a result the number of vendors in downtown Puebla, the busiest commercial area, increased exponentially. According to the 1969 census taken by the Labor Ministry, there were 228 street vendors downtown.[92] Federal secret police records estimated that in 1973, between 500 and 800 sellers installed semi-fixed stalls on the streets.[93] In 1977 there were approximately 1,200 sellers.[94] In 1979 around 3,000 people sold on the streets, and by 1986 at least 5,000 street vendors occupied approximately sixty blocks in the city center, mostly around La Victoria market. In contrast to these official sources, the UPVA leadership claimed 10,000 members by the mid-1980s.[95] Even taking the lowest, most conservative numbers before the 1982 crisis, between 1969 and 1979 the number of vendors increased tenfold.

The informal sector provided certain advantages that allowed men and women to support their families. Above all, people made at least modest profits in order to survive economically. Entry costs were relatively low; vendors managed their own time; and during the period covered in this book most did not have a boss overseeing and exploiting their labor.[96] Women could bring their children with them to work. It was typical to see children of all ages next to their parents on the streets. As they grew older, children went to school and continued selling. Gabina Rodríguez, a single mother of four, was especially thankful for this work. Early in the morning she bought produce from a wholesaler, and her eldest son helped carry it to her plastic mats, which another son had already prepared. As Rodríguez pointed out, "My children and their mom worked together." In fact the success of street vendors' economic activities often depended on their family members' labor. Their children also carried out social reproductive labor and even union-related work. In addition to economic gains for themselves and their families, some vendors felt personally empowered. As women earned their own money, they had the courage to leave or divorce their husbands or partners, especially if they were in abusive relationships.[97]

Despite its advantages and vendors' hard work, street vending barely allowed the sellers to survive economically, especially from the 1980s on. This fact was reflected in the places where they lived. Bejarano's home, for instance, is located in the northernmost section of Puebla, in a neighborhood that does not even appear on a printed map. Dirt roads are the only path to her home, and only after crossing a ravine that serves as an informal landfill with hundreds of exposed plastic trash bags. A dangerous one-lane dirt bridge crosses the ravine and leads to Bejarano's small cement home. She and her son built the house after many years of work. Across town Corona and Javier lived in a one-story house in which one of the rooms served as both their living room and bedroom. Their adult children and grandchildren lived with them there. Like many others who did not have any capital to spare, some vendors lived in squatter settlements and "self-help housing," referring to houses that inhabitants built by themselves; others rented rooms in *vecindades* (tenements) in central areas of town.[98] Like Bejarano, Corona, and Javier, most of the vendors shared accommodations with immediate and extended family. Despite all their political and modest economic gains, life had become increasingly difficult for them and their children.

SOURCES

This book relies primarily on four sets of sources: municipal archival documents, federal secret police reports, newspaper articles, and oral interviews. Unfortunately the UPVA does not have a formal archive, and some of the organization's documents were presumably destroyed in one of several police raids. A few scholars had access to some UPVA files directly from the leadership before 1989, but I was not so lucky. After 1989, when the union's main leader was incarcerated, the UPVA became increasingly distrustful of outsiders and reluctant to share internal documentation. However, given that municipal authorities oversaw the city's market activities and commerce on the streets, the municipality kept track of vendors' economic activities. For decades, vendors seeking a permit to sell on the street or inside special areas in markets designated for vendedores ambulantes wrote to the city describing the products they wanted to sell.

Fig. 2. Street vendors behind La Victoria market. Courtesy of Archivo General Municipal de Puebla, unnumbered image, Junta de Mejoramiento Moral, Cívico y Material del Municipio de Puebla, 1970s.

Sellers also wrote—or paid someone to write—petitions to authorities to lower their fees or waive them completely and complained about abusive fee collectors and the police. City authorities received letters from shopkeepers who aired their dissatisfaction regarding the presence of vendors outside their establishments. UPVA members also wrote to the city council. These documents, housed at the two locations of the previously named Archivo Histórico Municipal de Puebla and recently renamed Archivo General Municipal de Puebla, provide a window into understanding who these vendors were, the kinds of merchandise they sold, the problems they faced, and the strategies they used when dealing with authorities.

Besides written documents, city authorities also kept photographs of streets, makeshift markets, and the downtown area in general. Municipal photographers took many of these images as they followed mayors, important figures in the business community, and visits by presidents to the city. On other occasions authorities sent photographers to shoot scenes on the street that would be published in mayors' annual activity reports. Photographers captured vendors and sometimes the chaos they were alleged to cause.

Municipal and newspaper photographs are two of the few sources in which women and children actually become visible. They illustrate how vendors, particularly women, modified public spaces to carry out their reproductive labor, using empty fruit boxes as chairs for their children, as places for young ones to nap, and as tables on which they displayed their merchandise.

Newspapers allow us to explore how the state and middle- and upper-class groups depicted vendors. The most popular newspaper, *El Sol de Puebla*, closely followed many of their activities. Most of these articles portray vendors in a negative light. This is not surprising, as the newspaper served as a pillar of the state government that praised Puebla's government and vilified those who opposed it. Many of the articles written about UPVA vendors appear in the "Nota Roja," the newspaper's crime section, which focused on capturing what the editors considered the disorderly, chaotic, and dirty practices of vendors. In the best cases readers saw vendors sitting in the middle of the street or sidewalk selling their wares and read that vendors were "obstructing traffic," "posing a danger to cars," and "representing a danger for public health."[99] In the worst cases readers looked at unkempt and handcuffed vendors detained by police.

As the state did with many organizations and individuals across the country, federal authorities began spying on the UPVA and its most active leaders in 1975. The Ministry of the Interior's Dirección Federal de Seguridad (Federal Security Directorate, DFS) and the Dirección General de Investigaciones Políticas y Sociales (General Directorate of Political and Social Investigations)—the two intelligence services operating across Mexico—also kept track of Puebla's independently organized street vendors. Both agencies left behind an array of sources available to researchers at Mexico City's Archivo General de la Nación, at least up to 2015.[100] The DFS documents, now with restricted access, were an invaluable source for the almost daily political activities in which vendors and their allies participated. Mexican police surveillance documents traced men's more than women's political activities, and, possibly like other secret police archives in other parts of the world, these sources tended to "magnify resistance and dissent" and to overstate the threats of the infiltrated groups to justify promotions and funding.[101]

This book places vendors' voices at the forefront of the story. For instance, women shaped public spaces, helped organize the union, and worked hard to maintain it. Women were the most active in reconfiguring the streets into hybrid spaces that served as their work space, home, and political stage.[102] Unsurprisingly these activities are mostly absent from archival sources. Oral interviews thus provide an opportunity to understand how vendors identified themselves and the kind of labors they carried out. Talking with female vendors about their political participation in the union and outside of it is enlightening because traditional archival sources minimize or ignore women's participation in union organizing. Federal secret reports, for instance, tended to concentrate on the top leadership, which was mostly male. Undercover agents, or those who presumably transcribed the reports, hardly ever mentioned female rank-and-file members. When they did acknowledge women, agents did so in terms of the women's relationships with the men (for instance, "the lover of").[103] The minimization and oversimplification of female vendors in Mexican official documents requires scholars to document their lives and political involvement through the women's own voices. In archival documents men are the most prominent actors; in real life it was women's everyday actions that economically sustained their families and politically fueled the vendors' union. In some ways this methodological choice was a pragmatic one: those who were still alive or in good physical shape were the women.

THE BOOK'S STRUCTURE

The book unfolds thematically and chronologically. Chapter 1 provides a historical overview of Puebla's politics and street vendors before 1973. I highlight vendors' main problems and identify the groups that disdained them, along with their reasons for demanding their removal. I analyze the political and organizational traditions street vendors relied on before forming the UPVA and argue that the vendors were political actors: they wrote letters to authorities, requested protection from federal authorities when the local government threatened their economic survival, and held membership in official unions. Their actions had serious limitations; toward the end of the 1960s and the beginning of the 1970s, city authorities engaged in constant and often violent removal of vendors from public spaces, which pushed sellers to find a more effective strategy to secure their livelihood.

In chapter 2 I analyze the unique alliance between street vendors and working-class students. When vendors decided to organize the UPVA, they relied on the support of young left-wing students, who put into practice the ideology they had learned during the university reform movement. Students believed that only a coalition of underprivileged groups could bring about social change. I argue that students provided ideological and practical tools that helped vendors organize an independent union.

Chapter 3 shows that vendors found innovative ways to achieve some of their demands. The use of public space and private property was essential to articulate their problems and goals and to press authorities to resolve grievances. Vendors organized marches on important avenues, painted slogans on walls, and hijacked buses. Through cultural activities they built local and international connections that allowed them to voice their demands. Influenced by students who were inspired by Chicano theater, vendors created their own theater group in which they articulated their struggles on Puebla's street corners and on more formal stages in Mexico City. Vendors also participated in the making of a short film that won recognition in Germany. In this chapter I broaden the concept of union democracy by arguing that UPVA vendors created their own union democratic practices, a more expansive sense of belonging to a community of peers that protected them from police violence and provided them with a space where they could freely express their concerns and find ways to solve them.

Chapter 4 documents the violence that the state inflicted upon informal sector workers. President Echeverría's democratic opening in the first half of the 1970s did not mark an end to Mexican authorities' harassment of union leaders and members. Authorities continued a campaign against independent unions that included infiltration, intimidation, and violence. This chapter illustrates the many disappearances, illegal detentions, and incarcerations, along with the physical and psychological torture that leaders and rank-and-file members of the UPVA endured at the hands of state agents. The state's violent and authoritarian measures sought to silence the most militant sellers and undermine the UPVA's independence.

When violent repression failed to discourage sellers from selling goods on the street and from actively participating in their union, the state engaged in a different and ultimately more successful campaign against them and other working-class people in downtown locations. Chapter 5 enhances our understanding of urban renewal in an age of neoliberal reform in Mexico. I look at vendors during the mid-1980s, when authorities and city boosters applied to UNESCO for the title of World Heritage Site. I argue that, instead of promoting the supposed cultural heritage of Puebla's downtown, city authorities oversaw the development of major retailers connected to the global economy at the expense of street vendors and marketers.

Chapter 6 explores street vendors' responses to their removal and relocation to markets in the outskirts of the city. Observers believed that downtown street selling brought the vendors' union together and that dispersal would destroy the UPVA. But the union did not disappear. Instead it gained some strength by expanding its membership. As a result of the UPVA's popularity, local, state, and federal authorities engaged once more in a violent but failed campaign to destroy the union. The state incarcerated the street vendors' leader in 1989, sending him to a number of maximum-security federal prisons for twelve years. This was part of the fight against unions after Mexico's adoption of neoliberalism.

In the conclusion I analyze some of the UPVA's continuities and changes over time. I briefly note the events that occurred in downtown Puebla and at the Miguel Hidalgo market at the turn of the twenty-first century. UPVA members face constant competition from large supermarket chains that surround the market. In addition downtown has experienced the effects of gentrification. Within the past three decades UPVA members have faced rapid and incessant neoliberal reforms that the PRI and the PAN have carried out. Indeed in the Latin American neoliberal city, "all are free to participate in the area's renewal, but all must do so through formal channels and with formal shops, with taxes, high rent, and utilities."[104] These official channels remain largely inaccessible to the thousands of people who struggle to make a living, which means that they will most likely continue to seek the support of independently organized vendors.

1 PRELUDE TO INDEPENDENT ORGANIZING

In the mid-1940s María Teyssier, an upper-class widow in Puebla, bitterly complained that merchandise from street vendors was dirtying the walls of her downtown residence. According to two letters she wrote to city authorities, the fruit peels that vendors discarded and their children's defecation on the sidewalk were preventing her from opening the windows of her home.[1] She could not stand the stench. Teyssier was not the only one to complain. Speaking on behalf of a larger collective, Ernesto Espinosa Yglesias, a member of a wealthy family, wrote a long letter to municipal officials stating that the boys selling candy in front of two of his family's movie theaters were unbearable and that they used "indecent vocabulary." The patrons of the movie theaters should not have to endure such improper behavior. Vendors, he continued, also obstructed the free movement of pedestrians on the sidewalk who could be hit by cars when they walked on the street to avoid them. He demanded the relocation of these sellers to the other side of the street.[2]

These letters reflect elite definitions of the proper use of urban space in Puebla: streets and sidewalks had to be literally and symbolically clean, devoid of impurities and poor people. Like elites elsewhere in Mexico, Teyssier and Espinosa Yglesias emphasized the class and cultural differences that separated them from Puebla's urban poor who, in their view, caused so many problems. The cultural and social antipathy of the elite was only one of the many challenges vendors experienced when they sold in public spaces. As I explore in this chapter, vendors had to pay multiple fees to sell in public spaces, bribe market officials, and deal with beatings from police.

Facing the possibility that local authorities would side with the elites and remove them from the street, vendors remained active. Throughout the first six decades of the twentieth century they wrote letters and petitions to the city government, sought the protection of the Federal Supreme Court through *amparos* (legal instruments similar to writs of habeas corpus), and joined PRI-affiliated unions. These mechanisms, however, met serious limitations by the early 1970s, when local authorities, convinced that vendors had to leave the streets, tried to remove them through violent means. After discussing Puebla's politics during the avilacamachista years (c. 1937–73), I explore the major challenges vendors faced at that time. This is followed by an analysis of vendors' strategies for remaining in public spaces and a discussion of municipal authorities' responses to vendors' individual and collective actions. The chapter ends with an exploration of street vendors' frustrations with official unions affiliated with the ruling party.

TWENTIETH-CENTURY POBLANO POLITICS AND ELITES

By the mid-1940s, when Teyssier and Espinosa Yglesias wrote their letters of complaint, the city of Puebla was already dominated politically and economically by the *avilacamachista cacicazgo*.[3] This conservative, authoritarian political machinery was created by Maximino Ávila Camacho (hereafter Maximino), governor from 1937 to 1941 and the brother of President Manuel Ávila Camacho (1940–46). The cacicazgo, which outlived Maximino and his governorship and included six governors, union leaders, and all sorts of state officials, was characterized by a very close relationship between wealthy Poblanos and the state. Following the most violent phase of the Mexican Revolution, Puebla experienced much political instability; in the 1920s, for instance, the state had approximately fourteen governors.[4] In that context the city's capitalists welcomed the arrival of the venal, anticommunist, bullfight aficionado, and pro-business Maximino, who promised political and economic stability.[5] Indeed he was able to cement a relatively harmonious relationship among politicians, industrialists, and the local hierarchy of the Catholic Church. He was also able to tame organized labor and control the state university. [6]

During the years of the avilacamachista cacicazgo those who became political leaders rotated positions and were drawn from a small group of businessmen, relatives, and friends of the Ávila Camacho family. The elites were actually interconnected politically, economically, and socially.[7] For instance, the avilacamachista governor Gonzalo Bautista Castillo (1941–45) married the daughter of a wealthy entrepreneur, Rómulo O'Farrill, who was in turn married to one of Maximino's daughters, Hilda Ávila Richardi. The wedding ceremony of Hilda and Rómulo was presided over by Puebla's archbishop Pedro Vera y Zuria.[8] Decades later, in the early 1970s, Gonzalo Bautista O'Farrill, the son of Gonzalo Bautista Castillo, became Puebla's mayor and the last of the avilacamachista governors.[9] Marriages were not the only way to forge good relationships; some sought the governor's *compadrazgo* (fictive kinship or godparenthood). For example, Maximino became the godfather to the son of the industrialist Elías David Hanan. According to one of Puebla's chroniclers, the most prominent Lebanese, French, and Mexican industrialists attended the baptism.[10]

Textile industry owners of Spanish and Lebanese descent composed Puebla's elite, a closed social and economic group with direct participation in Puebla's political life.[11] Their wealth certainly preceded Maximino's tenure.[12] At the beginning of the twentieth century some of these industrialists expanded their fortune by investing in banks, haciendas, and several commercial activities.[13] Their economic importance continued throughout the twentieth century, thanks to local state support and a series of intragroup alliances and marriages.[14] For Poblanos of Spanish and Lebanese descent, as well as for a minority of individuals of French origin, maintaining their ethnic identity was crucial. They tended to marry within the same elite families—including Mexican families—or to look for spouses in their family's country of origin.[15] In later decades Spanish and Lebanese families began to intermarry, protecting their whiteness or their Lebanese identity, which became synonymous with their wealth. Unsurprisingly vendors in the city's public spaces ruffled the feathers of some of these people—especially those who still lived or had their business downtown.[16]

In addition to consolidating an alliance between state and capital, the avilacamachistas were able to control Puebla's state university.[17] Generations of students sympathized with popular plights, and the political elite sought to discipline and to neutralize them, as they did to organized labor. Thanks to regulations that Maximino imposed on the institution, Puebla's governors had a great deal of power over important university decisions, including the ability to designate its presidents (*rectores*). Maximino and the governors who succeeded him were famous for electing close friends and military men to administrative posts.[18] In the early 1950s, for instance, at least nine military officers occupied administrative positions in an effort to militarize and control the student population.[19]

Until the early 1970s men associated with the avilacamachista cacicazgo dominated the university administration. Indeed men who sought a political post at the local or state level often became university president first, and politicians often held administrative jobs or professorships. The importance of the state university had to do with the fact that, until 1969, it was the only university in town that both elite and nonelite students attended. The other two major institutions, the Universidad de las Américas and the Universidad Popular Autónoma de Puebla, opened their private doors to upper-class students in 1970 and 1973, respectively. As the most important institution of higher education, the state university was a space where "what was said and done shaped public opinion."[20] For this reason groups other than the political elite—such as the Catholic Church and progressive and right-wing organizations—sought to maintain a presence there.

During the avilacamachista years the Catholic Church and right-wing organizations became active in internal university matters. Archbishop Octaviano Márquez y Toriz, a fervent anticommunist, as well as the Frente Universitario Anti-comunista (Anticommunist University Front) and the Movimiento Universitario de Renovadora Orientación (University Movement of Renovating Orientation) fought hard—sometimes with violent means—to defend the conservative teachings of the Church. This included crushing communists and perceived communists, defending conservative sexual behavior, and combating what they perceived as pornography within and outside the university.[21] These groups could carry out their activities at the university because of their close connections to the avilacamachista administration.

The power of the avilacamachista cacicazgo and its conservative Catholic allies faced several challenges from progressive students and some faculty. In the early 1960s progressive and left-wing groups sought to reform and radically transform the university: getting rid of conservative, outdated rules and curricula and combating the right-wing forces that dominated the university. Committed to social justice, the proponents of university reform wanted to open spaces for traditionally marginalized students from urban and rural areas. Reform was a long process that was challenged by conservative students and administrators. The university became a violent battleground where the avilacamachista politicians fought their last battles to avoid losing control over the state and the university.

DOWNTOWN STREETS

While elites sought to maintain political and economic power, street vendors were trying to make a living in downtown public spaces. The city center's streets and sidewalks were the busiest commercial spaces. From the city's founding in the sixteenth century to the mid-1980s, Puebla's downtown housed most of the economic, educational, religious, and bureaucratic activity. According to a tourist guide published in 1968, municipal markets, department stores, specialty shops, restaurants, coffee shops, the post and telegraph offices, banks, bus stations, the state university, libraries, museums, cinemas, theaters, churches, tenements, and municipal and state government offices were all located in the heart of the city.[22] Some of these institutions were housed in the architecturally attractive colonial and nineteenth-century buildings that made Puebla's historic center famous.

All sorts of people carried out diverse activities in the city center: students attended classes at the state university's downtown campus;

politicians held meetings at the municipal palace and the congress; groups of peasants from rural areas carried out political demonstrations on the main avenues; and people traveling by bus from the smallest towns in the countryside and from the country's capital arrived at one of several bus stations. Religious Poblanos attended mass in the many churches downtown, and tourists visited Puebla's cathedral. Housewives and maids bought their household's daily consumption items at one of several municipal enclosed markets. And all of these people most likely bought something, even if just a snack, from street vendors.

Whenever possible peddlers preferred to sell in the city's main square, the *zócalo*, which is surrounded by the cathedral, see to the oldest Catholic diocese in Mexico, and—on the opposite side—by the Municipal Palace, seat of the city government. Aside from the square's commercial desirability, vendors had a historical reason to prefer the site, as people had sold here for centuries. Sixteenth-century inhabitants called the zócalo el Tiánguis, from the Nahuatl word *tianquiztli*, which means "market" or "place of commerce," and itself derives from the verb *tiamiqui*, meaning "to trade" or "to sell." In the colonial period vendors sold fruit, bread, clothes, and poultry on a daily basis; on Thursdays and Saturdays vendors from nearby towns were allowed to sell all sorts of merchandise.[23]

Another favorite space for vendors was at the three *portales*, the set of colonnaded arches surrounding the zócalo, characteristic of Mexican towns. These portales were built in the sixteenth century allegedly to accommodate vendors and protect them from the elements. In the modern period the portales were named after the leaders of the independence wars: Hidalgo, Morelos, and Iturbide. Vendors either hawked their products there or set up outside the entrance of established shops. In the late seventeenth century, for instance, in what is now portal Morelos, vendors sold flowers, and the area became known as the portal de las Flores. Despite the existence of the Parián market, vendors continued to sell used clothes and fabrics in the portal Hidalgo.[24] Municipal correspondence in the early twentieth century reveals that many vendors sold prepared food, forcing established owners of bakeries, restaurants, and *torterías* (sandwich shops) to share the portales with street vendors who had semi-fixed and mobile stalls under the arches and right outside their stores.[25]

Most vendors, however, sought to secure space outside the municipal markets, such as the one east of the zócalo, in El Alto, and on the west side in the Nicolás Bravo market. The majority of street vendors tried to find space outside the largest and most popular market of the city, La Victoria. Although it was mainly a food market, its marketers also offered ropes and hats, ceramics, notions, shoes, clothes, toys, flowers, live animals, and other merchandise. Street vendors tried to take advantage of the hundreds of pedestrians in the area.

STREET VENDORS' MAIN CHALLENGES

Vendors faced all sorts of problems trying to sell in public spaces. Like Teyssier and Espinosa Yglesias, many people fought for what they considered the fair and appropriate use of streets and sidewalks. To some Poblanos vendors represented economic competition; to the wealthy, vendors offended their supposedly refined cultural sensibilities and taste. Historically there was tension between the upper classes and the working poor in Puebla and elsewhere in Mexico.[26] Both groups had a different vision of what public spaces should look like and how people should use them. For instance, Porfirian and postrevolutionary elites in Mexico City wanted to ban street vendors, whom they associated with lack of hygiene, stench, and unsafe handling of food.[27] Privileged Poblanos wanted their streets to be orderly, clean, and accessible to and enjoyable for only a few. For the working class and the poor, the same spaces represented the only locations where they and their family members could make a living. Therefore one of the major challenges vendors confronted was the cultural antipathy and complaints from downtown neighbors and established business owners, usually members of the middle and upper classes who perceived themselves superior to the urban poor in every sense. Established business owners had more capital than itinerant vendors did, and they used it to furnish their shops and maintain their reputation. Street vendors represented an economic challenge, not because they were their direct competitors but because they were an eyesore.

From the correspondence members of the upper class sent to municipal authorities it is clear that they disdained the presence of vendors, along with their products and their clientele. They usually found vendors' practices offensive and even repulsive. In 1919 food vendors annoyed the French owner of La Princesa bakery, located under the portal Hidalgo. The baker stated that the enchiladas, beans, mole, and tacos that vendors sold right outside the bakery's entrance were "filthy merchandise" for which "Puebla's correct and educated classes" that shopped in his store felt "repulsion." In his view the vendors were "a danger for his refined female customers' dresses because vendors could dirty them with their foods" as the women entered his shop. Street vendors' children were an additional nuisance; the little ones "pitiably begged for money" from his wealthy customers. Clearly the vendors in front of his shop damaged its prestige and the aesthetics of one of the city's best sites.[28] The baker was not exaggerating. At the beginning of the twentieth century wealthy women, usually the wives of textile owners, showed off their best clothes when they ventured from their downtown residence to the street, perhaps on their way to some of the French-style department stores, such as Al Puerto de Veracruz, Las Fábricas de Francia, and La Ciudad de México. And when they went to church they covered their head with a Spanish mantilla.[29]

Similarly, in 1921 the heirs of Angel Díaz Rubín, a wealthy Spanish textile factory owner, wrote to the municipality, pointing out that vendors dirtied the streets surrounding the portales. Feeling entitled to speak on behalf of Puebla, these elites said "the city" hated the enchiladas vendors sold and the tables they set up for their clientele; the heirs wanted the police to remove all the vendors.[30] Although it is hard to believe that all Poblanos despised enchilada vendors, these men felt repulsed by the look and smell of working-class food. As a business owner once put it, street vendors were the "gente del pueblo," that is, low-class, ordinary people, uneducated and lacking in good manners.[31] As I will show, this perception continued throughout much of the century, and in the mid-1980s the vendors were relocated to the outskirts of the city, where they would become practically invisible.

FIG. 3. Vendors on sidewalks. Courtesy of Archivo General Municipal de Puebla, unnumbered image, c. 1960s.

Some viewed vendors as an urban danger, clogging the streets at the same time the number of cars was increasing. A man who lived downtown complained that a fruit stall occupied the sidewalk on his children's way to school. He was concerned his children would be hit by a car because the maids who accompanied them made them walk on the street.[32]

Street vendors around La Victoria also faced hostility from the established marketers inside. For the most part, established marketers sold the same kinds of products as their street counterparts, but at slightly higher prices. Unlike vendors, however, established marketers had to pay rent, electricity, and sanitation permits, among other expenses; they therefore saw street vendors as a financial threat. Municipal officers spent endless hours reading letters from dissatisfied marketers. For instance, in 1936 the members of a tortilla makers' union in La Victoria wanted to halt the sale of hand-made tortillas by itinerant vendors from the countryside who sold their products in the market's halls but did not have a stall. These peddlers had a devastating effect on their business because customers preferred the handmade tortillas to the union's machine-made tortillas.[33]

One of the hardest parts of the street-vending trade was finding and keeping attractive spots at which to sell. In addition to the complaints from shop owners and marketers, vendors dealt with a barrage of municipal officials who made it difficult for them to secure vending spaces. Municipal market administrators were in charge of regulating commerce inside and outside enclosed city markets. Working under their supervision, fee collectors and their aides collected the fees that vendors had to pay the municipality for the use of public space, even if public space meant one square meter on a sidewalk or a square meter on the floor of a market. The amount of money vendors paid to the municipality was dictated by regulations on the spaces that street vendors could occupy inside and outside markets, the hours they could work, the kinds of merchandise they could sell, and how they could display their wares.[34] The written market regulations were quite specific and rigid; in practice, however, municipal officials approached the regulations with great flexibility. In addition, the municipality did not update the regulations, making some clauses obsolete allowing officials to disregard others. In effect, market officials imposed their own, sometimes random rules on vendors.

Such practices, especially those of fee collectors, became a source of distress for vendors. Fees varied from street to street and product to product. While some fees were written in the market regulations, fee collectors charged vendors at will.[35] In 1947 market administrators earned 15 pesos per day, fee collectors earned 3.5 pesos, and collectors' aides earned 2.5 pesos.[36] It is possible that due to the low income of fee collectors and their aides they supplemented their wages by overcharging street vendors, demanding bribes, charging vendors several times a day, and seizing their merchandise or personal items if they failed to pay.[37] The seized products were supposed to be kept in the market administrator's office, but this was not always the case. According to one vendor I interviewed, Gabina Reyes, municipal inspectors always kept the best or most expensive merchandise for themselves: "Officials' wives always had fruits and vegetables in their kitchens because their husbands stole them from us, the vendors!"[38]

FIG. 4. A fee collector. Courtesy of Archivo General Municipal de Puebla, image 1006, Administración Municipal, 1975–78.

The many letters from discontented street vendors suggest that market administrators were aware of these corrupt practices and that they too pocketed the money. It is possible that market administrators demanded that fee collectors share that extra money with them.

This harassment of vendors was well known. A group of shopkeepers called municipal officials "immoral employees" because, in addition to pocketing vendors' fees, they also demanded bribes.[39] Yolanda Bejarano used to give fee collectors "gifts," such as some of the fruit she sold, in order to stay in good standing with them.[40] When vendors failed to pay fees or bribes to municipal authorities, they were forcefully removed by police officers. Vendors who resisted were beaten or dragged away, men and women alike. In the process vendors lost their merchandise and were detained. For those with small children, detentions were particularly vexing. Teresa Rosales remembers that inspectors and police seized her merchandise and arrested her several times; on one occasion she was pregnant, and on another she spent hours at the police station with two of her young children.[41] Paula Javier, another seller, said that after experiencing many incidents with the police, her children cried when officers and fee collectors approached her stand.[42]

By the early 1970s vendors faced authorities' physical violence more regularly. The use of "public force," as the police called it, entailed spraying tear gas, dragging vendors from their stalls, and beating them. Bejarano recalled, "Police treated us as if we were criminals."[43] Women and children were not immune to this treatment, which appalled vendors. In a letter to Mayor Carlos Arruti, a group of street vendors claimed that police beat female vendors "whose only crime is working to bring food to their children."[44] Vendor Blanca Pastrana's first experience with tear gas was when she was a little girl. Her mother was a street vendor, and Blanca went selling with her after school. One day, on her way to the stall, she saw police everywhere. She recalls feeling "something strange" and falling down. Luckily a neighbor dragged her inside her house to protect her.[45] City authorities publicly announced their use of violence against vendors; one newspaper published the mayor's declaration that, if vendors insisted upon selling in the streets, then "the problem must be repressed."[46] The mayor thus reduced vendors' economic subsistence to a "problem" whose solution was physical force.

Harassment of female vendors included sexual advances from the entirely male cadre of municipal employees. Bejarano said that police officers "touched the women" in the heat of the moment during police raids. She vividly remembered the fear she and other vendors felt on the night of October 28, 1973, when the police put a young girl inside a police truck while carrying out a violent raid: "The girl was very young, about eight years old, came from a small town, San Pablo del Monte, and she had her own stall; her mother also had a stall." The vendors feared that officers would rape her "because during the raid, officers were very high on drugs." The vendors followed the vehicle and rescued the girl. "She was all scared and crying."[47] On a different occasion, during a protest in front of about two hundred people, one unidentified vendor took the microphone and accused municipal officers of being "immoral subjects." These men, he argued, "extort vendors and sometimes try to abuse women by demanding that they provide sexual favors."[48]

Indeed officers perceived female vendors as "mujeres de la calle" (street women) who were available for men's pleasure.[49] There are historical reasons why women working outside the home faced severe criticism and harassment. During the Porfiriato (1876–1911) women working in factories were associated with disease and moral corruption, especially if they shared the shop floor with men.[50] In the 1940s Poblano women who labored in the textile industry were criticized by members of organized labor, who linked working-class women to the home and to motherhood.[51] In the late 1960s even female students witnessed the conservatism of urban Poblano families regardless of whether or not their family members were conservative, liberal, or even communist. Few women wore pants, as they would be criticized and called tomboys. Women who attended mass had to wear a veil and a dress whose hemline was below the knee. Society approved only certain jobs and activities, often related to the domestic sphere, as appropriate for women.[52]

Street vendors did not remain passive to the abuses they experienced. Instead they used several strategies to defend what they considered their right to make a living.[53] They petitioned market administrators and mayors, and if their petitions failed, they sought the protection of federal authorities through the legal mechanism of the amparo. Some hoped to be protected by their membership in official unions. Up until 1973 vendors' success at resisting abuse varied significantly.

LETTER WRITING

As individuals and as groups, vendors sent letters to municipal officials explaining their problems and demanding or proposing solutions. Scholars have demonstrated that even when vendors were illiterate, they were savvy in their letters or when they asked someone else to represent them.[54] Public scribes—those who wrote letters on behalf of the vendors—were analytical middlemen who played the role of negotiators between the government and vendors. They acted as the nexus for ordinary people to enter the realm of the "lettered city."[55] These paid writers of letters and petitions, who worked at desks in public spaces, were quite skilled in using language that best fit the narratives and discourse of the time.[56]

We have a good sense of the kind of rhetorical elements that sellers or their public scribes employed over time. In the late nineteenth century, for instance, vendors in Morelia presented themselves as "hard-working, moral, consumer-conscious sellers" who asserted their right to the use of the city as *vecinos* (respectable neighbors) and as citizens.[57] During the Porfiriato and early revolutionary period, Mexico City's female vendors defended themselves from removal by city authorities by constructing identities around their sexual morality, honor, and alleged weaknesses.[58] In nineteenth-century Guadalajara women "used the prevailing [gender] ideology of the times to their advantage when petitioning city hall" and described themselves "as vulnerable and helpless."[59]

In later decades male and female vendors in Puebla used some of the same rhetorical elements the vendors in Mexico City, Morelia, and Guadalajara had employed. These include a mélange of explanations to defend themselves against accusations coming from people who sought to impede their commerce or remove them. They used a gendered and class-based language, appealing to their constitutional rights and even to their Mexican nationality. Referring to their gender, female vendors tended to stress that they were "mujeres solas," women without anyone to help them economically.[60] Male and female street vendors situated themselves as responsible breadwinners of extended families, though they sought to communicate that they were very poor and alluded to their class status. In 1946 Teresa Nava asked authorities not to remove her stall because it was the only means she had to support her mother and her children. Some letters were quite intense. In 1945 Rita Zarate wrote a number of times, asking the mayor to allow her to sell on the streets: "My condition of mujer sola forces me to work to support my six children. People know how much I suffer. . . . Please [let me sell] in the name of your little caring mother [*hágalo por su linda mamacita de usted*]. I beg you, I am poor, sick, and I have such a large family [to support]." Men too presented themselves as helpless, emphasizing their extreme economic hardship. In 1946 Gregorio García petitioned for a commercial license to sell sodas and candy; he identified himself as a poor, small-size seller. Another vendor stated that he was very poor and wished to build a semi-fixed stall because he had few economic resources and supported a large family. Another claimed he was a publicly known poor person and wanted to sell candy and sodas.[61] In short, female and male vendors emphasized their poverty and asked authorities to reduce their fees, give them extra time to pay, or waive the fees altogether, and to grant them commercial licenses. They appealed to authorities using a vocabulary that exalted their good parenting and their economic difficulties.[62]

Despite their dramatic language, vendors were not writing fiction; their words reflected the reality of the harsh economic conditions they experienced throughout most of their lives. In interviews from the 1960s and 1970s women stated that the only way to sustain a family was by migrating to work in a large city like Puebla; they had left their children in the care of their parents and hoped to make enough money to bring their children to live with them. Clearly this was still an option for folks in rural areas during the Mexican Miracle, as opposed to later decades when the savviest option was to migrate to the United States.

Street vendors also claimed that selling legal products (*productos lícitos*) in makeshift markets and other public spaces was their constitutional right and an honest way to earn a living. They were relying on an older tradition that peddlers and other ordinary Mexicans had used since at least the nineteenth century. As the historian Christina Jiménez has shown, vendors' legal references and their claim of a right to trade and a right to make an honest living by engaging in any occupation they chose were based on rights guaranteed by the 1857 Constitution.[63]

Later Puebla sellers appealed to the 1917 Constitution, particularly to Article 4, which states, "No person [may] be prevented from engaging in the profession, industrial or commercial pursuit, or occupation of his choice, provided it is lawful."[64] In the early 1920s a group of shawl sellers wrote that the police accused them of cheating customers and prevented them from selling their wares, which they insisted was a violation of their "libertad de comercio" (commercial freedom), which Article 4 granted to all citizens.[65] Another group of sellers wrote a letter complaining about the market administrator who charged them an arbitrary fee for bringing products into the market from the countryside. The vendors identified these fees as the updated *alcabalas*, or colonial sales taxes, which the Mexican Constitution forbade.[66] In 1948 a street vendor, Luz Andrade, declared that she was removed by the mayor and other officials after eighteen years of having a stall on the street. She claimed that authorities violated her constitutional rights by impeding her from "working honestly . . . without any justification." After all, her stall was the only means by which she could support her family and pay for her children's education.[67]

In other letters vendors appealed to authorities on the basis of their shared nationality as Mexicans with the same rights and responsibilities. In 1950 a group of butchers who sold on the street defended their livelihood by arguing, "As Mexicans who fully exercise our rights, we can make a living choosing the profession that is better suited to our interests."[68] Vendors were also suggesting that authorities should defend Mexicans over the interests of foreigners. These ideas were not unique to street vendors. Market sellers in Puebla, and in other locations and times, also complained about foreigners.[69] In 1947 María Moreno wrote to the municipality combining several rhetorical elements:

> I am a very old woman with a large family to support. In order to face my humble condition, as I have always been poor, I was granted a permit to sell *tortas compuestas* [sandwiches] and coffee in the evenings. I have been selling for the past nine years and I have punctually paid my license and fees for the use of space. Today I am writing to you because my stall, that I have earned honorably, is in danger. A man of Polish or Russian nationality, feeling entitled because he is a foreigner, wants to remove us. He doesn't take into account that our nation has generously granted him asylum. . . . He thinks he has the right to remove us but he is not the owner of the public space, which belongs to the heroic Municipal government.[70]

Antonia Mendoza, who came from the countryside and sold flowers in Puebla, appealed to the memory of the Mexican Revolution when complaining that city authorities collected too many fees from street vendors. Referencing the 1910 Revolution was a strategy vendors had been using since the conflict began. In this case Mendoza went a bit further. With the revolutionary struggle and its gains still fresh in her mind, she wrote in a 1962 letter that the city government of Puebla was a shame and a disgrace to the spirit of the Revolution. She added that authorities did not care about the peasants' dignity. Indeed she equated the abuses of the local government to those of Porfirio Díaz (1876–1911), suggesting that the principles of the Mexican Revolution had been eroded.[71]

MUNICIPAL RESPONSES TO LETTERS AND PETITIONS

Responses from municipal authorities to vendors' letters varied. Sometimes they favored vendors; sometimes they simply ignored them; and sometimes authorities hurt vendors' economic interests. Until the late 1960s city government officials thought they had to respond to the interests of both street vendors and established business owners. Both groups actively demanded that authorities respond to their requests, and officials found themselves caught between the plights and constitutional rights of street vendors and the claims the established business community made for commerce without competition from informal economic actors. At the end of the day it was, as Jiménez notes, a political calculation.[72]

Several scholars have demonstrated that relationships between authorities and street vendors have not always been hostile.[73] Many of these relationships were complex and often were related to the political, economic, and even religious climate in specific locations and periods, as well as larger state and national circumstances. For instance, in mid-nineteenth-century Mexico City authorities approached vendors with a sense of compassion rooted in Catholicism.[74] Later on, Porfirian elites acknowledged the social function of vendors, who provided inexpensive food to the poor.[75] During the 1910 Revolution and its immediate aftermath, when the state needed political clients among the urban working class, authorities used a strategy of "balanced containment."[76]

On the local level certain political groups in Puebla tended to tolerate vendors' presence more than others did. Municipal market administrators and their subordinates, namely fee collectors and their aides, allowed vendors to sell in public spaces for profit because, as mentioned earlier, they benefited financially from vendors' fees and from the extra money that they extracted, including from bribes. In 1945 a group of sellers at the Nicolás Bravo market asked the market administrator to force street vendors to sell in the stalls inside the market, but the municipal administrator claimed "there would not be enough stalls in the market to house all of the street vendors."[77] The frustrated marketers wrote another letter and accused the administrator of lying, insisting that there were more than enough stalls for the peddlers inside the facility.[78] Vendors continued selling on the streets, and the administrator and fee collectors benefited financially. Mayors were ambivalent. They allowed vendors to sell in public spaces as long as the mayor's office did not face political and economic pressure from organized groups of established businessmen. But under pressure mayors removed vendors temporarily or denied them vending permits.

Puebla's authorities had several reasons to tolerate vendors. They provided inexpensive merchandise to the city's needy population and offered to sell small quantities at all hours.[79] Some vendors sold overripe fruits and vegetables to the poor for much lower prices.[80] It was a win-win situation: vendors did not lose all the money they had invested, and their customers did not go hungry. Clients could also negotiate the amount and price of merchandise they bought; haggling (*regateo*) was an advantage for those whose budget was tight. In short, street vendors subsidized food and other basic products, and authorities were well aware of this function.

Puebla's city government also tended to tolerate street vendors because it was less costly to allow them to stay on the streets and to collect their fees than to invest in building new facilities to accommodate them. Between 1966 and 1970 the local government did not spend a single cent in building any commercial facilities that could have accommodated street vendors.[81] This lack of public investment is part of a larger trend that goes back several decades. Despite petitions from working-class neighborhoods, the city government was unwilling or financially unable to build enclosed public markets. Residents in several neighborhoods asked authorities to build affordable markets nearby because markets represented a "social good" (*un bien común*): markets provided fixed spaces for vendors to make a living while also providing residents easy access to food and other basic products. Groups of neighbors even offered tracts of land to the municipality on which to build a market. The most persistent—and most frustrated—residents were those who lived in the Colonia Obrera Lázaro Cárdenas; they first requested the construction of a market in 1945, and their last demand occurred in 1968. In 1966 the group even offered a lot of two thousand square meters for the municipality to build the market. Two years later the municipality finally decided that it could not build the facility.[82] Similar cases occurred in Colonia Héroes de Nacozari, a railroad workers' neighborhood, and in Colonia Santa Cruz Angeles, where people demanded the construction of marketplaces on tracts of land they owned and that the municipality could use.[83] Authorities did not build a market in either of these cases. For decades they disregarded ordinary people's proposals on urban planning and decentralization of commercial activities.[84] In the meantime, and to the chagrin of many, vendors continued selling on downtown streets. Although they could make a living, they still had to pay fees and bribes and suffered harassment and violence.

Depending on the economic and political climate, the city government's tolerance of street vending had its limits. As mentioned, when organized groups of established business people—including sellers in enclosed markets—pressured the municipality, authorities either removed vendors temporarily or did not grant them selling permits. In an effort to counteract these decisions, street vendors used a legal mechanism, the amparo suit (*juicio de amparo*).

Historically the amparo was widely used, especially by indigenous groups seeking royal protection, in land cases since the late sixteenth century.[85] In its modern form the amparo requested the federal government to protect ordinary people from unconstitutional actions of the local government. The Federal Supreme Court was the body that decided whether or not local authorities violated people's rights. The amparo had its modern origins in Articles 101 and 102 of the Mexican Constitution of 1857, and later in Article 107 of the 1917 Constitution.[86] Since the end of the nineteenth century people from all social classes, not only the wealthy, used amparos to address a variety of offenses by the state.[87] Street vendors' illiteracy did not deter them from using this legal mechanism. In 1913 a female vendor of meat initiated an amparo suit because city authorities moved her from a makeshift market to another site where she had fewer customers. She stated that the removal was a violation of Article 16 of the 1857 Constitution: "My business is my only patrimony, and being removed is the equivalent of losing my property in benefit of the Municipality."[88]

The amparo did not guarantee that vendors would be able to sell their products on the streets. The process could be long, and the Federal Supreme Court could deny vendors the protection of federal government against local authorities. A 1952 amparo suit exemplifies the intricacies of this legal mechanism. In March of that year a group of three women and one man began an amparo suit against Puebla's mayor, Nicolás Vázquez, and two other city officials. These vendors sought to sell *aguamiel*, the nutritious maguey sap, at a semi-fixed stall on a street near La Victoria market and asked the city government to issue them a commercial license to do so. The authorities denied the request, claiming that aguamiel was an alcoholic beverage and that "selling [it] was a dangerous practice at work places, which resulted in pitiful accidents."[89]

The vendors decided to challenge the denial of the commercial license through an amparo. At least two of the women, Josefa Avila and Alfonsa Sastre, did not know how to write or sign their names, so they delegated Juana Torres, the third female vendor, to represent them. Evidently this small group of vendors had a lawyer who took their case. The vendors claimed that the mayor, the municipal general secretary, and the municipal chief of taxes and regulations were violating their right to make a living because the selling of aguamiel was legal and justified (*lícita*) and did not endanger the city's morality. In fact, they added, in Puebla there were many shops and stalls that sold aguamiel, pulque, and alcoholic beverages. The vendors and their lawyer presented a copy of a letter in which the municipal authorities had granted a license to other sellers of aguamiel only a few weeks earlier. The sellers also claimed that city officials violated Articles 4, 14, and 16 of the 1917 Mexican Constitution by not granting them a license. They emphasized that their product was legal and that their stall was far from any workplace.[90]

Although it seemed the street vendors were about to win the case, in June 1952 the Supreme Court of Justice unexpectedly denied them the protection of the federal government, ruling in favor of the city authorities. Despite a three-month-long legal engagement, the vendors could not sell their product, at least not legally.[91]

In 1959 another group of vendors failed to win an amparo against Puebla's mayor, Rafael Artasánchez Romero (1957–60), who had decided to remove them from the streets. The Supreme Court denied the vendors its protection, which allowed the mayor to proudly announce that—with the aid of the local business association, the Cámara Nacional de Comercio de Puebla—the municipality had temporarily removed peddlers from downtown.[92] After a while, however, the vendors went back to selling on the streets. For them it was a matter of economic survival.

There were also cases when the Supreme Court favored vendors but local authorities ignored the amparos and removed vendors or their merchandise. In 1969 tensions escalated between the municipal government and an increasing number of vendors. Stating that vendors caused "a lot of traffic and were a risk to pedestrians," Mayor Carlos Arruti (1969–72) carried out a temporary removal in March 1969. But once more vendors sought the protection of the federal government, and a number of them won amparo suits in June 1970.[93] Yet another campaign against them began immediately afterward, lasting from August to September 1970. Despite having the amparos in their hands, street vendors faced harassment and threats from police, fee collectors, and the Agrupación de Locatarios libres del Estado de Puebla (Association of Free Stall Owners of the State of Puebla), one of the charro organizations that represented marketers at La Victoria and collaborated with authorities to remove vendors from the streets.[94] Authorities arrested vendors, confiscated their merchandise, and sent police to guard the streets. Clearly amparos did not help them much.

OFFICIAL UNIONS

By 1973, when Poblano street vendors decided to form an independent union, some of them had already participated in at least one of the official unions affiliated with the PRI. Street vendors in several cities across Mexico had organized collectively since the 1920s. One of the first unions in Mexico City, for instance, was organized by newspaper sellers, the Unión de Expendedores, Voceaderos y Repartidores de Prensa del Distrito Ferderal (Union of Newspaper Sellers).[95] By 1930 at least two unions represented sellers, stall owners, and vendors in Morelia: the Union of Independent, Small-Scale Employees and Owners and the Union of Small Business Owners.[96]

With all its limitations, unions represented one of the most common ways for ordinary people to achieve some of their demands and to defend themselves from powerful people. While organized workers in the formal economy formed unions to ensure their wages, benefits, and respect and to protect themselves from employers' unfair policies, vendors organized unions to secure access to public spaces in order to make a living. During the time covered in this book, street vendors were not wage earners and did not have employers; thus they were not "workers" in the eyes of the state and labor law and could not form *sindicatos* (trade unions). They could, however, form *uniones* or *agrupaciones*, voluntary associations to defend their economic interests.[97] When the ruling party began establishing a corporatist structure, these vendors' organizations had to join state-sponsored organizations. At different times Puebla's vendors' unions held membership in the Confederación Regional Obrera Mexicana (Regional Confederation of Mexican Workers), the Federación Regional de Obreros y Campesinos (Regional Federation of Workers and Peasants, FROC), and ultimately the Confederación Nacional de Organizaciones Populares (National Confederation of Popular Organizations, CNOP).[98]

Some of the official unions that vendors joined included established small entrepreneurs such as market vendors and established business owners. These were groups whose very different interests were at odds with each other. Established market vendors, for instance, perceived street vendors as their economic competitors. One of these unions to which vendors belonged was the Unión de Comerciantes e Industriales en pequeño de la Ciudad de Puebla (Union of Merchants and Small Industrialists of the City of Puebla), which was affiliated with the CNOP.[99] By 1964 the FROC and the Confederación Revolucionaria de Obreros y Campesinos (Revolutionary Confederation of Workers and Peasants, CROC) were able to recruit three hundred street vendors into their unions.[100] The fact that charro unions included antagonistic groups suggests their ineffectiveness in legitimately fighting for the interests of their members.

A profound sense of disillusionment and frustration grew among street vendors toward official unions and their charro leaders, who tended to cooperate with authorities and failed to defend members' interests. In that sense PRI-affiliated unions of street vendors were not dissimilar to blue-collar workers' official unions. Both had charro leaders who seemed to be more preoccupied with securing support for politicians' campaigns than actually defending workers' rights.[101] Part of the disillusionment had to do with charro practices, which included exorbitant fees, support for

PRI politicians, and coercion against militant vendors. On one occasion street vendors complained because the official leadership made them pay 75 pesos to produce banners thanking President Gustavo Díaz Ordaz for his generosity in allowing them to sell on the streets. Vendors most likely realized that the president had nothing to do with the decision and that the fee was a waste of money they certainly could not afford and that could have been used for a different purpose. From the perspective of the official union, praising Mexico's executive was a common clientelistic practice. When authorities granted street vendors stalls in markets, they forced the vendors to join the CNOP; those who refused were forbidden to sell their merchandise. In 1969, for instance, the avilacamachista governor Rafael Moreno Valle (1969–72) granted a group of militant vendors the use of land to set up a makeshift market. Immediately the CNOP launched a campaign to recruit them into its ranks. The vendors who refused to join the ruling party's organization were expelled from the market.[102]

Cooperation between authorities and official charro leaders was common. Correspondence between leaders of the FROC-CROC and Puebla's mayor in 1969 shows that the leaders reassured authorities of their commitment. The leadership wrote, "The FROC will not intervene in defense of vendors, because [vendors] need to be disciplined, obey, and pay their fees to the government that you [mayor] represent."[103] The discipline these leaders advocated was vendors' removal from the streets, which was a constant and very realistic threat to militant vendors. The most leaders did for the rank and file was to negotiate with authorities in order to extend the time vendors could sell in public spaces.[104]

Official leaders expected vendors to show their political loyalty and support for all of the PRI candidates and politicians on the local, state, and federal levels. PRI-affiliated leaders forced vendors to vote for the official party's candidates. In 1977 Luz María Lara, a PRI-affiliated union leader in Puebla, openly admitted that the street vendors in her organization always had to vote for PRI candidates.[105] The rank-and-file members also had to show up at political campaign rallies or face punishment, including expulsion from the union, thus decreasing their chance of selling on the streets.[106] Some leaders literally dragged people to these events, and for that reason they were known as *acarreados*. During these mandatory events the rank and file carried official banners, applauded, and shouted "Viva" to the PRI candidates.[107] At campaign events for mayors, governors, and Mexico's presidents, PRI-affiliated members had to be present showing—or at least faking—their support. Vendors' attendance at these political events was a condition for maintaining union membership.[108] Whereas factory workers may have treated these rallies as well-deserved breaks from work, for street vendors they represented a financial burden because they were unable to sell their goods. Generally speaking, charro leaders in Puebla did not challenge authorities and did little for their members.

Street vendors hoped that if official unions could not do much for them, an independent union might. Vendors agreed they needed to avoid charro leaders in order to guarantee their permanency on the streets and their access to markets. As we will see, encouraged by students, street vendors committed to build a union free of charros and free of caciques, or "petty caciques," as Alan Knight calls them.[109] This independence meant that the vendors were not affiliated with any PRI workers' confederation or any popular organization under PRI's control, and were thus independent from the state.[110]

CONCLUSION

Middle- and upper-class people disdained street vendors because they represented the gente del pueblo: the poor, uneducated, and unrefined masses. Privileged people preferred not to see or deal with the urban poor. They preferred an orderly city and a clean downtown devoid of vendors. In the view of the elites, vendors culturally degraded the city. Their foul language, unruly children, and cheap merchandise literally and figuratively dirtied the city's walls and sidewalks. For established businesses, especially for marketers, vendors selling inexpensive merchandise represented an economic challenge.

Nevertheless, until the late 1960s complaints to municipal authorities from elites usually fell on deaf ears. Mayors realized that sellers fulfilled the important function of providing inexpensive products to the urban poor and the working class, and fees and bribes complemented the low wages of low-ranking municipal employees. In addition, authorities did not have any intention of building new markets. Only when the municipality felt threatened by business groups did it respond by removing vendors from downtown, especially from the streets that surrounded markets. These measures were only temporary, however, and vendors quickly went back to selling on the streets and sidewalks.

During removals vendors experienced physical violence and harassment from police and other municipal officials while their goods were seized. But street vendors did not passively accept this treatment; they cited their constitutional rights and petitioned authorities to allow them to make a living by trading on the streets, used amparo suits to demand the Federal Supreme Court protect them against local government abuses, or asked their official union to advance their demands. However, each of these approaches had serious limitations, and by the early 1970s vendors clearly saw the need to organize independently from official, charro unions. Downtown streets had become hot with political activism among left-wing and progressive actors at Puebla's state university; with their help, street vendors began to focus on organizing collectively into an independent union to protect their right to make a living without the harassment of local and state authorities.

2 VENDORS AND STUDENTS IN THE 1970S

After thirty years of living together as parents of six children, Teresa Rosales, a lifelong street vendor, and Bulmaro Vega León, a former student-teacher at the Universidad Autónoma de Puebla (Autonomous University of Puebla, UAP), decided to formalize their union and get married. When Rosales met Vega in the early 1970s she was a young single mother of three who had migrated to the state capital from the impoverished town of Tepeaca, Puebla. At sixteen she had become a fruit vendor, the only economic activity that allowed her to take care of her children, including a newborn, while making a living. Like many other street vendors who tended their merchandise on sidewalks, Rosales faced several violent removals at the hands of police officers until she and her fellow vendors began organizing the UPVA. Born in Tecamachalco, Puebla, Vega (1945–2011) was a physics student at the Universidad Nacional Autónoma de México (National Autonomous University of Mexico, UNAM) and a self-proclaimed Maoist. After witnessing the 1968 massacre at Tlatelolco in Mexico City, he moved to Puebla to continue his studies and engage in activism. He became a student-teacher at a state university-affiliated high school, worked as an organizer for several independent unions, and joined the street vendors' struggle.[1]

Rosales and Vega's relationship was emblematic of a larger alliance between street vendors and left-wing, working-class students who interacted on the streets, shared common experiences, and worked together to create the UPVA in the fall of 1973.[2] Like other unions that emerged during the labor insurgency of the 1970s, the UPVA was independent of the PRI. Unlike the others, its members worked in the informal economy. The alliance with young left-wing students helped vendors create and shape an independent and democratic union. Street vendors became the ideological and political heirs of Puebla's students in the 1970s, who in turn had inherited their political culture from the national student movement of the long 1960s (c. 1956–71).[3] From their student allies vendors borrowed ideological and structural traits, as well as organizational strategies, political practices, and negotiation skills that helped vendors build an organization independent from the ruling party.

This unique vendor-student alliance represented a political challenge to local and federal authorities and a threat to conservatives at Puebla's state university.[4] Locally the formation of strong links between students and vendors occurred at the very moment when the most conservative political forces of Puebla's PRI since the 1930s, the avilacamachistas, were experiencing a political crisis in relation to the federal government that ultimately led to their fall.[5] From 1970 to 1973 two avilacamachista governors, Rafael Moreno Valle (1969–72) and Gonzalo Bautista O'Farrill (1972–73), carried out repressive campaigns against progressive students and administrators at the UAP, including acts of violence that resulted in the death of half a dozen people. As Wil Pansters has shown, a coalition of students, street vendors, and other popular groups made public the state repression against members of the university community, an act that helped undermine the remaining power of the avilacamachistas, especially vis-à-vis the administration of President Luis Echeverría Álvarez.[6]

The murder of university students and administrators in 1972 and 1973 by avilacamachista gunmen called into question the president's so-called democratic opening, a set of political and labor policies to clean up Echeverría's image after his participation as secretary of the interior in the 1968 Tlatelolco massacre in Mexico City.[7] Through the democratic opening the president tried to distance himself from the Díaz Ordaz administration (1964–70) by becoming more tolerant of student demands and by recognizing independent unions. In 1973 popular groups in Puebla, while distrustful of Echeverría's policies, at least expected the president to act against Governor Gonzalo Bautista O'Farrill who, in their view, had masterminded the assassination of students and administrators in 1972 and 1973. The governor's historical connections with former president Gustavo Díaz Ordaz made it easier for Echeverría to depose Bautista O'Farrill in May 1973. This executive order represented a fatal blow to the avilacamachista cacicazgo.

At the national level the alliance between students and a segment of the informal economy challenged the way the PRI state had compartmentalized Mexican society, dividing it into discrete sectors so that, in theory, the government could control it more effectively. Traditionally the ruling party had placed organizations of workers, peasants, and popular groups, including street vendors, into one of its three main confederations: the CTM, CNC, and CNOP, respectively. By doing so the PRI kept unions and other organizations within the party, but at the same time kept them apart from one another. Like other groups across the country, street vendors and students challenged this structure by reaching out to each other, by working together to form the UPVA, and by refusing to join the PRI's ranks. Creating and sustaining a political alliance of this sort was possible thanks to students' and vendors' grassroots organizing. The so-called democratic opening therefore served only as the background to these events. While to a certain degree Echeverría's policies allowed the existence of independent unions, these organizations had to act very carefully within a climate of local repression against activists and organizers.

STUDENTS AND VENDORS

Students and vendors shared common characteristics that facilitated their political alliance. The group of students who got involved with vendors either belonged to or identified with the working class. Interviews with former students reflecting on their lives in the 1970s reveal that they were often the children of low-wage factory workers, service sector employees, teachers, and workers in the informal economy.[8] While slightly better off than street vendors, working-class students still struggled financially.

The schools they attended and their neighborhoods and homes attest to their social status. A student leader from one of the UAP's high schools described his background and that of his friends: "We want to make it clear that we are the children of workers . . . [and we] the workers are the most *jodidos* [poorest]."[9] A former teacher at this school remembered that some of these working-class students could not afford shoes and came to class barefoot.[10]

The students who joined the street vendors' struggles attended the newest of the state university's preparatory schools, the Preparatoria Popular Emiliano Zapata (called Prepa Zapata).[11] As part of Puebla's university reform movement, begun in 1961, a group of progressive professors created this high school specifically for nontraditional, working-class students whose academic record was below average and who had not been accepted to the other state university-affiliated high school, the Preparatoria Benito Juárez. Giving working-class students an opportunity to study at the Prepa Zapata provided them with the training to pursue a college degree at the UAP and then, at least in theory, advance up the socioeconomic ladder. The Prepa Zapata opened its doors with scant financial resources in the second semester of 1969, receiving 617 students.[12] By January 1970 it already had 830 students enrolled, a sign of pent-up working-class demand for higher education.[13] During the first three years the approximately eighty-eight teachers who taught at the Prepa Zapata worked for free because the university did not have a budget assigned to this new school.[14] Their teaching was a commitment to transform the university system into one that served the needs of an increasing urban and working-class population.

Before enrolling at the Prepa Zapata, students had attended public elementary and secondary schools such as the Escuela Flores Magón, which, in an ironic twist of history, was a public night school for workers and their children. Some of these children held jobs during the day to bring money home. One of the students who later joined the vendors' struggle was José Luis Díaz, whose single mother had moved with two of her children from the town of Mizantla, Veracruz, to the city of Puebla. At age fourteen Díaz began working in a textile factory during the day and attended the Flores Magón at night. Like many migrants, both vendors or blue-collar workers, Diaz's family did not have a permanent residence; instead they lived with another family member in Puebla. Díaz would later contend that he empathized with street vendors because they both lacked a stable home.[15] Omar Castro also became involved with the vendors' struggle; he too was a nontraditional student who attended the Flores Magón and later the Prepa Zapata. Every summer he worked in the muddy, humid forest in the Can-Cún area to help sustain his family.[16]

In addition to sharing a similar class background, both young students and street vendors faced the challenge of trying to incorporate themselves as recent migrants into the dynamics of urban life; students sought secure places to study, and vendors sought secure places to sell. Both groups were part of the urban poor and the working class who fought for alternatives to survive in an urban setting that marginalized them. For the students, defending the existence of the Prepa Zapata was a constant challenge. Threatened by the admission of lower-class students to the university system, conservative and elitist groups at the UAP tried to close down the Prepa Zapata; they wanted to reserve the university as a space for the children of the upper and middle classes. Equally important, the teachers and professors who supported the creation of the Prepa Zapata were members of left-wing groups, including the Partido Comunista Mexicano (Mexican Communist Party, PCM). Conservative groups accused all of these progressives of being communists, and thus a danger to the university and to society.[17] The support that poor students received from progressive groups within the university was an affront to those who sought to protect their class status from the "dangers" the masses presumably posed to middle- and upper-class students.[18] For instance, conservatives stated that the Prepa Zapata students suffered from mental disabilities, which explained their low grades, and also blamed their teachers for promoting prostitution and drug addiction among students.[19]

Conservatives also had political reasons to dislike the Prepa Zapata. The high school represented an achievement for the professors, teachers, students, and administrators who had supported the left-leaning university reform movement. As part of this reform, progressive groups opened the doors of higher education to urban and rural workers and their children by providing a public high school with different shifts that allowed them to attend school after their work day ended. In this sense the Preparatoria Popular Emiliano Zapata lived up to its name; it was "popular" because it was accessible to the working class. The emergence of the so-called popular high schools was part of a broader effort also occurring in Mexico City. Indeed the supporters of the university reform movement were responding to a national trend: a constant flow of rural migrants to urban areas who did not find study spaces in the cities. In the case of Puebla, up to 1969 the state university had only one public high school, the Preparatoria Benito Juárez, which was not large enough to receive an increasing number of students; in that year over a thousand students could not attend because there were no seats available.[20] Officially recognized in 1973 as a university-affiliated school, the Prepa Zapata represented a success for the progressive reformers.

The first students to attend the Prepa Zapata began to make the school their own by getting rid of some bourgeois activities that were common at the UAP. They banned the famous hazing rituals (*novatadas*) that were so popular among conservative college students in Puebla. Novatadas derived their meaning from the word *novatos* (new students). Novatadas have a long history in Mexico and elsewhere. Hazing rituals were often public or semipublic practices in which senior students forced new students to act as subordinates.[21] In Puebla these practices regularly had the support of conservative university authorities. The mostly male student body considered them rites of initiation, rituals to welcome new students to the university setting. These activities included the *paseos de perro*, the parading of new students (also known as *perros*, "dogs") through the streets nearly naked; *los corridos* (the runaways), in which senior students forced freshmen to steal cigarettes and drinks for them; and the *empeño de perros* (pawning of dogs), in which new students were forced to treat senior students to meals at fancy restaurants. Having no money to pay the bill, the new students had to work in these restaurants until someone paid the bill and "retrieved" the students. While in other university settings and at other times, such as the 1940s and 1950s in Mexico City, students enjoyed hazing rituals and even employed them to demonstrate their adaptability to urban areas and demonstrate their masculinity, other students strongly contested and despised these practices. Not only could working-class students at the Prepa Zapata not afford these practices, but these practices put them in danger of arrest in the repressive early 1970s.[22]

In this context the Prepa Zapata students and their teachers fought to maintain a space in the university system by keeping the school open and working together to improve it. In addition to its institutional survival, the Prepa Zapata was one of the most marginalized of the public schools in the city. Its classrooms used to be labs for chemistry majors, a program that had been relocated to a new campus on the periphery of the city. Classrooms were dark, humid, and not suitable for a high school.[23] Lacking benches and blackboards, students sought to ameliorate their school's conditions by asking for monetary assistance from the community. They organized informal fundraising campaigns on buses, on street corners, and in markets in what they called *boteo* because they used empty cans (*botes*) to collect money. In interviews former students remembered that the urban working class was the one group that typically shared its scant resources; for instance, the students received small but constant contributions from street vendors.[24] Students and vendors spent long periods of time in public spaces—often in the same streets—where they developed a shared distrust of authorities, especially when they confronted police repression. Students in the long 1960s were not only fundraising on the streets to improve their school condition but also rallied downtown for other purposes.

Since at least 1961, when university reform started, and well into the 1970s Poblano students protested a combination of local and national problems that included repression and lack of democracy. Students recalled the railroad strikes of 1958–59 and the political prisoners from those conflicts, who were still in jail almost a decade later. Indeed students made one of the railroad workers' demands their own: freedom for political prisoners. In 1964 some students had attended with their parents the protests against Puebla's governor Gen. Antonio Nava Castillo, whose business ambitions led him to acts of repression against his detractors. In

1968 some Poblano students sympathized with and supported students in Mexico City and directly or indirectly witnessed the increasing repression of the time. Others, especially female students, became more involved in politics. The Poblano students who participated in the local 1968 student movement organized brigades that made and distributed fliers, produced banners, collected money, and went to public demonstrations in Mexico City like the Great Silence March of September 13, 1968.[25]

These were the political activities that put New Left students at odds with authorities and in close contact with vendors. And authorities did not hesitate to use violence to remove students and vendors from the streets. In the case of the students, state repression was particularly acute from 1970 to 1973, as these were the most politically contentious years of university reform in Puebla.

UNIVERSITY REFORM

The fight over the Prepa Zapata's creation and survival occurred within the context of university reform. In the early 1970s young people in Mexico's province were still engaged in university reform movements that had started in the 1950s. At the UAP reform began in 1961 and consisted of various changes whose main objective was to transform the university into an institution that was attuned to Mexico's social needs. The leaders of university reform were progressive students, professors, and administrators who fought for the education of the popular masses and for the improvement of the institution by updating its curricula, modernizing the libraries and laboratories, and increasing the faculty's wages, among other changes.[26] These progressives, some of whom were members of the PCM, wanted to transform the university into what they deemed a "popular, democratic, and critical" institution ("universidad popular, crítica y democrática"). In order to make it popular (belonging to the common people), reformers sought to increase the number of students from working-class backgrounds; thus the Prepa Zapata was created. Another strategy was to establish alliances with independent unions such as electrical workers and automobile workers at the Volkswagen plant. These alliances sought to bring much-needed support to university reform as well as continue creating a student presence in the political life of the city.

Conservative administrators, professors, and students sought to neutralize the progressives' efforts to democratize the university. In the early 1970s they relied on support from Puebla's Catholic Church hierarchy, business associations, newspaper editors, and the avilacamachista machine, namely Governor Rafael Moreno Valle (1969–72) and his successor, the ultraconservative Gonzalo Bautista O'Farrill (April 1972 to May 1973). Conservative groups tried to maintain their eroded power by denigrating and physically assaulting progressive groups and by creating a "moral panic." In a media campaign they called the progressives communists and accused them of introducing drugs and pornography to Puebla.[27] More important, conservative forces engaged in violent attacks against left-wing students and administrators, who were gaining more power within the university and were challenging the dominant position of the avilacamachistas. And the PRI regime had no monopoly on violence. Right-wing groups also employed "agent provocateurs and intermediaries inside the schools."[28]

REPRESSION

During the UAP's reform movement, students and administrators became targets of repression. Since 1964 progressive groups had been gaining popularity and power, a process that climaxed in 1972. In June Sergio Flores Suárez, a member of the PCM, became the UAP's interim president. Three months later he was chosen as UAP president for a three-year term.[29] His election was a huge victory for left-wing groups at the state university. For the first time in the history of the university, a member of the PCM, not an avilacamachista civilian or military officer, occupied the highest post in the administration.

The election of Flores did not go unchallenged. In what seemed to be a desperate effort to destroy progressive and left-wing tendencies at the UAP, Governor Bautista O'Farrill and his allies ordered state agents to attack students and key administrators they perceived as a political threat. Joel Arriaga was a former student who participated in the 1968 student movement in Mexico City and was later imprisoned at the Lecumberri Prison; he was an active member of the PCM and the founder of Puebla's communist youth (*juventud comunista*).[30] As part of Echeverría's democratic opening, federal authorities released him from prison in 1972.[31] Arriaga was committed to the education of the urban and rural popular classes, and he went to Puebla and became the director of the Preparatoria Benito Juárez. On July 21, 1972, unidentified gunmen shot and killed him in Puebla, while he and his wife were in their car, stopped at a traffic light. Some people linked his assassination to Governor Bautista O'Farrill, Archbishop Octaviano Márquez y Toriz, and right-wing students from the Frente Universitario Anti-comunista.[32] All of them, however, claimed that they had nothing to do with Arriaga's murder, which has remained unsolved.

State and right-wing groups' violence did not end with the killing of Joel Arriaga. Months later, on December 20, 1972, gunmen killed Professor Enrique Cabrera, who had a long history of left-wing activism at the UAP and who had coordinated student political activities in rural areas. The height of the violence, however, took place on Labor Day, May 1, 1973. By then the governor had increased the number of police officers patrolling the university and its surroundings, and the number of detentions for minor political activities, such as allegedly possessing Marxist literature, had risen.[33] Instead of killing administrators, Bautista O'Farrill targeted young college and preparatory school students. During Labor Day commemorations four students—Alfonso Calderón Moreno, Ignacio González Román, José Norberto Suárez Lara, and Victor Manuel Medina Cuevas—were shot to death by snipers. Two days later police and paramilitary groups killed another five students. One of them, an eighteen-year-old high school student named Gilberto Chávez Ávila, was savagely beaten to death on the street.[34] According to the governor, "The police carried out the order to kill anyone who threatens public peace or who attempts to kidnap police officers."[35] By murdering these students, Bautista shamelessly hoped to thwart other students' left-wing political activism.[36]

In this context of violence and heightened police presence, students feared for their lives every time they took to the streets to rally. But repression did not deter them; it further politicized them. They called for popular groups to join them and to protest these authoritarian and violent acts. Students called Bautista O'Farrill a fascist and issued fliers and made speeches in which they identified the governor as the culprit in the killing of the students, Arriaga, and Cabrera. In a propaganda piece students portrayed Bautista O'Farrill as Adolf Hitler.[37] Students also organized a series of protests in which they demanded the investigation of Arriaga's assassination; for example, on July 26, 1972, a few days after Arriaga's murder, they organized a march attended by some fifteen thousand people.

Vendors, peasants, taxi drivers, and electrical and railroad workers joined the students. These events were open to all, allowing many to air their own demands. For example, street vendors demanded that authorities decrease the fees they paid to the city government for the use of public space.[38] This was only one of many events in which street vendors, not yet formally organized, recognized the advantages of collective action and alliances with other groups.

Puebla's state-led violence during 1972 and 1973 apparently unnerved President Luis Echeverría, who decided to depose Puebla's governor in May 1973.[39] Bautista O'Farrill was the third and last of Puebla's governors deposed by the executive. For all the power Mexican presidents had, they removed governors only in extraordinary circumstances, when the governors failed to preserve political stability between the local and federal governments. Governors usually found themselves in trouble when they disregarded presidential policies and when they used their power excessively.[40] Bautista O'Farrill fulfilled all these criteria. The repression and murders of students and administrators undermined Echeverría's rhetoric of a democratic opening. Moreover Bautista O'Farrill belonged to the last vestiges of the avilacamachista cacicazgo, a group that had been at odds with the Echeverría administration. Puebla's political elite, which was closely associated with the avilacamachistas, had criticized and labeled Echeverría's close aides communists. The executive decision to depose the governor stemmed from Echeverría's tendency to destroy his political

enemies.[41] A new group of politicians who were not part of the avilacamachista machine took power after the fall of Bautista O'Farrill. The new
governor, Guillermo Morales Blumenkron (1973–75), was supposedly
more conciliatory and loyal to the president, and his administration ended
the repression of students. Later targets of violence were not students,
but their allies, the street vendors. Regardless of which group was in
power, repression remained a constant feature of the vendor experience.

POLITICIZATION OF STUDENTS

Material experiences, namely class background, migration, marginalization
in the urban setting, and repression, partially explain the political alliance
between students and street vendors. The eclectic left-wing ideology that
students acquired at the university helps us understand their involvement
with street vendors in the long term. The political climate brought on
by university reform provided a radical setting wherein students and,
later, street vendors became further politicized. The UAP offered various spaces where students questioned and advanced ideas about social
change. Progressive sectors at the university, among them affiliates of
the PCM, New Left activists such as self-identified Maoists, hosted a
number of activities that were open to students and the general public.
Some of the most progressive minds of the time presented talks at the
university and were welcomed by crowds. For example, a leading Mexican
liberation theologian, Sergio Méndez Arceo, called the "Red Bishop" of
Cuernavaca diocese in the state of Morelos, visited Puebla's state university
several times. In 1970 he was invited by leaders of one of the popular high
schools to take part in a series of activities commemorating the Cuban
Revolution.[42] He delivered at least one speech in front of hundreds of
students. Immediately after his talk was a question-and-answer session,
which lasted over three hours. One of Méndez Arceo's main messages
was that, unlike capitalism, socialism is compatible with Christianity.
Socialism, he argued, is more akin to the Christian principles of true
fraternity, peace, and justice.[43] Other priests, who were forced by the
conservative hierarchy to leave the Catholic Church because of their
political views, also visited the university. In June 1971 Felipe Pardiñas,

a former Jesuit, gave a talk to students in which he discussed Mao's ideas on the people's revolution.[44] The Belgian monk Gregorio Lemercier was also invited; he was based in Cuernavaca and had close connections with Méndez Arceo.[45] Inviting militant priests to campus was a radical act, especially because many students, professors, and administrators were conservative Catholics who, together with the religious hierarchy in Puebla, perceived liberation theologians and their sympathizers as communists and attacked them accordingly through the press.[46]

Méndez Arceo and liberation theology in general had an ideological impact on students, who appropriated the language of liberation for their own political purposes. The word *liberation* itself was used by students in Latin America in their rhetoric of dissent.[47] Fliers and pamphlets that students produced in the early 1970s exemplified the extent of this influence. In a flier that publicized the visit of the Red Bishop to the UAP in 1970, students from one of the groups that planned events and spread propaganda, the *comités de lucha* (fight committees, or committees of struggle), drew a church tower beside the following text: "The rich won't be saved. Just like Mary, we must recognize that God walks along the poor and the humble on their way to their own LIBERATION. . . . The rich and powerful [should] reflect on their acts and be liberated from the sin of exploitation. . . . This is the true road that Christians follow. We, the workers, the peasants, and the students have chosen this road."[48] Students were class-conscious and understood university reform as a class struggle between the poor and the rich, and some used the language of liberation theology as a way to communicate their message.

By reversing the Catholic language of obedience and passivity, students expressed their criticism toward the conservative Catholic hierarchy and its strong relation to politically powerful elites, including the president. Students appropriated Catholic prayers, altered them, and mocked the Church, the PRI, and President Luis Echeverría Álvarez (LEA):

Padre LEA
Padre LEA que estás en los Pinos
Muy publicado sea tu nombre

Y disfruta de tus viajes
Asi en México como en el extranjero
El PRI nuestro de todos los días
Quítanoslo hoy
Y perdona nuestros impuestos
Asi como nosotros perdonamos a tus trinqueteros
Y no nos dejes caer en la debaluación [*sic*]
Y libranos del santo clero.⁴⁹

Our Father LEA
Our Father LEA who is in Los Pinos,
widely published is your name.
Enjoy your trips
in Mexico and abroad
Take away the PRI this day
And forgive us our taxes
As we forgive your scammers
And lead us not into devaluation,
And deliver us from the holy clergy.

NATIONAL AND LATIN AMERICAN POLITICS

Contemporary political events in Latin America also contributed to the politicization of students. Since the triumph of the Cuban Revolution of 1959 the university's progressive sectors had become loyal supporters of the new revolutionary regime. In many ways this support was symbolic. Throughout the 1970s the university showed dozens of films and documentaries produced on the island and students gathered to discuss them. In 1970 the Prepa Zapata commemorated the third anniversary of Ernesto (Che) Guevara's death; students showed their creativity by writing poems that praised his revolutionary deeds.⁵⁰ In September 1971 leaders at the Preparatoria Populares organized Las Semanas del Guerrillero Heroico (Weeks of the Heroic Guerrilla), a series of talks and Cuban films in homage to Che.⁵¹

University students also learned about the right-wing regimes in the Southern Cone and their human rights abuses. On September 11, 1974, exactly a year after the military coup in Chile ended the democratically elected socialist government of Salvador Allende, a group of approximately three thousand students, teachers, workers, and "gente de condición humilde" (humble people) marched on the streets of Puebla in solidarity with the Chilean people and against the military junta.[52] Progressive faculty took their teaching outside the classroom, and the "gente de condición humilde," which in this context referred to the uneducated and poor, had a chance to learn and reflect about Latin American politics.

National politics and recent Mexican history also shaped the political consciousness of the youth. Contrary to the Pax Priísta, which proposed that the 1940s to 1968 was a prolonged peaceful period, students were aware of the past and present social discontent and political struggles in urban and rural areas all over the country. These included the Jaramillistas of Morelos, the railroad strikes of 1958–59, the teachers' strikes of 1958, rural rebellions in Guerrero, medical doctors' strikes, and student movements throughout the long 1960s.[53] For instance, family members of Rubén Sarabia Sánchez (known as Simitrio), a student who became the main leader of the UPVA, had participated in the railroad workers' movement.[54]

The students at the UAP became the ideological heirs of these movements, especially of the student movement. Poblano students used many of their predecessors' organizational strategies and forms of protests. Students at the UAP inherited the "new student culture" that began with the 1956 strike at Mexico City's Instituto Politécnico Nacional.[55] As the historian Jaime Pensado has shown, from the mid-1950s on, students used new forms of "direct action" when many other passive ways of negotiating with authorities had not been successful. These innovative and confrontational strategies included organizing informational brigades and *mítines relámpago* (brief political rallies or quick political meetings); hijacking buses, especially the Las Palmas, one of the most popular routes at the time; and taking over buildings.[56] Just like their counterparts in Mexico City, Puebla's students organized into brigades (small groups in charge

FIG. 5. A bus painted with a student slogan: "Luis Echeverría Álvarez [LEA] assassin." Courtesy of Archivo Histórico BUAP, Colección Vida Universitaria, 25AU-05/919, box 3.

of a specific task). They used the buses as barricades to block traffic and as a political stage, climbing on to the roof to addressing fellow students and the general public. They painted the buses (the so-called *pintas*) with slogans, demands, or criticisms of authority. The university building most often targeted for takeover was El Carolino, the heart of the downtown campus, a former Jesuit convent that housed most departments and administrative offices at the UAP. Students conveyed their messages through mítines relámpago at schools, open-air and enclosed markets, and the zócalo.[57] Street vendors incorporated these same strategies for their own struggle.

The social unrest that continued into the early 1970s in Puebla was also fueled by the memory of the Tlatelolco massacre in Mexico City. On October 2, 1968, the Mexican state killed students and bystanders gathered in the Tlatelolco Plaza in Mexico City protesting police brutality, violations of the Constitution, and the single-party rule of the PRI.[58]

The massacre inspired student activists to continue fighting against state authoritarianism, a fight that had begun in the mid-1950s.[59] Although it was not a complete turning point for student reform in Puebla, Tlatelolco was fresh in the minds and experiences of the young people involved with vendors and other workers. A former student argues that for Poblano female students, Tlatelolco represented a departure as more and more women participated in political activities at the university. These newly politicized women questioned and challenged more forcefully the notions of the patriarchal, authoritarian family and unequal relationships within couples, and they pushed the boundaries of conservative sexual behavior, especially in relation to marriage. Some of the female students joined their *compañeros* in fighting against repression and protesting the suffering they experienced under the leadership of an intolerant local government.[60]

Certainly after Tlatelolco the state continued to police students, and the number of student detainees increased.[61] Bulmaro Vega León, the union organizer and a former student at the UNAM who married the street vendor Teresa Rosales, was detained in its immediate aftermath. Rosales and close friends said Vega had been lucky to escape the massacre, allegedly by covering himself with the body of a dead student. Instead of quitting his activism, Vega moved to Puebla to organize vendors and welders.

TEACHERS AND PROFESSORS

UAP's high school teachers and professors played an essential role in politicizing students. In the early 1970s, thanks to university reform, left-wing faculty had academic freedom and were able to expose students to revolutionary writers such as Marx, Engels, Lenin, and Mao. These radical philosophies gave students hope; Marxism in particular stressed the importance of collective action against inequality and oppression. Equally important, the students would later introduce these texts to the vendors.

One of these young teachers was Bulmaro Vega León. A genuine working-class intellectual, Vega read political science, theory, and history texts late into the night. Always surrounded by books and pamphlets, he taught at the Prepa Zapata and introduced his high school students to the ideas of Marx and Mao.[62] One of his students said, "Bulmaro taught us the basic tenets of Maoism."[63] In the 1960s, prior to moving to Puebla, Vega studied in Mexico City's UNAM, where Maoist circles were very active. One of them was the Sociedad de Amistad México-China (Mexico-China Friendship Society), which was founded in 1957 by Luis Torres Ordoñez. An active member was Esther Chapa Tijerina, a professor of microbiology at the UNAM, who organized appealing talks on Chinese affairs and whose ideology called for a prolonged people's war and on studying Mao's thought. One of the Society's main activities consisted of distributing Chinese literature in Mexico. Among the publications the Society distributed were the *Peking Review*, *China Reconstruye* (China Reconstructs), *La Nueva China* (the New China), and *China Popular* (Popular China). The *Peking Review*, a weekly Chinese news magazine discussing international relations, was one of the magazines that students in Puebla read and discussed with vendors.[64] According to a former student, Mao's Cultural Revolution influenced students to form study groups and to visit the Chinese embassy, where they received pamphlets, posters, and books filled with Maoist ideas.[65]

When teaching, Vega was a pragmatist who stressed that students needed to apply Maoism flexibly to social conditions in Mexico. Vega was not the exception; other Maoists in Mexico and Latin America "domesticated" Maoism to fit local conditions.[66] Vega believed that an alliance linking formal and informal workers, as well as peasants and factory workers, could challenge the state, disturb the status quo, and ultimately achieve radical change.[67] These ideas appealed to some of his students in the Prepa Zapata because of the inequality they experienced and observed on the streets. These students began to situate themselves politically as Maoists and called themselves the *mamecas*. They were mainly working-class students who disengaged from the PCM, which represented the institutionalized and traditional left. The mamecas believed that once PCM members had taken over the state university administration, they sold out and no longer cared about the common people outside the university. As Maoists these students felt more authentic and more closely related to the masses. The Prepa Zapata students did not get paid to live among the poor or the masses and did not have to become proletarian.[68] They were already proletarian.

In addition Maoist students did not follow the narrow directives imposed by the PCM at the UAP; they were disillusioned when the university administration under the PCM did not support vendors.[69] These young Maoists perceived street vendors as a mixture of urban and rural folks who could achieve social change through their involvement in student-led popular groups such as the Frente de Autodefensa del Pueblo, an organization that UAP students had created. The historian Mathew Rothwell is correct in suggesting that "by the time that Mexico's long 1960s began, Maoist ideas had gained sufficient traction in Mexico to play a significant role in the social movements of the period."[70] These young students helped organize vendors and even made vendors memorize Mao's *Little Red Book*.

Students and vendors were the emerging actors of the New Left, which, according to Barry Carr, stood in opposition to "a despotic state," was ideologically diverse (in this case drawing on Maoism), incorporated women in greater numbers, and had new ways of struggle.[71] Equally important, the New Left supported independent unions because of their historical fight for democracy.[72] With or without knowing it, students and vendors shaped the political contours of the long 1960s.

THE STUDENT-VENDOR ALLIANCE

While some students acquired a left-wing ideology in the university setting and classroom, street vendors faced economic problems on a daily basis, hardships that made them aware of the need to organize effectively and to search for allies. As I discussed in the previous chapter, by the early 1970s police repression and harassment, removals, constant seizures of merchandise, expensive fees, bribes, and charro leaders had forced Puebla's street vendors to seek effective ways to defend what they considered their right to a downtown space where they could sell their merchandise and survive economically. Vendors saw students as possible allies. They had interacted with students during the university reform movement, donating money for material improvements to the Prepa Zapata. Students showed up on street corners in their *mítines relámpago*, and vendors reciprocated by joining students' marches. Each group had something to gain from the other.

The event that made students most famous on the popular political scene was the *lechero* conflict. Small milk sellers on bicycles, the *lecheros*, sold thousands of liters of raw milk to approximately twenty thousand families. Governor Antonio Nava Castillo, another avilacamachista, along with a group of politicians and businessmen, sought to open a large pasteurization plant and to monopolize the distribution and commercialization of milk. Threatened with the loss of their livelihood, the lecheros resisted the governor's plan and university students supported them. On October 13, 1964, the lecheros organized a peaceful march, pressuring the state to provide them with a loan to open a pasteurization cooperative.[73] University students joined the march, which the government opposed with violence. Governor Nava Castillo ordered the police to use tear gas and arrest dozens of protestors. The next day the police attacked students at the university for their participation in the march.[74] After this episode students and milk sellers became allies and together organized more demonstrations against the governor, which in turn led to more violence. On October 28 the police rounded up and beat a brigade of young students when they painted slogans on the walls (*pintas*) against the government.[75]

President Adolfo López Mateos (1958–64) objected to these violent acts against the milkmen and students; the authorities had had disagreements with Nava Castillo before this. On October 29, 1964, facing pressure from milkmen, students, and the federal government, Nava Castillo stepped down.[76] Afterward students established other links with other labor unions and popular organizations. In 1967, for instance, they provided support to workers at Camisetas de Puebla, a maker of T-shirts, where twenty-five workers were fired unjustly.[77] These connections were necessary for students to gain support for their university reform.[78] Throughout the mid-1960s and 1970s different groups of Puebla's students allied with railroad workers of the Consejo General Ferrocarrilero (Railroad General

Council), with independent teachers from the Movimiento Revolucionario Magisterial (Revolutionary Teachers Movement), with peasants
of the Confederación Campesina Independiente (Independent Peasant
Organization, CCI), and with street vendors. Indeed Puebla's progressive
student movement became the center of a number of Poblano resistance
groups.[79] Certainly not all university students supported the plight of
the working class. Conservative university students were immersed in
their own fight against what they considered left-wing students' threats
to morality and to the teachings of the Catholic Church.[80]

The students' reputation for militancy traveled by word of mouth.
In 1970 a friend from Zumiatla, Puebla, who belonged to the CCI, told
Juana Sánchez that students at the state university helped poor people.
Sánchez was one of the many street vendors whose livelihood was at stake
on a daily basis. In her memory of those days, many problems haunted
her sleep; most of all she worried that her meager sales were not enough
to feed her family. Although almost all of her ten children sold goods on
the streets, they were constantly losing their merchandise during police
raids. She needed to change this situation. One morning she and one of
her daughters entered the UAP in search of students who would support
her and her fellow vendors. She was clear and firm: "I'm a street vendor,
I'm illiterate and I know that you help the poor. Inspectors constantly
take away our merchandise and we lose everything. We need help."[81]

The young students that Juana addressed were receptive to her plight
and decided to help. Over the next few days students and about four
hundred vendors held meetings at El Carolino, the main university building, in which both groups strategized how to best approach authorities.
According to secret police files, students helped the sellers draft their
proposals to local authorities, which included the retrieval of seized
vendor merchandise from market managers and police, the ability to sell
in streets around La Victoria market, and freedom for the vendors who
were arrested for selling fruits and vegetables in public spaces.[82]

The student-vendor alliance was mutually beneficial. In the early 1970s
vendors helped students take over buildings and hijack buses, and both
attended marches, meetings, and sit-ins. At the beginning of 1971, when

FIG. 6. Downtown protest by students and vendors. Courtesy of Archivo General Municipal de Puebla, image 927, Administración Municipal, 1975–78.

college and high school students took over El Carolino, the students relied on street vendors to feed them.[83] A former student, Maria Luisa, recalls "Keeping us [students] fed and warm was an essential task for the success of the university reform." According to students, vendors were able to sneak in small boxes of fruits and women prepared *tortas* and tacos. Yolanda Bejarano recalls how her mother, who was also a seller, used to give students cigarettes and coffee to cheer and warm them. She was such a thoughtful older woman that students and activists nicknamed her *la abuelita*, the affectionate term for "grandmother." Everyone knew her and her house because she provided shelter to students who were hounded by the police and who sought a safe place.[84]

Street vendors also participated in the many marches that students organized. Together students and vendors protested the murder of students at the UAP in the early 1970s. Street vendors became quite vocal about their support and commitment to the students and Puebla's politics. In a 1974 meeting to protest the murder of the student Guillermo Ramírez Alvarado, a female vendor publicly declared that all vendors were eager to do whatever it took to solve the murder case.[85]

THE MAKING OF THE UNION

The idea of organizing an independent street vendors' union with the support of students did not materialize until the end of October 1973. As mentioned earlier, the politicians who took power in Puebla after the fall of Bautista O'Farrill were more conciliatory and ended the repression of students and university authorities, but the situation was very different with respect to street vendors. Although the use of force by local authorities against vendors was nothing new, the situation became more explosive. At 1 a.m. on October 28 hordes of police began expelling hundreds of vendors from downtown streets. Officers tore down and torched dozens of stalls. Over the course of a few hours the police destroyed merchandise and beat sellers, forcing men, women, and children to run for their lives. From the vendors' perspective, the timing of the raid could not have been worse. The Day of the Dead, All Souls' Day on the Catholic calendar and one of Mexico's most sacred religious holidays, was approaching, and vendors had anticipated busy days of selling the traditional items people placed in the altars to their dead: flowers, incense, bread, fruit, and candles. As was customary, the vendors had slept on the street with their families to secure the best spots to sell their merchandise. Yet city authorities cared little for vendors' needs and safety. According to witnesses, officers drove their cars on sidewalks, killing three people and injuring many others. The most disturbing casualty was a vendor's baby, who burned to death after police set merchandise and stalls on fire.[86] According to Bejarano, some of the vendors knew that something bad was about to happen:

> A very old fee collector told us that they were going to beat us up. We used to sell outside of Almacenes Muñoz, and we were waiting for them [collectors] to come charge us the fees, but the old man said we were going to be beaten. On the corner of 8 Poniente Street, they

killed [vendor] Mr. Erasto Cabrera, and on 3 Norte Street, they killed the child. He burned. We could only see part of his blanket [on fire]. We were beaten really bad. I ended up in the hospital, but hospitals refused to take us in. [We] vendors went to the university and students came with us and made sure that hospitals took care of us. There I met Javier Elivar, a medical student; he was the one who made sure that they took me in. They only put on a bandage and didn't even give me a painkiller and the bandage was loose. He [Elivar] told me, "Don't worry because your injuries are seeking revenge [No te preocupes porque tus golpes están siendo bien vengados]."[87]

Elivar's words were prophetic. Instead of leaving the streets in defeat, the vendors struck back during the last days of October. In an impressive act of resistance, female and male vendors armed themselves with sticks and Molotov cocktails. They set police cars on fire and beat police officers. Bejarano remembers, "Police were being beaten up. Streets were blocked so they [vendors and students] could get the police officers. On October 28, the compañeros burned police trucks on 8 Poniente and 3 Norte streets, right where vendors had died. . . . We became fearless because we realized that we could defeat the police." After the violent confrontation, and with the help of sympathetic students, between five hundred and eight hundred vendors set up their stalls on the sidewalks. They were determined to reoccupy their vending spaces, and they were ultimately successful.[88]

Vendors set up their stalls on downtown streets surrounding La Victoria market all the way to the Cinco de Mayo market, the busiest and most commercially active spots in town. Vendors sold there for thirteen years, from the fall of 1973 to the summer of 1986, without facing major violent removals from authorities. Collectively street vendors secured the public spaces necessary to make a living. However, they had no desire to engage in a prolonged campaign of violence; instead they had to find ways to defend themselves systematically for the long term. For this reason they did not think twice when students encouraged them to form a union to defend themselves against local politicians, economic elites, police, and abusive fee collectors.

Organizing the union was not an extraordinarily difficult task; vendors, especially the women, had already developed relationships with one another for many years.[89] They had confronted similar problems—removals, harassment, and violence from municipal officials—many times before. And vendors and students had been working together for the past three years during the university reform movement.

THE FORMAL ORGANIZATION OF THE UPVA

A few days after the October raid around four hundred vendors decided to form a union with the ideological and practical support of the students.[90] The students were enthusiastic about becoming leaders and offering ideological guidance to the vendors. The formation of the union gave students a chance to put into practice what they had learned in the classroom, and street vendors were open to learning new political skills and ready to continue their economic struggle.

Initially vendors called their union the Unión de Vendedores Ambulantes Emiliano Zapata in honor of the revolutionary leader and in recognition of the students of Prepa Zapata. They changed it to Unión Popular de Vendedores Ambulantes, later renaming it UPVA–28 de Octubre in remembrance of the violent police raid in October 1973.[91] Over the years the organization became known as "la 28" or "la 28 de Octubre." The choice of name was crucial because vendors were giving their organization political significance, keeping alive the memory of the repression they had suffered at the hands of the government.

The vendor union had three immediate goals. First, vendors demanded that local authorities allow them to keep stalls for UPVA members in downtown streets without police crackdowns and seizure of merchandise. This would allow vendors to make an honest living, as guaranteed in the 1917 Constitution. Second, members demanded an end to fees and bribes to local authorities. Third, vendors, especially women, demanded that authorities build at least one enclosed market downtown where they could rent fixed stalls, be protected from police removals, and have basic services—running water, a roof, electricity, and bathrooms—to facilitate their productive, reproductive, and political labors.[92]

FIG. 7. Touring a possible site for an enclosed market. Courtesy of Archivo General Municipal de Puebla, unnumbered image, Administración Municipal, 1975–78.

BUILDING THE UNION STRUCTURE AND IDEOLOGY

Vendors and students wanted the UPVA to differentiate itself from charro unions, which were affiliated with the ruling party, the PRI, which in turn selected union leaders who, in many instances, did little to defend the interests of the rank and file and who occupied the same position for long periods of time. Official union members did not participate in decision making and lacked a mechanism to voice their concerns. In order to avoid these traits vendors and students created a different structure for the UPVA. Both vendors and students wanted an organization that truly defended vendors' interests, in which vendors could elect their own representatives and shape the union's political orientation.

To start, leaders of both groups recruited as many vendors as possible to participate in union activities. They formed different commissions for various tasks: conflict resolution, negotiation, finance, politics, and culture. The political commission was in charge of drafting vendor demands and making arrangements to meet with local authorities to present those demands. At the beginning of 1975, for example, the political commission demanded that municipal authorities build an adequate and functional market in downtown.[93] The conflict resolution and negotiation groups aimed to preserve harmony within the union. The finance commission took care of collecting and administering union fees. The cultural commission was in charge of promoting art. These commissions allowed many vendors to be part of a community of peers. For UPVA members like Teresa Rosales, union democracy meant taking part in the day-to-day union activities, learning skills, and participating in political acts. Rosales fondly recounted her time on the propaganda commission, where she learned how to use the printing press to produce fliers to hand out to fellow vendors. This was an activity she never thought she could perform. Rosa Martínez remembered the pride she felt when her compañeros elected her treasurer. Within her section she was the only person who knew how to read and write, a crucial fact in her election. Union democracy meant that she could directly participate in the commissions.[94]

To break away from one of the charro leadership characteristics the union would hold regular elections. A former student who was involved in the organization of the union recalled, "We didn't want *caudillos*. We needed to rotate the leadership positions because *caudillos* sold out."[95] The student used the term *caudillo* to refer to the authoritarian behavior of the unelected charro leaders. To avoid falling into the same trap, vendors elected their own representatives, and those elected could hold their leadership position for only six months; after that period elections for new representatives took place. Leadership positions included street coordinators who were in charge of gathering information about vendors' needs and problems in each street. They also publicized the UPVA's events and marches and encouraged people to attend. These coordinators attended the General Assembly, a forum where they and other members of the UPVA met to expose vendors' problems and find solutions. Street coordinators also organized smaller assemblies where they informed vendors about the issues discussed at the General Assembly. By 1977 a typical General Assembly was attended by about twenty street coordinators; in 1979 by around fifty; and in 1980 by approximately seventy.[96]

With this model, street vendors were adopting organizational practices and structure from the student movement. UAP students had met in general assemblies during university reform; they themselves had borrowed the structure from their counterparts in Mexico City, who created assemblies as alternative and democratic organizations during their movement in 1958.[97] The vendors' assemblies were quite inclusive. In these meetings vendors and their leaders discussed a broad range of topics. It was important to establish democratic features within these assemblies; therefore all participants could vote, pass resolutions, and suggest discussion items for the next assembly. The general assembly was also a place for solving grievances. When Bejarano was a street coordinator, her compañeros gathered in an assembly, discussed a mistake she made with union fees, and decided to expel her from the position. "The fact that vendors had a voice in union activities was a democracy," Bejarano said.[98] At one assembly with more than fifty street coordinators, their leader, Simitrio, proposed an increase in the union fees to five pesos a week. The coordinators rejected the proposal, leaving the fee at two pesos. The money paid for UPVA expenses and helped support other organizations such as the Unión Campesina Independiente (Independent Peasant Union) of northern Puebla, Consejo General Campesino (General Peasant Council, CGC), and the Casa del Estudiante Poblano in Mexico City. Simitrio accepted the coordinators' decision.[99] The union's political and financial independence from the PRI allowed vendors to decide what to do with the fees they collected, and it democratically set low fees that vendors could afford.

IDEOLOGICAL TRAINING

One of the main strengths of the UPVA is that it remained independent of the PRI. In a country famous for the ruling party's co-optation of unions, this success was due precisely to the alliance that the vendors had forged with students. Students exposed street vendors, especially the leadership, to left-wing political ideologies, which helped vendors make sense of their day-to-day reality and become even more critical of the state and especially of the PRI. After a long day of selling, some vendors sat

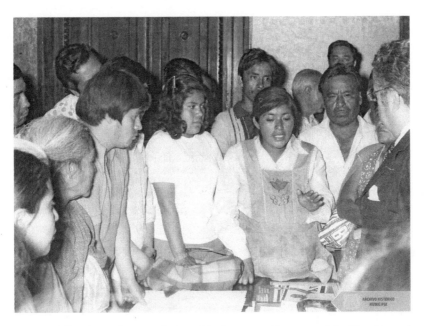

FIG. 8. A female vendor negotiating with the mayor. Courtesy of Archivo General Municipal de Puebla, image 1100, Administración Municipal 1972–75.

down with students who taught them theory and political skills in study groups, what they called *círculos de estudio*. These study groups were open to all vendors but tended to attract the most intellectually curious among them.[100] To overcome the illiteracy of many participants, students and literate vendors read aloud and explained the theories, especially the ideas outlined in Mao's *Little Red Book*.[101] The students who organized these readings, the mamecas, were those who attended the Prepa Zapata and were students of Bulmaro Vega. While these sessions could be exciting to the vendors, Bejarano admits that reading Mao over and over, even learning it by heart, bored her to tears.[102] As a result the student leaders of the study groups began reading and discussing daily newspapers to keep up with local and international events, and often tied local, national, and international struggles to the theories discussed in the groups, a process that made theoretical learning more palatable to the vendors. The study circles' emphasis on education was in part a reflection of the participation of students and teachers in the street vendors' struggle. Grassroots education politically empowered members of the UPVA.

One of the most important outcomes of the study groups was that vendors learned to speak formally in public and to debate. They put these skills into practice in negotiations with municipal authorities, in meetings, and in public speeches. According to Bejarano, "There were many meetings with government officials in which Simitrio, one of the UPVA's leaders and former Prepa Zapata student, did not talk at all; he allowed vendors to talk even if we made mistakes. Vendors got educated and politicized because of the study groups that we organized. Anyone who wanted to participate could do it." Another vendor, Rosa Martínez, proudly stated that through the study circles the union "taught [her] how to speak in public." Indeed such meetings were powerful and provided vendors with a sense of confidence while gaining new political skills.[103]

Training in the study groups, which later was led by a "cadre of intellectual vendors" instead of students, was very useful for the UPVA's rank-and-file members. One vendor recalled that during the first meetings in the early 1970s, people tended to talk over each other, to interrupt, and to scream; in the study circles they learned to be patient and attentive and to express their ideas in a clear and orderly fashion. For some women that meant a lot. Before becoming a vendor and union member, Martínez had been a housewife whose abusive husband did not allow her to even open the door when strangers rang the bell. She increasingly lost her ability to make decisions and did not talk with anyone outside her household.[104] Through her union activity Martínez learned to speak up, to defend her fellow vendors, and to experience a liberating new social life: "I am telling you, I learned a lot with the UPVA especially because my husband was always vigilant and violent. I was used to being silent. When we had a guest, he always told me, 'What the fuck are you doing here? Go inside because this person is talking with me.' If I didn't obey, he beat me. . . . [In the union] I had different positions. My compañeras [comrades] chose me because there were many who didn't know how to read or write and could not be representatives. I could. I was treasurer, secretary, and negotiator."[105]

Referring to the work of the study circles, Bejarano stated that they "trained good cadres," including La Tía (the Aunt). "She was a peasant but if you talk with her today, you would hardly see any traces of the peasant that she once was. She and her husband were trained at the UPVA." Bejarano continued, "In the UPVA, there were many people from the town of Sarabia. In that town people expelled the corrupt town's priest because people got politicized. They got educated because we organized the study circles and anybody could participate. At the beginning we didn't read anything beyond Mao's book, but then we demanded more, and then we began focusing on problems that we had in real life." Pointing out that La Tía's background was rural and very modest, Bejarano argued that the union's study groups provided the skills to communicate efficiently and pointedly with authorities and fellow vendors, who traditionally had looked upon them with various degrees of contempt.[106] At any rate, Martínez, La Tía, Bejarano, and many other female and male vendors participated in study circles, which was a learning and empowering experience for them all.

A final important characteristic of these study circles is that they occurred on the street, outside La Victoria market and at the UPVA's makeshift market. Vendors participated in and shaped the popular public sphere in the streets. This was a major achievement for the urban poor, some of whom were of rural descent and illiterate. In this way vendors were able to use the streets for democratic purposes until 1986.

BROADENING STREET VENDORS' ALLIANCES AND DEMANDS
One of the most important legacies of the student-vendor alliance was that it broadened vendors' political activities and demands. From their interactions with students, vendors learned about the strategic importance of making alliances with other sectors of society for both ideological and practical purposes. For independent unions to survive, become visible, and achieve their demands it was necessary that they support one another. For this reason street vendors became involved with independent peasant groups, participating in marches and protests. The vendors were particularly supportive of the CGC of Tecamachalco, Puebla, and also attended events organized by the CCI of the Sierra Norte. They demanded that the

government stop kidnapping and imprisoning peasants in the northern part of the state. In August 1977 the UPVA leadership investigated the case of seven CGC members the police beat in the middle of the night and detained in their homes, and UPVA members organized a march to protest the treatment.[107]

Street vendors became involved in other actions that went far beyond their own immediate economic and political concerns. In 1974, for instance, vendors participated in a march commemorating the death of President Salvador Allende of Chile and condemning the military coup. When Nicaragua's Ernesto Cardenal visited the UAP, vendors heard him speak and asked Puebla's citizens to support the Nicaraguan population in their struggles against U.S. imperialism. On still another occasion vendors collected clothes, medicine, and nonperishable food for the poor in El Salvador.[108] These activities, some of which were connected to the university, had radicalizing effects on the vendors. They learned about events outside Puebla, sympathized with the people involved, and became aware of the struggle of people throughout Latin America. And they began to imagine that a different society was possible.

Years later and without the support of students, vendors continued to carry out political activities that focused on communicating the struggles of people in Central America. For instance, on October 28, 1981, during a UPVA commemorative march, vendors read aloud a flier alluding to Salvadoran archbishop Oscar Romero's words: "When all peaceful means have been exhausted, the Church considers insurrection moral and justified."[109] The leaders explained that Romero, killed in March 1980, had sought an end to injustice in El Salvador and had believed in workers' organizing as the only way people could end their oppression.[110]

Vendors also participated in overseeing local elections, when, as usual, the PRI imposed its own candidates. In these events vendors openly voiced their political views. They denounced the state and its effort to divide the working class and urged the poor to make alliances to defend themselves against abuse by the authorities, corruption, and antidemocratic behavior. In a meeting that protested the 1974 election of a PRI boss (cacique) in the neighboring town of Cholula, a female vendor addressing about four hundred people insisted that all the people in the meeting, which included vendors, students, peasants, police officers, and members of official unions, were brothers and sisters with a common enemy. She said they all should be united because the PRI and their allies exploited them all.[111] All of these political activities went beyond the immediate concerns of the vendors. They tried to create bridges between different groups in society to effect some change.

LIMITATIONS TO UPVA'S INDEPENDENCE

Certainly there were limitations to what the UPVA, as a union independent from the PRI, could achieve. UPVA members secured downtown public spaces for thirteen years, from 1973, when they formed the union, to 1986, when local authorities removed all vendors from the city center. For the most part city authorities respected the union and realized that the united group defended its interests and could protect its members from the police and fee collectors alike. UPVA members stopped paying fees to the municipality for the use of public space. Instead they paid fees to their union, which were considerably lower than the money they paid to the city and in the bribes to officials.

Like any other independent union, the UPVA did not receive any subsidies, material benefits, or financial contributions from the ruling party.[112] The UPVA leadership had to rely solely on members' fees for all the organization's daily expenses as well as legal incidentals. Throughout the years these union dues became a problem and an issue of concern for many members. According to Bejarano:

> We paid five pesos every week [in the late 1970s]; two of those five pesos went to Simitrio's family expenses [when he was in prison], and three went to the union for publicity. If we calculate, he got a lot of money, but analyzing the situation, it was a fair deal because he was like the union's lawyer, organizer, and negotiator. After all, we secured a place where we could sell for five pesos a week. In contrast, fee collectors charged us daily, plus the bribes we gave to the police, and the merchandise they took, which represented more than money.[113]

As Bejarano mentioned, besides reducing the amount of money they paid to secure their spots, the fact that vendors could keep their products safe meant a lot to them. Their merchandise represented all the capital they invested and the labor of choosing, acquiring, transporting, sorting, and displaying their merchandise. It was all the vendors had.

The thorniest, most complicated issue the UPVA faced was convincing the city government to build a market for union members. During the first half of 1974 the municipality responded to vendors' demands and granted them a "market."[114] Unfortunately the so-called market consisted of an empty lot located only three blocks from the La Victoria market in a space that was once a junkyard. Vendors called their new market El Corralón (the Yard) because of its previous use. There were four walls around the lot, one of which was collapsing.[115] At El Corralón the municipal officials simply painted the walls and hung a cheap publicity placard stating, "Popular Market: We encourage people to buy [in this market]." A photograph published in *El Sol de Puebla* shows only a few vendors selling in the lot, many unaccompanied children sitting on the dirt floors, and small amounts of merchandise.[116] Another picture shows that the lack of a roof and the penetrating sun rays forced vendors to use their scant resources to build their own roof.[117] These photographs suggest that most vendors were out on the streets vending and left their children at El Corralón to make sure that authorities would not take back the lot. At least authorities could not claim that vendors did not have any intention of using this space. Vendors pressed them to install bathrooms, ceilings, entrance doors, cement floors, and water. Vendors also wanted office space for their union.[118]

City authorities had no obligation to provide for members of independent unions. But in March 1975 Mayor Eduardo Cué Merlo publicly and proudly announced that the municipality was about to begin the construction of all basic services necessary for the proper use of the market. He even announced that the market would be finished within three months and that the municipality would invest 750,000 pesos, a significant amount of money that he believed was worth spending because it was beneficial to the needy classes, "las clases necesitadas."[119] However, his populist rhetoric did not match reality as the construction work took years, and the resulting facility was still of low quality.

CONCLUSION

The alliance between students and vendors took place simultaneously with progressive reforms at Puebla's state university and during President Echeverría's democratic opening. At the university students acquired a left-wing ideology and faced repression, which further politicized them and urged them to form alliances with popular groups. Students, especially those who began to identify themselves as Maoists, saw vendors as allies and potential actors for effective political change. Vendors who faced multiple problems on a daily basis approached students for organizational help and support in what became a mutually beneficial relationship. Vendors helped students with their university reforms, and students provided guidance to organize and structure vendors' union. Also, by promoting this alliance and others of its kind, students were able to strengthen the university reform that ultimately made possible the progressive takeover of the UAP's administration and, indirectly, the fall of the last of the avilacamachista governors.

In the context of the so-called democratic opening, street vendors built an independent union that defended their economic interests and developed internal democracy. Establishing democracy was very important to street vendors and their student allies. Both groups sought to differentiate themselves from traditional charro unions that often lacked democratic features and paid lip service to their members while actually serving the state and employers. In the context of the new labor insurgency of the 1960s and 1970s, vendors joined the ranks of unions in the formal economy and challenged the corporatist structure of the PRI. They demonstrated that it was not only in factories or fields where people organized independent unions.

Vendors were successful in forming their independent union and forging internal union democracy thanks to their reliance on the political culture and practices of the student movement. The UPVA provided political spaces such as general assemblies and commissions and positions such as street coordinator through which vendors could voice and solve their problems. Male and female vendors felt empowered by the characteristics and structure of their union. One of the legacies of the student-vendor alliance was the creation of the study groups where vendors acquired ideological training and new political skills. Vendors incorporated into their actions the lessons and legacies of their experiences with students during the university reform of the long 1960s. Together students and street vendors challenged the corporatist structure of the PRI by refusing to accept the traditional division of the society into sectors. Vendors also broke away from the features typical of official unions by electing their own leaders for limited terms only.

Vendors participated in the public sphere in their discussions of left-wing texts, in their reading and interpretation of the news, and in their discussions with students. They built a "popular public sphere" on the streets and at their makeshift market. El Corralón became what Margaret Kohn calls a "radical democratic space," a political site "outside the state where the disenfranchised generated power."[120] At El Corralón vendors met with a wide range of people; blue-collar workers, peasants, teachers, and others came to El Corralón to discuss mutual problems, to find support, and to create links of solidarity.

As I argue in the next chapter, vendors also used innovative strategies that combined elements and forms of the student movement to empower themselves more directly and to democratize their union further. They became political performers: actors and directors creating new scripts and finding their way out of old, predetermined roles.

3 STAGING DEMOCRACY AT HOME AND ABROAD

In the summer of 1974 Chicano and Latin American theater companies from more than a dozen countries met in Mexico to participate in a distinctive festival, titled One Continent, One Culture for a Free Theatre and for Liberation. UPVA street vendors joined more than seven hundred participants on different stages in Mexico City, Teotihuacán, and El Tajín. The event was organized by the Chicano Teatro Nacional de Aztlán (National Theater of Aztlán, TENAZ) and the Mexico City–based Centro Libre de Experimentación Teatral y Artística (Free Center of Theater and Artistic Experimentation, CLETA). TENAZ was a network of theaters in the United States, Puerto Rico, and Mexico that was founded in 1971; it held annual festivals in which groups from Latin America and Europe engaged in "performances, workshops, and critiques."[1] TENAZ and CLETA expected that the two-week-long event would bring together people from all over América who "fight for their liberation against yanki [sic] imperialism—Chicanos, Indians, Mexicans, Latin Americans, Anglos." Organizers also wanted participants to identify with their indigenous roots and traditions.[2] In Teotihuacán Puebla's vendors shared the same stage as Luis Valdez's Teatro Campesino (Farmworkers' Theater), a group that had originally formed in 1965 among farmworkers in Delano, California. Even without having a direct link to the Chicanos prior to Teotihuacán, the vendors were indirectly influenced by their work. During the festival Chicanos performed a

Maya-inspired production, *El Baile de los Gigantes* (The Dance of the Giants). Paula Javier and Adolfo Corona were two members of the UPVA cultural commission who attended the festival. The vendor theater group presented a short play titled *Vendedores Ambulantes* (Street Vendors). Their messages and performance were so clear and poignant they attracted the attention of Theodore Shank, a professor and theater director at the University of California, Davis, who was in the audience. In one of his articles in the *Drama Review: TDR*, Shank detailed eight of the sixty presentations that included dance, music, and theater. He wrote that, unlike other groups in this event, Puebla's vendors "dr[ew] directly from their own daily experience in presenting their relationship to the establishment. . . . The peddlers are played straight and come across sympathetically."[3] The vendors of Puebla had arrived on the international stage.

I argue that, through their independent union, vendors used alternative mechanisms, such as theater, film, marches, and parades, to exercise forms of direct democracy. These activities were very important in a country with few communication channels for ordinary people. The theater performances, for instance, became an act of role reversal. It was usually students, city authorities, and even official union leaders who taught vendors how to act on the political stage, and it was the more educated, the better off, and the more powerful groups who defined vendors and what they did. In the early 1970s, however, vendors began reversing those political practices and creating their own scripts. They first defined themselves as workers, then introduced their labor and their problems to others. More important, UPVA vendors directly criticized state authoritarianism by exposing its restrictions on the use of public space, its corruption, its monopoly over the media, its manipulation of elections, and its many forms of violence toward ordinary citizens.

To broadcast their messages and protests vendors appropriated public spaces and used them as a political stage; this represents one of the most democratic features of their union activities. UPVA vendors transformed and broadened what Habermas calls the "public sphere" (*Öffentlichkeit*).[4] The sort of democracy that vendors were practicing did not happen in the bourgeois public sphere, such as cafés, salons, and PRI venues, but in makeshift markets, at the union office, on street corners, and on sidewalks. It was in these spaces where vendors, students, blue-collar workers, and peasants came together to express their problems, to find solutions, and to show solidarity and support. Men and women participated in union activities, often accompanied by their family members. Women, for instance, attended marches with their children wrapped in their *rebozos* (shawls) and hanging from their shoulders.

Together vendors pushed several boundaries. In a climate where undemocratic official unions prevailed, media vilified street vendors, and police violence was rampant, women, the urban poor, and people of indigenous descent were not supposed to be using the streets of Puebla's so-called historic downtown to carry out antigovernment protests. Yet UPVA members were able to exercise direct democracy through their union. Vendors were free to create alternative ways of resistance, which made the UPVA different from official unions controlled by the PRI state. For vendors, union democracy meant more than just participating in the election of leaders, voting to pass resolutions, and engaging in strikes; it also meant more than bread-and-butter issues in the formal sector, such as wage increases for members. Although these elements were important for determining union democracy and militancy, they fell short in expressing what exercising democracy meant for organized members of the informal economy who could not stop production to fight for better conditions. It was necessary for UPVA members to create alternative protest strategies that went beyond strikes.

THEATER ACROSS BORDERS

In 1973 about half a dozen street vendors in the UPVA's cultural commission, led by the Prepa Zapata students José Luis Díaz and Omar Castro, created a play, *Vendedores Ambulantes*. Inspired by Luis Valdez's Teatro Campesino, the students convinced the vendors that theater could be an effective way to communicate their problems to a larger audience. At the Prepa Zapata, Díaz and Castro had participated in a university-based theater group organized by their instructor Ericka Treviño, who introduced her students to the Chicano theater movement. Treviño's group symbolized a breakthrough in the University Theater. According to Miko Viya, a Puebla chronicler, the University Theater, founded by the rector Gonzalo Bautista O'Farrill in 1953, staged mostly Western European plays.[5] In contrast, and in the context of Puebla's university reform movement, Treviño's plays criticized authority figures such as Puebla's Catholic Church hierarchy, conservative university administrators, and local politicians.[6] Castro explained, "We used to create plays representing peasants' occupations of lands, and about how the Prepa Zapata was created. We were influenced by the Chicanos."[7] The Chicano struggle was known in Mexico due to migration networks.[8] Although referring to middle-class students, the historian Eric Zolov notes that "Mexico's proximity to the US generated a cross-fertilization of imagery, musical styles, and ideas that were also central to the formation of a transnational New Left sensibility."[9] Certainly Poblano students developed this sensibility and in turn convinced vendors to stage a play in the same subversive and rebellious spirit.

Certain elements of Teatro Campesino were especially attractive to UPVA members and suited them perfectly. The theater expert Jorge Huerta explains that Teatro Campesino was a political act of the people, and its message was more significant than its medium. One of the most important elements of the Teatro was the *acto* (brief sketch or skit with a political message), which Luis Valdez defined as an improvisation of the collectivity based on the participants' lived experiences. Valdez saw the acto not as "a part of a larger theatrical piece, like an act of a play, but a complete statement in itself."[10] An acto had five goals: "inspire the audience to social action, illuminate specific points about social problems, satirize the opposition, show or hint at a solution, and express what the people were feeling."[11] Teatro Campesino also had pragmatic characteristics that fit the vendors' situation: it was ambulatory; the actors were workers themselves; the plays were short, improvised, collectively created, and carried a political message; the plays did not need complicated or expensive scenarios and venues; and few decorative elements were necessary.[12]

Like their counterparts in Teatro Campesino, street vendors were not professional actors; indeed a family of vendors led the UPVA cultural commission in charge of theatrical productions. The Corona family, consisting of three siblings and their partners, together created the 1973 play, *Vendedores Ambulantes*. Also like their counterparts in the United States, some of the street vendors in the cultural commission were illiterate and thus could not write down the script, or "book," of the play. Without an official book, the vendors were free to improvise by adding or deleting parts every time they presented it.

Similar to California's farmworkers, street vendors were clear and succinct in identifying their main problems and successfully conveyed them to audiences. This was one of the characteristics that attracted the attention of Shank when he first observed the play. As discussed in chapter 1, a major concern for street vendors in the early 1970s was constant police violence, harassment, and the financial abuses of fee collectors. The play included a portrayal of a government infiltrator who disguised himself as a union organizer in order to discover and stop the vendors who wanted to create a union.[13] Vendors were well aware that their union was under the watchful eye of local and state authorities; what they did not know at the time was that the federal government too was spying on them.

In their play the street vendors ridiculed authority, a position they shared with Teatro Campesino. They mocked police officers by playing them wearing upside-down chamber pots instead of helmets. But vendors also pointed to the narrow class differences between themselves and police officers, who were overwhelmingly from the working classes and shared with vendors the fact that the political elite exploited them both. In their play and elsewhere street vendors called on police to recognize their oppression and to realize that police and vendors were brothers. Vendors sought to convince police officers that the fact that they could exercise violence did not mean they were not also victims of those in power. In short, vendors sought to raise the consciousness of the police, to convince them to wake up from their confusion and be sympathetic to the plight of the poor. It was a very ambitious goal and, unfortunately, a futile one.

Vendors also portrayed the unequal gender and power dynamics of

FIG. 9. A female vendor and her child in a play. Photo by and courtesy of Theodore Shank.

the street vending population, in which males were usually those with power and females were beaten and harassed by the police. In the play two or three male vendors played police officers and fee collectors; they were violent, lowbrow, and rude and always ended up beating the vendors, who for the most part were played by women.

The female vendors who participated in the play had their own unique problems and concerns as women and mothers. They brought their young children with them to the streets and worried about their safety. After all, these children witnessed their parents' economic struggles and police violence. In large part because they could not afford day care, the women brought their children to rehearsals too. Soon they realized their children added a poignant layer to the performance. In one acto, vendors acted out police attacks: three female vendors sit on the ground vending their merchandise; a hostile inspector arrives to charge them for using public space; the vendors refuse to pay, and the inspector calls the police, who beat the vendors.[14] The children cried and screamed when they saw the police officers abusing their mothers.[15] A photograph taken by Shank and published in the *TDR* captures the violence as female vendors cover their toddlers with their own bodies while the police officers beat them.

Just as female vendors had done in their letters to authorities, women now performed their role of economic struggle as poor Mexicans and as mothers who had to feed their family. Violence and removals further damaged vendors' economic survival. In the play the women scream at the officers, "Why did you take my merchandise? How will I feed my children?" Exploiting their role as mothers was a powerful way to portray the vendors as sympathetic economic actors, even to those who opposed street vending. Nobody liked to see little children going hungry after a day of work and seeing the police beat their mothers.

Fees and physical violence were not the only problems the women faced. Sexual harassment was also a common experience. As discussed in chapter 1, fee collectors and police equated the women with *mujeres de la calle*, prostitutes whom they could easily harass. The theater expert Shank took note of this gendered message: "Several women, kneeling on the ground, each with a few limes, carrots, or onions arranged in front, call out prices, attempting to attract customers. One of them has a baby. A man enters, tells them they must have a permit to sell there, and begins to attack them by kicking at their merchandise. One of the women gives him a little money, and he lets her stay. He offers to let another sell if she will come home with him. She refuses, and he chases off all the women."[16]

In addition to protecting their children and their merchandise, the women in the play had the chance to defend their reputation, to show audiences that they were decent women. The play suggests that, although vendors needed to provide for themselves and their families, the women did not sell or barter their bodies to officers in exchange for a space in which to sell. They were poor women, sometimes even desperate, but they were not prostitutes.[17]

Following the Teatro Campesino's premise that theater must go to the people, vendors took their play to sidewalks, street corners, public markets, classrooms, and towns in the countryside.[18] *Vendedores Ambulantes* was quite portable: it did not need a setting, backdrops, lighting, or sound effects, and the actors did not need makeup or costumes. It was easy for vendors to portray themselves and their workplaces.

It was important that the play reach a broad audience, including fellow vendors, so the Corona family also staged it on the streets where their fellow vendors sold their wares. Vendors usually performed one short act on street corners where even drivers stopped at a red light could see their messages. The entire play was presented at the university-affiliated high schools or outside of Puebla. For instance, Díaz described left-wing priests in the countryside inviting a performance, especially where people were petitioning for land or fighting against local authorities and caciques. According to Díaz, these priests found *Vendedores Ambulantes* an inspiring piece in which common people expressed their daily battles against authorities.[19]

Like its own actors, the theater of the vendors had become ambulatory, performed for a working-class audience, the common people, the uneducated, the young and the old. The audience consisted of children, housewives, market people, and random pedestrians. These were people who had not been exposed to theater and could not afford ticket prices. In early 1970s Mexico only the educated, the wealthy, the middle classes, and those who lived in urban areas had access to commercial theater. Puebla's vendors did not intend to profit from the performances; their goal was to draw attention to their plight, and they sustained their group by donations.

Vendors gained recognition for their work by bringing their theater to more sophisticated and formal stages. Students like Díaz introduced the vendors to university-based theater groups and encouraged the UPVA cultural commission to schedule performances in the country's capital. Considering themselves public representatives of their fellow vendors, the Corona family collected money to travel to Mexico City's Instituto Politécnico Nacional (IPN).

According to Paula Javier, the IPN jurors awarded a prize to *Vendedores Ambulantes* for authenticity. After all, the vendors were playing vendors, wearing their own clothes and carrying flattened burlap bags on which to display their merchandise. Indeed the characters looked "so real" that IPN employees momentarily prevented them from entering the theater, believing that they were simply a group of street vendors trying to get into the building to sell merchandise.[20]

Javier was proud of their performance at the IPN: "Our play won the first prize among popular theater groups and it won people's sympathy. There was also an opportunity to act abroad, but we always thought, 'How are we going to leave our stalls?' . . . Unlike students who played the roles of railroad workers, we were authentic and represented daily life. We were the original ones."[21] Indeed at the IPN and the festival in Teotihuacán, *Vendedores Ambulantes* was one of the few plays in which the actors themselves were the subjects of the performances.

While the street vendors enjoyed their participation in the UPVA cultural commission, they also faced financial challenges that prevented them from continuing. Due to the UPVA's independence from the PRI, vendors did not receive any material support to finance their cultural activities. The group raised funds to pay for short trips, and the recipient communities provided lodging and food, but often the vendors did not have enough money to pay for the return bus fare. Adding to the financial difficulties that these travels entailed, the time dedicated to acting detracted from selling. Javier daydreamed about the various places she could go to perform, but wondered, "Who is going to sell while I am acting?"[22] This was a harsh reminder that, above all, vendors had to make a living and the performances were detrimental to their sales.

Unlike their counterparts in California, Puebla street vendors did not have a guide like Luis Valdez to educate them about the theater. Theirs was a much more modest project, with high school students serving as their teachers. Problems arose from this lack of expertise. For one, the theater group was short-lived, and the street vendors did not create any more actos.[23] Nevertheless they deserve much credit. Their group, if short-lived, remained independent from any institution (the state, the university) or political party (PRI, PAN). Its only commitment was to the vendors' struggle, and it provided them with a space in which to vividly portray the difficult realities of their daily lives.

THE STREET VENDORS' MOVIE

At the end of 1973 Arturo Garmendia, a photography and film instructor at the UAP's Escuela Popular de Artes, captured some of the vendors' theatrical acts in a low-budget short film, also called *Los Vendedores Ambulantes*. Garmendia was sensitive to the common people's struggles and state violence. He had produced short documentaries about the 1971 student repression in Mexico City and about peasants in Chiapas. Believing that social issues could reach broader audiences through short films than by other means, Garmendia approached the vendors to see if they would be interested in collaborating with him on a short film about their struggles.[24]

Because of his connections to the university, vendors perceived Garmendia as an ally and agreed to participate in the project. The camera, film, and editing process were subsidized by the UAP.[25] The result was a twenty-minute-long, black-and-white documentary, which the vendors later called "la película de los ambulantes," literally "the street vendors' movie." Garmendia shot some acts of the play and combined them with scenes of vendors at work on the street. He also recorded scenes of people who had built their one-room homes from scratch and scrap on the outskirts of the city. Garmendia sought to emphasize that both the vendors and the *colonos* (tenants) were economically marginalized groups that appropriated public areas to sell or to live in order to survive in an urban setting.

Interestingly, while the play portrayed women exclusively as vendors and men as police officers and authority figures, the young vendor Olga Corona is the protagonist in the short film.[26] Garmendia was sensitive to gender issues, realizing the omnipresence of female vendors and their activism in confronting the police and organizing. He perceptively chose to include the interventions of Adolfo Corona's sister, Olga, who explained the street vendors' main problems.

The documentary's narrator introduces the street vendors, mentioning their background and presenting them as subjects in a state of in-betweenness. They had migrated from rural areas, yet they were not peasants because they did not own any land; in fact "they were dispossessed of their lands." Street vendors were marginalized within the urban setting, yet "they [had] not entered the ranks of the proletariat because they [had] been expelled from the factories." A contemporary film critic who analyzed the documentary concludes, "Despite its simplicity, it was an ambitious film." He lauds its portrayal of the vendors' struggle for "its rediscovery of community value, its social-psychological drama toward liberation, its unique and alternative techniques that showed the sociopolitical imagination of common people."[27]

The film emphasized state repression. Vendors re-created the October 28, 1973, police seizure and subsequent burning of their merchandise and stalls. Left-wing university administrators allowed Garmendia to film the scene on one of the patios of El Carolino, the main university building.[28] Vendors felt vindicated by participating in the production of the documentary, particularly by reenacting these violent scenes, which had been ignored by local mainstream media and the state. Yolanda Bejarano, who had witnessed the events on that late night, remembered that after the stalls were burned, "the firefighters came to clean, and at sunrise the streets were all clean. That is the reason why that history did not happen. That night never happened in Puebla."[29] Those who tried to suppress the event could not know that the story would be told in a documentary seen by many people around the world and that the prestigious National Autonomous University of Mexico would keep a copy of it at its film repository.

In Mexico City, Garmendia had met the representative of the Goethe Institute, who was interested in showing documentaries in Germany that represented people's struggles. Garmendia mentioned the short film, and months later, in 1974, *Los Vendedores Ambulantes* was awarded first prize for best political and educational film by the Ministry of Education and Cultural Affairs of North Rhine-Westphalia at the International Short Film Festival, Oberhausen. The selection committee lauded "the value of visual media to communicate [the] vendors' message" and acknowledged "their fight for social justice." The film was awarded 5,000 DM.[30]

Unfortunately the vendors did not benefit financially from the prize. What happened to the money remains a mystery.[31] Disputes regarding its whereabouts created friction among the vendors, who suspected each other of stealing it. Yet despite the lack of monetary compensation, vendors were proud of the prize and their participation in the film. Paula Javier found a practical use for the documentary; she showed it for years to street vendors and marketers, believing the fight against state repression and for economic justice had the potential to politicize them.[32]

"LA LLORONA"

Vendors found other creative ways to express their hardships and political views. In addition to producing the play and participating in the documentary, sellers also composed what they called the "Street Vendors' Anthem." This was a short song they created to celebrate their independent union and their activism, conveying their history and political stand vis-à-vis the state. Like the play, the song had no single author. Instead vendors composed the song as a group without recording the lyric. They continued playing it on special occasions for decades.

Vendors cleverly used the melody from a melancholic Mexican folksong, "La Llorona" (The Weeping Woman or The Wailing Woman). La Llorona is the main character of a centuries-old legend. While there are many versions and uses of La Llorona, in Mexican and Mexican American folklore the weeping woman cries for her children whom she killed after her lover abandoned her. She then wanders by riverbanks and lake shores, looking for her children's bodies for all eternity.[33] In the traditional stories she is invisible, a deceiver, unredeemable, selfish, vain, whorish, dangerous, and, above all, a bad mother.[34]

Joining the ranks of all those who have used La Llorona in their songs, vendors borrowed certain conventional characteristics of the weeping woman. They probably chose La Llorona because she resembled the state: an unreliable and treacherous entity that sought only certain political reforms and could take the vendors as its prey. They portrayed the Mexican state as a threat, an entity that could betray, abandon, and ultimately kill. But vendors did not portray themselves merely as victims; they first introduce themselves to La Llorona by declaring that they are courageous and are not associated with the ruling party. They briefly tell La Llorona about their struggle and acknowledge the students' participation in their movement. While La Llorona is a villain, just like the state, male and female street vendors, as part of *el pueblo* (the people or the working-class), are willing to take her on. They refuse to be La Llorona's children.[35]

> Los ambulantes de Puebla, Llorona
> No nos la sabemos rajar
>
> Los ambulantes de Puebla, Llorona
> No nos la sabemos rajar
>
> Ya desde el '73 Llorona comenzamos a luchar
> Al surgir el movimiento, Llorona, fue el ambulante de Puebla
>
> Y el primero fue el estudiante, Llorona,
> Que nos respondió como hermano
>
> Porque exigimos mercados, Llorona, se nos llama comunistas
>
> Pero un orgullo tenemos de no haber sido PRIístas
>
> Ay de ti, Llorona, tan gobiernista
>
> Y al pueblo, Llorona, le tocará quitarte lo reformista
> Ay de ti, Llorona, tan reformista
>
> The street vendors of Puebla, Llorona,

don't sell out

The street vendors of Puebla, Llorona.
don't sell out

Since '73, Llorona, we began to fight
When our movement started, it was the street vendors of Puebla

And the first to respond to us was the student, Llorona,
Who is like a brother

And when we demanded markets, some people called us
   Communists[36]

But we are proud of never being part of the PRI

You, Llorona, did sell out to the government

The people will fight against you, Llorona, because you are just
   reformist
Poor you, Llorona, who are so reformist.

Vendors sang "La Llorona" at marches, meetings, and social gatherings. Sometimes guitar players enhanced the melody, which already had a melancholic character. The music was sad and the lyrics portrayed courageous vendors who had organized and challenged the state, suggesting that the vendors' struggle was filled with moments of success, challenges, and defeats.

PINTAS

In the absence of a free press the walls of the city turned into the newspapers of the poor. In a practice called *pintas* the walls of downtown buildings and the sides of public transportation buses on busy streets became places where vendors painted all sorts of political messages. Public space and private property were thus essential venues for articulating vendors' grievances and goals to authorities.

Street vendors now had a union, but the informal nature of their work meant the usual means of striking and stopping production were not available to them. And there were limitations to singing songs, performing theater, and screening films, as these could communicate their messages only to sympathetic audiences who took the time and energy to listen. So vendors had to resort to other ways of protest, which they borrowed from the student movement: engaging in pintas, hijacking buses, and occupying streets. Vendors were well aware of the dynamics and symbolic meanings of certain streets and employed that knowledge to protest against authorities.

In countries like Mexico where mainstream media are owned and manipulated by the state and economic elites, it was very hard for the common people, especially marginalized groups, to convey their message through official media. For instance, the major newspaper in Puebla, *El Sol de Puebla*, constantly attacked UPVA street vendors. Indeed the paper had been functioning as a pillar of Puebla's government since it was launched in the early 1940s by Maximino Ávila Camacho.[37] *El Sol*, as people commonly called it, portrayed vendors as dirty, backward, and the source of violence and even gangsterism. The newspaper failed to report the police violence against vendors on October 28, 1973. For this reason vendors found other outlets to express their ideas, demands, and criticisms.

At night, using thick paintbrushes and oil paint, small groups of UPVA vendors—usually young men and women who could write and run fast—painted short messages and slogans on the exterior walls of buildings on busy streets.[38] The work was obviously dangerous; they had to work quickly to avoid police. Sometimes the leadership punished vendors who did not attend union meetings by making them do the pintas.[39]

Vendors first engaged in the pintas with students. In 1970, for instance, both groups worked together painting over PRI political propaganda during Echeverría's campaign for the presidency. Students and vendors painted slogans that portrayed the election process as a farce in which Efraín González Morfín, the PAN candidate, played a puppet: "Don't vote." "If you vote, you become an accomplice of the electoral farce." "Neither Echeverría, nor González Morfín—active abstention." "Death to LEA [Luis Echeverría Álvarez]." "LEA will be imposed on the people."[40]

At the end of April 1974 groups of street vendors, students, and peasants invited the public to participate in the commemoration of May Day. In addition to posting small propaganda signs on trees and in shop windows, they carried out pintas on the walls surrounding La Victoria market:

We will not forget the May 1st Massacre [of 1973 in Puebla].
Power to the people.
Death to fascist governments.
Death to LEA.
Join the March on May 1st.[41]

Pintas represented a political challenge to the state monopoly over expression and representation.[42] Vendors could shape or at least attempted to shape the public sphere.

MARCHES

Street vendors engaged in dozens of marches in which hundreds of UPVA members and their supporters voiced their demands. The UPVA became famous for the frequency of their marches, for the number of participants, and for the disruption they caused. Marches, like most protests, had several objectives. The first was to communicate vendors' problems to society and to authorities. Usually these marches occurred after vendors failed to negotiate their demands with politicians, such as the release of incarcerated leaders. A second objective was to make themselves visible and their demands and criticisms known to the rest of society. As the UPVA continued to grow throughout the 1970s and 1980s, it could mobilize thousands of people who marched on dozens of downtown streets, paralyzing downtown traffic. They used public spaces to participate in acts of democracy. As the architect Clara Irazábal points out, "Public space is essential to the maintenance of democracy in making it possible to publicize dissent."[43] But the ability of vendors to protest in downtown spaces became increasingly limited after the mid-1980s, when Puebla's city center became a UNESCO World Heritage Site and Mexico adopted neoliberal policies.

By organizing marches, vendors also sought the support of other groups, including university students. They wisely chose symbolic and politically charged spaces. They connected their workplaces to the sites where local and state governments drafted policies and made decisions that affected vendors' daily lives and ways of survival. For instance, before authorities removed and relocated street vendors from the downtown area in 1986, UPVA members began their marches at the state university (at El Carolino) or at the UPVA headquarters at El Corralón, the makeshift market. They marched down a number of important streets and finished in front of the municipal palace, at the zócalo, the main plaza right at the heart of the city.[44] Like most main plazas in Latin America, this zócalo is surrounded by the cathedral, symbolizing the power of the Catholic Church, and by the Municipal Palace. Like the zócalo in Mexico City, Puebla's main square became "a symbolic space where . . . unions, . . . local urban and civic organizations, and religious groups have literally found 'common ground.'"[45]

Marches usually began around 4 p.m. and lasted several hours. Sometimes vendors formed separate columns for men and women. Female vendors and children marched in the front; that way they would be the first ones attacked if the police became violent, and observers would be more likely to expose the abuse.[46] Marchers stayed downtown, where most political and commercial activity took place, ending in front of the Municipal Palace and the zócalo. A UPVA commission, usually the political or negotiation commission, met with the mayor or other municipal officers to request a solution to their problems. Once the meeting was over and vendors believed it had been successful, they abandoned the area and unblocked the surrounding streets.[47] By communicating with local officials the vendors launched a direct challenge to the clientelistic and corporatist character of the state. As members of an independent union and acting as a collectivity, they did not need middlemen, such as charro leaders, to negotiate on their behalf.

Pedestrians and authorities read vendors' messages on the large banners vendors carried while marching. Along with the walls of buildings, banners were one of the few means through which vendors could directly communicate their problems and demands. Unlike the professional, homogeneous, factory-made banners that charro unions used when they participated in official acts, vendors used their own symbols and vocabulary, which sometimes included profanity. The following are examples of banners:

> [They] seize our merchandise, which is our children's bread.
> [Mayor] Arruti: charro leaders manipulate you.
> Class brothers, this is your struggle.
> Stop the beatings of vendors.
> Down with the charro leaders.
> Peasant and Worker: support our struggle to survive.
> We want a functional market.
> We want justice, no more promises.
> Long live Lucio Cabañas. Long Live Genáro Vázquez.[48]

While carrying these banners, vendors also chanted offensive criticisms: "Quién es el ladrón del pueblo? Será melón, sera sandía, sera el pelón de Echeverría?" (Who steals from the people? It must be the bald Echeverría.)[49]

Archival photographs show that vendors positioned pickup trucks in front of and following the marchers as protection. Loudspeakers in vans were used to talk to authorities who refused to formally meet with the vendors. Even if local authorities still refused to pay heed to their demands, the vendors at least attracted the attention of pedestrians. Vendors certainly attracted the attention of the federal government, whose agents recorded details about those who spoke.[50] These marches also drew municipal photographers.

Due to their independence, UPVA vendors were free to make alliances with diverse organizations challenging the corporatist nature of the Mexican state. When vendors marched, members of other independent organizations joined them, which troubled local and state authorities. The state tried to disrupt these marches; it was common practice for the judicial police to block highways to prevent the movement of vehicles transporting protestors and to send the protestors back to their place of origin.[51]

Marches sometimes took place with the sole purpose of quickly conveying multiple messages to UPVA members and their supporters. These marches were then combined with *mítines relámpago*, "hit-and-run" rallies of the kind that students at the IPN in Mexico City had been staging since the mid-1950s.[52] In January 1971 students and street vendors tried to reach out to people in marginalized neighborhoods, inviting them to join their protests against the rising cost of living, especially the high price of sugar. Later, when the UPVA organized its own mítines relámpago, a small group of vendors met with others to communicate urgent messages such as the time and location of an upcoming meeting. In April 1974 a group of vendors encouraged non-UPVA vendors to join their union and demand the local government build a "popular market" free of charro leaders. Four years later around three hundred people—mostly UPVA members and peasants from the Consejo General Campesino—organized a march in which vendors announced that they were still fighting for the release of their leaders from prison and confirmed that they were not going to leave the streets and relocate elsewhere.[53] These mítines were the fastest and most efficient way to communicate messages to a large community of vendors who were located on different streets.

FOOD COMMISSIONS

Female vendors were in charge of bringing food for the participants when marches lasted several hours or even a day. This was often the case when vendors participated in protests in Mexico City. Sometimes their demands were not heard by local and state officials, which prompted UPVA members to travel the 149 kilometers to the country's capital and occupy part of the zócalo for several days. Lacking financial resources, street vendors could not afford prepared food from local merchants for a prolonged period of time. For that reason the UPVA leadership created the food commissions to feed the participants. These food commissions reflected the gender values of the mostly male leaders, as they assigned only rank-and-file female vendors to this activity. Women brought large amounts of food to Mexico City's zócalo and cooked breakfasts, lunches, snacks, and dinners for the participants. Vendors brought pots, pans, plates, and all sorts of kitchen utensils in addition to hundreds of tortillas, canned food, water, and coffee. One of the vendors who participated in the food commission described how much work it was to prepare three meals for the comrades who attended the meetings and marches. Work never ended for these women.[54] Even if the men rarely acknowledged it, the reproductive labor of women played an important role in the organization. Female vendors fed others so that the men could engage in formal political work.[55] In interviews women did not indicate that they thought of this kind of labor as political work; it was simply the work women did. In contrast women and men valued their participation in the play or documentary as both cultural and political.

Participating in marches that took place outside of Puebla, however, was an eye-opening experience and an act of self-reflection. Certainly not all women went along only to cook. Going to the country's capital was a big step for Rosa Martínez, who was born and raised in a small town next to Cholula, Puebla, and had never traveled. She had never seen a subway, and some of the subway stations had escalators, which she had no idea how to use. She was proud that she learned how to ride them. Going to Mexico City also represented freedom and self-sufficiency. When she was a child, her parents were too poor to go anywhere. For most of her young and adult life, before she became a vendor, Martínez had been married to a man who did not allow her to go outside the home and who limited her contact with other people. Going to marches and socializing with UPVA *compañeros* and *compañeras* who supported her in her struggle was tremendously valuable for her. Martínez's participation in the union allowed her to travel, to learn from others, and to find a community of peers. She also participated in acts that she never thought she could do, like hijacking buses on behalf of her union.[56]

HIJACKING BUSES

Hijacking buses was another political practice that street vendors learned from students, and it had symbolic and practical purposes. Visible, large, and mobile, buses offered an ideal place for the vendors to paint their slogans. Equally important, the buses served to transport vendors to marches. Ironically the PRI used buses to transport *acarreados* (dragged artificial supporters) to all sorts of political events. Since the PRI-led regime had close political connections with the owners of buses through the Alianza de Camioneros de la República Mexicana (National Alliance of Mexican Bus Operators) as well as their CNOP leaders, it was relatively easy for the PRI to borrow these vehicles for their political events.[57] First, a group of vendors got on a bus and asked the other passengers to get off, explaining that they were going to use the vehicle for a march. Vendors would then load the bus with fellow UPVA members and supporters from other organizations and transport them to marches within or outside of Puebla.[58] Vendors recalled that the people who rode the buses were supportive of them and willingly got off to catch the next bus, and sometimes the bus drivers volunteered to drive.[59] Perhaps it was in their best interest to safeguard the bus they were driving.

The first time vendors hijacked buses was in the immediate aftermath of the police seizure of merchandise on October 28, 1973. With the aid of student supporters, street vendors employed the hijacked vehicles to block streets and corners of the areas where they were planning to set up their stalls. These bus barricades kept police cars from driving over the stalls as they had done on the night of October 28. In many future protests vendors used bus barricades to block streets and disrupt traffic in order to make themselves visible. On May 16, 1974, vendors parked five buses in front of the municipal palace after a march and threatened to remain there until the mayor addressed their demand to build a market.[60]

COMMEMORATIONS

Vendors also protested the state's monopoly on official celebrations and commemorations. The PRI state and the media deleted from the historical record events in which the state used violence to clamp down on ordinary people's struggles. Street vendors sought to counteract these omissions through their independent union. They created their own historical narrative and emphasized the role they played through an alternative commemoration of events. Some were symbolic and unique to vendors, while others spoke to a larger community. An example of the former is the vendors' commemoration of the violent police raid and the burning of stalls that took place on October 28, 1973. Every October 28 vendors organized a march in the main streets of Puebla, followed by festivities in their makeshift market and at the Mercado Hidalgo, where most UPVA members relocated after 1986. People enjoyed free food, mariachis, and wrestling matches at the festivities. These parties were free and open to all. More important, they gave vendors a sense of belonging in their union by commemorating vendors' common history of facing obstacles.

On other dates vendors paid tribute to people who fell victim to state repression and were absent from official commemorations and history. For instance, vendors commemorated the Tlatelolco massacre of October 2, 1968. The Mexican state denied the killing of students and bystanders on October 2, and the mainstream media, for the most part, did not report it. Back in the fall of 1968, with the Olympic Games around the corner, the state and media were highly interested in portraying an image of order, enthusiasm, and modernity in Mexico City and across the country. After all, Mexico was the first Latin American country to host the Games.[61] Two exceptions were the widely circulated newspaper *Excélsior* and magazine *Siempre!* But their coverage was limited to interior pages. The state omitted the massacre in history textbooks and did not build a single monument to the victims. For the most part, society did not know about or chose to ignore the killings, disappearances, and detentions.[62] No politician commemorated the event until October 2, 1998, when Cuauhtémoc Cárdenas Solórzano, the first mayor of Mexico City from the opposition Party of the Democratic Revolution, ordered "that all flags be flown at half-staff . . . to honor the dead."[63]

While officials were slow in honoring the dead, Puebla's street vendors had been joining independent organizations and unions in Mexico City in acts of public commemoration on this date for several years. The state disliked these groups emphasizing such an inconvenient history. Fearing acts of state repression in the country's capital, in 1979 vendors decided to commemorate October 2 locally, in front of the municipal palace at Puebla's zócalo. The UPVA leadership invited independent organizations from the states of Veracruz, Morelos, and Mexico to join them.[64] In commemorating October 2 the street vendors refused to be silent accomplices of the state. They refused to forget the dead, the disappeared, the incarcerated, and those who were tortured in police stations and secret detention centers.

LABOR DAY PARADES

As early as 1975 street vendors had participated in the Labor Day parade, giving new meanings to this co-opted celebration.[65] Labor Day commemorates the Haymarket tragedy of May 1, 1886. On that day Chicago workers had organized a series of strikes for the eight-hour day and were violently attacked by the police. The first Labor Day parade took place in 1890 in Paris and has since become a militant celebration around the world.[66] In Mexico unionized and nonunion workers first participated in the Labor Day parade in Mexico City in 1913, during the government of Victoriano Huerta.[67] It was a massive and militant event that included recently created unions and mutualist societies and challenged Huerta's regime.[68] In the early twentieth century women workers—seamstresses, market women, and prostitutes, among many others—also participated, expressing their demands as female workers excluded from many unions.[69]

Over the years the Mexican state and the ruling party appropriated this celebration and neutralized its militant character. The state dictated the script that workers had to follow; unionized workers affiliated with any of the PRI umbrella labor organizations, such as the CTM, CROC, and CROM, had to march in their city every May 1. In Puebla the official Labor Day parade took place on the widest and most important streets, where thousands of unionized workers solemnly marched under the excruciating sun, saluting union leaders and high-ranking state officials, showing—or at least pretending to show—their respect and recognition to their mostly charro leaders. These politicians and leaders sat on shaded elevated seats as a marker of their high status, observing the rank and file marching in front of them.

By joining the Labor Day parade, street vendors publicly inserted themselves as workers and an intrinsic part of the labor movement. Since they were not invited into the official parade, they joined the independent unions, forming an independent group (a *columna independiente*) that marched behind the official unions. The independent unions included university workers, the Sindicato Unitario de Trabajadores de la Universidad Autónoma de Puebla (Unitarian Union of Workers of the Autonomous University of Puebla); the Central Campesina Independiente; and the democratic branch of electrical workers, the Sindicato Único de Trabajadores Electricistas de la República Mexicana (General Union of Mexican Electrical Workers).[70]

The independent unions, including street vendors, sought to counteract the presence of charro unions by participating in the official PRI-supported parade. In street vendors' view, charro leaders forced the rank and file to support the PRI candidates by loudly chanting their names. The independent organizations wanted to deliver a different message; they marched in the official Labor Day parade in order "to give it back its historically proletarian and combative character because the official parade only served to show reverence to the bourgeois state apparatus that has transformed this celebration into a manifestation of the control that the bourgeoisie has over the charro unions." During the 1975 parade street vendors sought to emphasize the repressive nature of the Mexican state by commemorating the second anniversary of the assassination of the five UAP students who were killed on May 1, 1973, by the "most reactionary government of Puebla," that of governor Gonzalo Bautista O'Farrill.[71]

Street vendors also participated in the 1981 Labor Day parade in Mexico City, which they saw as an opportunity to present their demands to a larger audience and to make themselves visible to other independent groups. Invited by the Unión Obrera Independiente (Independent Workers Union, UOI)—the umbrella organization to which the Volkswagen independent union belonged—the UPVA sent street vendors in about ten buses that the UOI provided. Vendors brought banners on which they wrote their demands: a central market for UPVA members and the end of state repression against vendors and peasant organizations.[72] Besides the symbolic nature of their participation in the parade, street vendors sought to maintain links with the UOI.

UPVA members had participated in the alternative Labor Day parade in Puebla at least since 1976. This parade was highly symbolic; only independent unions participated, and it followed a different route from the official PRI workers' parade. It typically started in popular locations such as markets, parks, or plazas and ended in front of the municipal palace. Organizers chose the route carefully so that participants did not have to salute authorities or show support for any politician. Street vendors brought their children with them; infants usually slept wrapped in their mothers' rebozos, and older children walked along their parents. The independent parade became a grassroots parade that had a more festive and informal character. More important, it was a more inclusive parade that portrayed people as workers, parents, and members of the independent union movement. The historian John Lear writes, "The struggle that began in 1913 between workers and the post-revolutionary state to appropriate and reclaim the meaning of May Day (as well as the streets and plazas of the city) has continued ever since."[73]

CONCLUSION

For street vendors, democracy was more than the election of leaders or votes in assemblies; it was determined by the political and cultural practices that members introduced to the union.[74] Whether it was by performing theater, painting slogans on walls, or hijacking buses, these men and women learned how to organize, how to represent themselves, and how to directly participate in the country's political life. This involvement was particularly important in places like Mexico, where democratic participation was accessible to only a few.

UPVA vendors exercised forms of direct democracy by creating and re-creating the political and cultural practices they had learned from protests during Mexico's long 1960s, specifically during Puebla's university reform in the early 1970s. For instance, vendors learned how to carry out pintas and hijack buses before they organized the UPVA, and they continued these practices for political and pragmatic reasons. Walls and the sides of buses became vendors' means to communicate specific messages and demands. Vendors and their sympathizers traveled to the many marches that the UPVA organized in Puebla and other cities. Thus vendors used public spaces and privately owned objects to engage and transform the political arena.

Exercising democracy and building an independent union were important successes for a group of ordinary people who had been politically, socially, and economically marginalized by the state and the upper classes. Vendors built a community of peers who protected each other from police violence and allowed them to make a living. They created an organization in which they could express their problems in their own words, provided solutions, and became active participants. The union, however, reflected the traditional gender values of many of their members and leaders. In the food commissions, for instance, only the women worked long hours to provide food for the compañeros.

Nevertheless, and unlike the official unions that were affiliated with and co-opted by the PRI, members of the UPVA created alternative ways to make their voices heard and to sustain their activities. In a climate of state repression against independent unions, vendors found ways to make themselves sympathetic to larger audiences that would support their cause, or at least attract public attention to their constant struggle to make a living. The UPVA theater group was perhaps the most effective strategy to present vendors as hard-working Mexicans who simply sought to sustain themselves and their children.[75] Doing so under the repressive conditions in Puebla was hard: their earnings were meager, and they had to deal with harassment, fees, bribes, and physical violence by authorities. Their performance was an affirmation of their daily experiences. The play, like the letters they had written since the nineteenth century, allowed vendors to participate in and shape the popular public sphere. This time, however, vendors did it directly, without intermediaries, using their own bodies and language.

The creativity and activism of the UPVA allowed vendors to join a larger community of independent unions and militant organizations that challenged the state. Vendors and other independent union members inserted themselves as the makers of an alternative historical narrative and emphasized the role they played in it. Although the PRI state's official history chose to delete Mexico's repression against its own citizens, UPVA members sought to remember and make the repression public. Vendors commemorated events that the state had left out of the official calendar, such as the Tlatelolco massacre. They engaged in a larger, decades-long national struggle against the authoritarianism, violence, and corruption of the Mexican state. The activism of the vendors and the challenges they posed to the PRI-led regime, however, generated even greater state violence.

4 THE DIRTY WAR ON STREET VENDORS

On October 11, 1977, *La Opinión*, a major newspaper in Puebla, published an article on the disappearance of two-year-old Oscar Vega Rosales. According to the newspaper, his mother, the vendor Teresa Rosales, was walking on a downtown street, with Oscar following a few steps behind her. When she turned the corner, she looked back, and he had disappeared. She looked for him everywhere, but not finding him she notified the police.[1] The account in *La Opinión* differed remarkably from Rosales's own account and from secret police documents. The newspaper suggested that Rosales's lack of care was to blame for her son's disappearance, and it omitted the political context in which the event took place. According to federal police files, on October 5, 1977, around 4 p.m., marching UPVA members demanded that authorities free their leaders, who were jailed under accusations of homicide. Like many of the UPVA marches at the time, this one was attended by about five hundred people, including students, peasants from the Consejo General Campesino de Tecamachalco, members of the Partido Revolucionario de los Trabajadores (Workers' Revolutionary Party), the Frente de Acción Solidaria (Solidarity Action Front), and railroad workers.[2] The UPVA issued the following announcement: "We, the street vendors, have decided to take Puebla's streets indefinitely as a sign of protest against authorities, and against the detention of our leaders. . . . We believe that our leaders' imprisonment is an act of provocation to encourage a battle between the police and vendors with the objective of destroying our organization.

Authorities are unable to provide a solution to our demands; instead they kidnap, threaten, imprison, and seek our removal from the streets through violence. . . . Stop the repression."[3] Rosales says she left her fruit stall at El Corralón, the makeshift open market, to join her fellow vendors. She left Oscar under the care of her oldest son, who was ten; like many vendor families, the older children often babysat younger siblings. After the march ended around 6:30 p.m., she went back to her stall and realized that Oscar was gone. Her worst fears had materialized. According to Rosales, months before the child's disappearance local authorities had threatened to hurt her family if she and her partner, Bulmaro Vega, continued their activism. Both had been active in organizing vendors and welders from a local factory.[4] Rosales and Vega believed their toddler's disappearance was related to these threats and their refusal to comply. She claimed, "My child was taken away from me to clamp down on the movement. Authorities came to see me at the stall and offered me money. 'What do you want, *morena*? Money?' I just wanted my son back. This history of the movement was forgotten."[5]

We will never know the complete story of what happened to Oscar Vega Rosales. Time has passed, the official records are silent, and the different memories of the event are irreconcilable. No one in the story is free of ulterior motives in how they present their version. In the end that is precisely what was so terrifying about Mexico's Dirty War: it erased normal standards of human interaction and left in their place fear, frustration, and anxiety about the unknown.

In interviews vendors interpreted the disappearance of Oscar as an act of psychological torture against them and, by extension, against the UPVA itself. Vendors and their leaders distrusted local and federal authorities and had little doubt that this was an act of intimidation against them. Although the available sources are imperfect, we can piece together extant evidence to explore why vendors thought the Mexican state carried out such harsh expressions of cruelty. Local, state, and federal authorities perceived the UPVA and its alliances with students and other independent unions as threats. We know this because the archival record offers a considerable amount of evidence of infiltration, detention, and interrogation. But government records within a regime marked by authoritarianism and corruption inevitably contain omissions. Scholars can fill these gaps with interviews and reports by third parties—in this case Amnesty International—to understand how the experience of UPVA members fit into a broader pattern of abuse and repression. In addition historians and journalists have demonstrated the many instances in which the Mexican police and military terrorized those who challenged the status quo.[6]

In this chapter I argue that guerrilla leaders, left-wing students and intellectuals, and trade union organizers in the formal sector were not the only ones violently repressed by the state during the Mexican Dirty War. Members of the informal economy—who in this case had organized an independent union—also felt the wrath of the authorities. Agents of the state harassed, arbitrarily incarcerated, and tortured vendors; the state also employed tactics such as the infiltration and systematic monitoring of the UPVA, which the historian María L. O. Muñoz has called a "form of terror."[7] All three levels of the state—local, state, and federal—were involved in the fight to neutralize the most militant sellers and to divide, weaken, and ultimately destroy or co-opt the street vendors' independent union. Because of the repression they endured and the legal tricks to incriminate activists, vendors distrusted authorities.

INFILTRATION

The Mexican state used infiltration as a technique against perceived and real threats. Federal authorities spied on the UPVA leaders and its most active members, as it spied on many other organizations and individuals across the country.[8] At the same time it was spying on the UPVA, the state monitored dozens of independent and militant organizations and individuals who had allied with the UPVA; as a new generation of historians has concluded, unions, political parties, guerrilla groups, politicians, priests, students, teachers, professors, medical doctors, and even state institutions themselves came under the close surveillance of the interior secretary's secret police.[9] Officials gathered information in thousands of files in what the historian Alexander Aviña calls "the archive of counterinsurgency," which "was designed for the counterinsurgent organization of knowledge that facilitated the policing and surveillance of individuals and organizations deemed national security threats."[10] Two agencies tracked the daily activities of the UPVA: the Dirección General de Investigaciones Políticas y Sociales (General Directorate of Political and Social Investigations, DGIPS) and the Dirección Federal de Seguridad (Federal Security Directorate, DFS). The DGIPS traced its origins to 1918, when President Venustiano Carranza created it under the name Confidential Services. The agency went through several changes in functions, staff, and titles until it was expanded in 1947 and adopted its current name. The DFS was created by President Miguel Alemán in the same year.[11] In addition to keeping the president informed about the subjects and groups under surveillance, it was in charge of "persecuting, punishing, and eliminating the state's enemies."[12] The U.S. Federal Bureau of Investigation trained some of the first DFS agents.[13]

The first DGIPS reports on the UPVA date back to vendors' participation with students. DGIPS records on the UPVA tended to be more detailed than those of the DFS. This information allowed the state to know exactly what leaders were doing, their political routine, and their location. It is likely that the two agencies relied on informants, possibly UPVA members. That is what one vendor supposed. A politically active vendor using the nickname "María Quesos" speculated that one of her compañeros could have been an informant. She claimed he almost never missed a meeting, and when he did he always asked her for details. She found his excessive questioning a bit strange.[14] Other vendors said they knew the identities of the intelligence agents and even said hello to them, as they were such frequent visitors in their meetings and at protests. Agents knew that vendors were aware of the spies. It is also possible that several people who infiltrated the meetings worked for different institutions. In one DGIPS document a federal agent reported, "An incident occurred when an unknown person was writing the names of the committee's members when he was caught and expelled from the meeting. It seems that he was working for the PRI."[15] In a 1976 DFS document the UPVA leader Simitrio stated that the government tried to infiltrate agents in order to create artificial divisions within the UPVA.[16] As discussed in chapter 3 and recorded by Theodor Shank, vendors' plays portrayed the police as spies as early as 1974.[17]

Mexico's presidents and Puebla's governors could rely on the information the Ministry of the Interior gathered on street vendors. In 1975 the DFS began a file on the UPVA titled "Mercado Popular 28 de Octubre."[18] Intelligence agents recorded most of the UPVA's activities: general assemblies, internal meetings, marches, and meetings with other organizations. These agents took detailed notes, almost daily, about the number of people in attendance, the names of the speakers, their messages, and the duration of each event. Spies also recorded the route of marches and the content of banners and chants and transcribed the content of fliers. After processing the information, these agents reported it back to their bosses in Mexico City, and reports were available to authorities in Puebla who requested it. For instance, in 1979 Puebla's governor Alfredo Toxqui Fernández de Lara requested that Assistant Secretary of Interior Javier García Paniagua prepare a document on the history of the UPVA. Toxqui received a concise, yet detailed five-page document prepared by DFS agents.[19]

Historians have observed that such documents reveal the assumptions the two state agencies held. In the case of the UPVA, intelligence agents considered only a small set of acts and actors political. In meetings, for instance, while the "majority of the attendees were women and children," agents were mostly interested in the male leadership.[20] Reports hardly ever mention women. Even if women participated in political activities, the agents did not know or did not normally record their names, with the exception of a few women associated with the top leadership. For rank-and-file participation, spies wrote only "unidentified female vendor." An even more sexist remark occurred when one agent referred to Teresa Rosales not as a leader, an activist, or a vendor but as "the lover of Bulmaro Vega," ignoring the considerable role she played in UPVA activities at all levels.[21] Intelligence agents did not record all UPVA political activities, perhaps because they did not consider them political enough. For instance, the UPVA's theater group, half of which was composed of female vendors and their children, escaped agents' notice.

Regardless of these blind spots in surveillance, infiltration allowed the authorities to gather precise information about the UPVA and its leaders, members, and supporters and to spread rumors to create internal conflicts and divisions. It would have been relatively easy for the state to abduct Rosales and Vega's toddler and spread the rumor that the couple had staged the disappearance.

Oscar's parents had a history of activism that made them targets of state repression. They were among the four hundred other vendors and students who organized the UPVA in the fall of 1973, four years before their child's kidnapping. As discussed in the previous chapters, the street vendors' union was an affront to the state because of its refusal to affiliate with the PRI, its challenge to state corporatism, and its ability to reach out to other independent unions and organizations. By 1977 Vega was one of the main leaders in the union, and the state's file on him had existed for eleven years.[22] Vega was a self-identified Maoist who sought to build alliances among street vendors, peasants, and factory workers. Part of the rank and file, Rosales too had been active in a variety of UPVA duties, such as participating on the propaganda commission and supporting sympathetic groups.

State repression was not new for Rosales or Vega. Rosales had witnessed the infamous police raid on October 28, 1973. Many times she was dragged by the hair by police while defending her merchandise, and she was detained while pregnant and with her young children.[23] Vega had been in prison a number of times. When he was a physics student at the UNAM, authorities arrested him twice—in September and October 1968—and again on October 8, 1970, when he was carrying propaganda from the Cuban embassy. He was arrested yet again in August 1977; this time he was severely tortured.[24] For these reasons both parents were certain that government agents had kidnapped their son to inflict psychological torture on them and, by extent, other UPVA members.

DETENTIONS AND INCARCERATIONS

In 1977, only three years after the creation of the UPVA, organized street vendors were active in bringing together groups of blue-collar workers, service sector employees, and peasants to rally against authorities' and employers' abuses. By then El Corralón, the UPVA's headquarters, had become a democratic space. Local and regional independent organizations met there to discuss their problems, receive support, and take action. Groups of peasants from northern Puebla—along with bus drivers, nurses, teachers, telephone workers, and members of the CCI—gathered at El Corralón. These organizations were analytical and critical, and they voiced their concerns to the Mexican government.

Street vendors had become visible and outspoken political actors at the local and state level, supporting a number of workers in the region who defied the state and their employers. Such activism and alliances challenged state authoritarianism. For example, on February 18, 1977, street vendors joined telephone workers' protests demanding the restitution of eight employees who were fired by the state-owned company, Teléfonos de México.[25] In the same month vendors supported seventeen drivers for the private bus company Autobuses Estrella de Oro, which ran from Puebla to Tlaxcala, who had been fired because they were organizing an independent union. Vendors joined the drivers in a strike at the bus depot.[26] The UPVA leadership believed that people fighting for independent unions deserved their support, even if they had to deal with police brutality, arrests, disappearance, and imprisonment.

In August 1977, two months before the disappearance of Oscar Vega Rosales, local and state authorities unleashed their first major assault against street vendors since 1973, arresting and imprisoning four UPVA leaders in an effort to neutralize the independent union. Authorities accused the men of homicide and related crimes, but the police relied on illegal actions and twisted the law.

According to police reports, at 4:00 a.m. on August 10 street vendors' merchandise was stolen by an unknown man whom authorities called "unidentified person no. 98." The leaders of the UPVA, who allegedly had been drinking the whole night, caught him in the act. Simitrio, one of the most charismatic leaders, and three others brought "unidentified person no. 98" inside the UPVA's makeshift market and headquarters. According to official interrogation reports, these men kicked and beat the thief before dumping him outside the locale. The Red Cross picked up the man, who allegedly died at University Hospital because of the beatings he had received.[27]

In a rare case of efficiency and speed, Puebla's judicial police—led by Lt. Col. Felipe Flores Narro, known for his repressive techniques—investigated the crime against "unidentified person no. 98." On August 22 officials detained UPVA leaders Simitrio, José Luis Hernández López (aka El Polo), and José Martínez Balladares (aka El Zacaola).[28] At the time of their arrest the authorities had known the exact whereabouts of each leader; Simitrio, for instance, was commuting to work on a public bus.[29]

A few days before arresting Simitrio, El Polo, and El Zacaola, police officers had illegally detained Vega. According to Rosales, someone rang their doorbell late at night. When Rosales opened the door a young man claiming to be a student begged her to ask Vega to tutor him for an upcoming exam. Vega, who taught at the Prepa Zapata, went out to talk with the student. He did not return that night or in the following days. Concerned, Rosales and her children—along with Vega's mother, Cristina León de Vega—went to the newspaper offices to report his disappearance after searching for him at several hospitals, the Red Cross, and the police station. The two women declared that Vega was a "good son, a magnificent spouse, a peaceful man who didn't even carry a knife to defend himself."[30] They learned later that the so-called student was simply bait to lure Vega from his home; waiting outside for him were a number of judicial police officers.[31] Authorities later declared that Vega was detained for information.[32]

THE INTERROGATION

In the detention of Vega and the UPVA leaders the police used legal and illegal procedures. According to police records, authorities interrogated each of the UPVA leaders on August 23, 1977; the following information is from their report. El Zacaola was sleeping inside the makeshift market when he heard someone screaming around 4:00 a.m. and realized that Simitrio, a street vendor named Darío, and El Polo were beating a young man who was about twenty years old. Vega was the next one to be interrogated. While he had not witnessed or participated in the event, he allegedly informed officers that a third person had told him that Simitrio, Darío, El Zacaola, and El Polo had beaten the man. He declared that the accused had also been involved in other illicit activities. El Polo told authorities that, as the UPVA makeshift market's night watchman, he had witnessed and participated in the crime. He accused Simitrio, Darío, and a street vendor known as "El Güero el de los peines" of beating the young man. All of the men were drunk. El Polo hit the man only in the face and kicked him once; Simitrio and Darío took the man outside the market, and the Red Cross later picked him up. The last man to be interrogated was the twenty-year-old UPVA leader Simitrio. He confessed that he and the others had beaten the man.[33]

TORTURE

Undermining the reliability of all this testimony are indications that local authorities tortured at least Vega and El Polo while they were detained. The goal was to make them confess to a crime they may not have committed and to incriminate their peers. According to Amnesty International, torture is a common practice in Mexico. Officials often torture people immediately after they are arrested as "a routine accompaniment to interrogation." Men, women, and children of low socioeconomic status have been the victims of torture; some, like the UPVA leaders, are independent political activists, students, and dissident union members. Most are tortured to coerce them "to confess to criminal charges . . . [and] to make them give information about suspects."[34] The political scientist Beatriz Martínez de Murguía has found that in Mexico torture is commonly used to obtain false confessions and to blackmail and is tolerated by "police bosses."[35]

At a UPVA general assembly a month after Vega's detention, he told participants he was tortured by judicial police officers.[36] His family took him to the hospital immediately after his release to recover from the injuries.[37] Yolanda Bejarano, who witnessed Vega's release, said the police forced him to lie on the ground: "Bulmaro was tortured a lot. They put a chair on top of each hand and they jumped on the chairs. My mother wanted to take care of his injuries, but he said 'I am burned in my manhood.'"[38] He was ashamed to be seen by the women, as he had received electric shocks to his testicles. Electric shocks were part of the "repertoire of terror" the Mexican state implemented during the Echeverría administration and continued to use afterward.[39] *La Opinión* reported that "Vega show[ed] no brain coordination after the beatings he received in the head while he was detained."[40]

Shortly after Vega was interrogated, he was set free. His hospital stay helped him recover from the physical torture, and he continued his work with the UPVA. The other men remained in detention, waiting to be sentenced.

Street vendors claimed that judicial police agents had beaten El Polo too during his detention, injuring his spinal cord, and denied him medical attention as he lay suffering.[41] In her research on torture Martínez de Murguía has documented a network of complicity among police officers, agents of the Ministerio Público (Office of the State Prosecutor), and doctors; agents of the ministerio turn a blind eye to torture and doctors falsify their reports.[42] The beatings and electric shocks that El Polo and Vega experienced are the most common methods of torture, according to Amnesty International. Other methods include "death threats, mock executions, threats of enforced disappearance, near asphyxiation using plastic bags, and threats against detainees' families."[43]

Why did authorities detain Vega, who had nothing to do with the alleged crime against "unidentified person no. 98"? Because they intended to use him to crush independent unions. Vega and Simitrio were the top leaders of the UPVA at that time; imprisoning them would weaken the union, as would physically coercing one of the leaders to implicate the other.[44] A newspaper article referred to Vega as the "advisor of the archmilitant welders' union" and described him as "agitating" the welders to strike.[45] Authorities probably believed that once the so-called agitator was neutralized, the whole union would die off.

In the meantime the other three men—Simitrio, El Polo, and El Zacaola—were "presumed responsible" for the homicide. El Zacaola was set free after authorities removed his charge of concealment, but in September 1977 Simitrio and El Polo were sent to Puebla's state prison, the Penitenciaria del Estado, even before they were sentenced. Vendors decried this as an unacceptable and illegal maneuver by the state. Authorities, however, claimed that the transfer was for the detainees' own safety.[46] The men would spend over a year in prison.

Vendors had to pay a lot of money to set their leaders free. El Polo's bail was set at 50,000 pesos on December 15, 1978, more than a year after his sentencing. Simitrio was the last to be released from jail, on February 6, 1979, after being imprisoned for eighteen months; his bail too was 50,000 pesos, which the vendors paid. Then, when he was about to be freed on bail, the state accused him of stealing and injuring (*robo y lesiones*). Now vendors had to pay an additional 20,000 pesos. The union gathered the money from dues contributed by approximately two thousand vendors.[47] Altogether the rank and file paid 120,000 pesos to free their two leaders. This created some animosity among vendors, who felt the brunt of the state's indirect method of extracting financial resources.

MORE DETENTIONS

Once more vendors took to the streets to expose and demonstrate against the local government's lack of transparency and the unjust imprisonment of their leaders. During the eighteen months this conflict lasted—from August 1977 to February 1979—street vendors organized dozens of marches to demand their leaders' freedom. The vendors and their supporters claimed that authorities lacked sufficient evidence to charge them. Nobody knew for certain if "unidentified person no. 98" had died, or if he was an agent provocateur paid by the state. According to secret police files, vendors argued that their leaders were in prison because they were political activists. Anselmo Torres said, "The police illegally detained these men as a strategy to intimidate them so they would stop fighting in democratic and popular struggles." A student sympathizer nicknamed "El Botas" called the leaders' imprisonment a "repressive act with a political character."[48]

UPVA members did not protest alone; they relied on the help of organized peasants and students from Puebla and surrounding towns. These supporters were as vocal and pointed as the street vendors. They too believed that the UPVA leaders were political prisoners.[49]

These marches were dangerous because they were the easiest, most common way for authorities to detain organized street vendors and their supporters. Authorities accused them of several crimes related to their protests, such as "attacking means of communication," delivering propaganda, and hijacking buses. "Attacking means of communication" meant that UPVA members obstructed streets or major roads when they marched and protested. These kinds of crimes belonged to the federal realm, and thus the federal police could take action against the vendors. The state judicial police also arrested a number of street vendors for minor offenses, such as distributing propaganda before or during the marches. Other offenses included the hijacking of buses. On September 18, 1977, for example, a group of vendors traveled to the town of Atlixco, Puebla, to distribute UPVA's propaganda and ask the citizens to attend their marches. Federal police agents were waiting for them when they returned. The authorities intimidated and arrested the vendors, including Teresa Rosales and Micaela Daniel (aka La Patricia), who were pregnant. While the police granted Rosales her freedom, La Patricia and the men remained in prison for almost six months, charged with hijacking buses.[50] Shortly after La Patricia was released from jail, she delivered her baby, whom she named Libertad.[51]

Authorities often arrested vendor sympathizers who were leaders or spokespersons of other unions and organizations, especially if they came from cities and towns in other states. On September 18, 1977, judicial police officers arrested two Oaxaqueño students, Jesús and Saúl Vázquez, who had gone to Puebla to join a UPVA march, and accused them of "attacking means of communication and damaging private property." In September 1977 ten to sixteen vendors and their supporters—some railroad workers among them—were arrested because they hijacked buses and blocked streets. Because state officials kept them incommunicado, their families and fellow vendors feared their compañeros had been disappeared. Officials used this classic scare tactic in order to spread fear among protestors. Most of the detainees would later be found in the detention cells (*separos*) at the judicial police headquarters.[52]

Detentions intimidated vendors, made them distrust authorities, and diverted energy from protests. The UPVA had to form several commissions devoted solely to the search for detainees or to meet with authorities to negotiate their release. Vendors organized even more marches to press for their compañeros' freedom, distributed fliers conveying the injustices in these cases, and approached the most sympathetic newspaper in town, *La Opinión*, to voice their dissatisfaction with what they considered the illegal detentions.

The detentions dragged on for months and created divisions within the union. UPVA leaders disagreed on the best strategy to press authorities to free detainees. A moderate faction wanted to accept any conditions imposed by the government in order to negotiate the freedom of their compañeros. The more radical group, headed by Bulmaro Vega, wanted to continue pressing the government to free the leaders without compromise. Vega believed that Governor Alfredo Toxqui's dictator-style government and the injustices that his administration committed against the UPVA and other independent groups could potentially backfire and put him in a vulnerable position with the federal government. Vega knew that the executive branch had deposed two previous governors, and he believed the street vendors had enough power to defeat Toxqui. Other divisions arose regarding the money the rank and file paid to support the marches and free the incarcerated leaders. For instance, over the sixteen months that Simitrio was in prison, some vendors refused to pay more fees, which they could barely afford on their already meager income. A crisis among vendors erupted when, on January 16, 1979, Simitrio's son died while he was in prison. Some vendors argued that the UPVA should have provided monetary assistance to Simitrio's family to save the sick child.[53]

LOOKING FOR OSCAR

By the time Simitrio was released from prison, Vega and Rosales had been looking for their child for over a year. Immediately after Oscar's disappearance, the couple had the support of UPVA members and the state university. On the evening of October 5, 1977, and during many days that followed, Rosales's fellow female vendors helped her search for her son. Yolanda Bejarano remembered that she and the other women

FIG. 10. Protesting the disappearance of Oscar Vega Rosales: "Exigimos la liberación [de] Oscar Vega Rosa[les], Juan Chaves Hoyos [*sic*] [y] Fidel de la Luna" (We demand the liberation of Oscar Vega Rosa[les], Juan Chaves Hoyos [*sic*] [and] Fidel de la Luna). Courtesy of Archivo Histórico BUAP, Colección Vida Universitaria, 25AU-05/45, box 1.

"looked for Oscar everywhere, and we even cried together." They searched downtown streets, markets, and tenements. They even emptied a well, thinking that Oscar may have fallen in it and drowned.[54] State university officials produced fliers, which students posted everywhere they could. The UPVA held events at which members carried banners with the name of the child, demanding that the state immediately "re-appear" him.[55]

Puebla's police claimed that they too were looking for Oscar. However, the record shows they did very little to investigate the disappearance of the boy, especially when compared to their aggressive investigation a few months earlier into the alleged homicide of "unidentified person no. 98." According to Rosales, the police on the case were slow, inefficient, and highly corrupt. When someone claimed Oscar was at the U.S.-Mexico border, near the cities of Matamoros and Brownsville, the judicial police drove Rosales there, accompanied ostentatiously by several police cars. But Oscar was nowhere to be seen.[56]

Oscar Vega Rosales's disappearance was an unquestionably horrific experience for his family. Rosales felt tremendous guilt for leaving her two children alone while she went to the march. When Oscar disappeared, she was a few months pregnant with her fourth child, but instead of gaining weight during the pregnancy, the anguished Rosales was very skinny, and her skin had a greenish tint. Her little girl was born anemic, and her other children also suffered.[57] The eldest still feels guilty because he fell asleep when he was supposed to be watching his little brother. All of the couple's children were afraid of being kidnapped. One daughter was sent to live with an aunt for safety. They all felt neglected by their parents, who were focused on finding the child.[58] Rosales's income declined during this period because she spent time away from selling. As for Vega, his son's disappearance destroyed him physically and emotionally.[59]

While there is no hard evidence that authorities kidnapped Oscar, police did abduct a number of children and young people during Mexico's Dirty War in an effort to terrorize their activist family members.[60] At the end of June 1971, for instance, the state tried to intimidate Genaro Vázquez, a Guerrero-based teacher and guerrilla leader, by kidnapping his eight-year-old son, Genaro Vázquez Solís, and fifteen-year-old niece, Blanca, along with his wife and sister-in-law. Vázquez was the founder of the group Asociación Cívica Nacional Revolucionaria, whose members later took up arms and kidnapped state officials and businessmen.[61] The children were taken by state agents after the two attempted to escape heavy police surveillance around their home in Guerrero. The boy was set free after some hours of interrogation, but Blanca was held in captivity for over two weeks.[62]

Worst of all, state officials "with free [rein] to eradicate guerrilla movements" even tortured minors in order to punish their parents.[63] An example is the White Brigade, which President José López Portillo (1976–82) created as a counterinsurgent organization whose goal was to eliminate urban guerrillas. Without providing many details about her or her husband's participation in the Movimiento de Acción Revolucionaria and the Liga Comunista 23 de septiembre, Bertha Alicia López de Zazueta (aka La Chilindrina) accused the White Brigade of detaining her and her family in April 1979 at the Campo Militar Número Uno in Mexico City, an infamous clandestine location, where hundreds of people were tortured and killed. Lopez's fourteen-month-old daughter, Tania, was given electric shocks all over her tiny body, while her parents were forced to watch. Allegedly, a police boss took Tania to live with his family. Some time later, after Lopez had left the Campo Militar, she retrieved Tania and took her case to the United Nations.[64] Rosales and Vega were not alone in their suspicions that state agents took their child to punish their own political activism.

Authorities also used scare tactics on detained male political activists by threatening to torture and rape their female family members in front of them.[65] Women were sexually tortured using heinous methods.[66] This type of depraved state violence contradicts one of the myths of modern Mexico, the Pax Priísta, which claimed that unlike contemporary military dictatorships in Latin America—especially in Argentina, Brazil, and Chile—Mexico was a peaceful and democratic country in which the PRI state did not persecute, imprison, torture, or disappear political activists and labor organizers. Although Vega and Rosales doubted that the state had their toddler in the Campo Militar, they shared many concerns with other parents whose children disappeared: Were their children alive? Were they fed? Were they sick? Were they dead?[67]

Indirectly, Oscar's disappearance made street vendors aware of the struggles of other people and groups victimized by the kidnappings and disappearances. Vega and Rosales actively participated with other parents and family members whose sons and daughters had gone missing in Mexico and other parts of Latin America. The couple joined organizations that focused on finding disappeared people and fighting for the liberation of political prisoners. Vega joined the Comité Nacional Independiente, Pro-Defensa de Presos, Perseguidos, Desaparecidos y Exiliados Políticos (National Independent Committee in Defense of Prisoners, Persecuted, Disappeared, and Political Exiles).[68] This committee was created by a former president of the Universidad Autónoma Benito Juárez de Oaxaca, Felipe Martínez Soriano, whose daughter was kidnapped and tortured for almost a week because agents of the López Portillo administration linked her father to the Unión del Pueblo, a guerrilla organization.[69] Vega also became Puebla's representative in the Frente Nacional contra la Represión (National Front against Repression). In light of this, Vega planned to produce a new theatrical play about the conditions in which political prisoners lived. He had been a political prisoner in 1968 and 1971 and had firsthand knowledge of what occurred inside these prisons. His objectives were to gain sympathizers and demonstrate that vendors were also targets of Mexico's Dirty War. According to secret police files, he claimed that it was necessary to let people know that the Mexican government was actively repressing popular movements of independent groups of street vendors, workers, and campesinos. He stated that the government kept political prisoners in Sinaloa, Guerrero, Morelos, and Oaxaca, where many workers, peasants, students, and teachers went missing because they resisted the charro leaders.[70]

Vega traveled to South America and attended a number of congresses. In Mexico he publicly accused the judicial police of kidnapping his son in order to destroy the street vendors' union. For him the Dirty War against street vendors did not end with Echeverría's so-called democratic opening that claimed to tolerate the existence of PRI-independent organizations. Vega argued that repression had actually increased during the administration of President José López Portillo (1976–82).[71] In the meantime Rosales and other street vendors attended meetings with Martinez's Committee in Mexico City and Tuxtepec, Oaxaca.[72]

Rosales also joined other women of the Comité Eureka, then known as the Comité Nacional Pro-Defensa de Presos, Perseguidos, Desaparecidos y Exiliados Políticos (Pro-Defense Commission of Political Prisoners, Persecuted, Disappeared, and Exiled People), created and led by Rosario Ibarra de la Piedra. Ibarra formed the committee in 1977 with other Mexican mothers of the disappeared after her own son, Jesús Piedra Ibarra, went missing.[73] The police had taken him away, accusing him of participating in the Liga Comunista 23 de Septiembre. Then he disappeared.[74] These mothers staged hunger strikes, and Rosales joined one in Mexico City.[75] While this committee eventually won the freedom of 148 political prisoners, violence continued in Mexico. In 1981 members of a different organization calculated that there were still some four hundred disappeared who had never been found.[76] They declared that the state repressed all of those who fought for democracy and that torture and kidnappings continued in Mexico.[77] This group's members had no doubt that the state abducted Oscar Vega Rosales because his father was a UPVA leader.[78]

Nine years after his disappearance Oscar was suddenly found. One day in March 1986, while Rosales was attending a UPVA assembly, some compañeras approached her hysterically and told her that someone had found her son. "Little Oscar has appeared!" one of them shouted. The boy was at the Salvation Army in a shelter that the institution owned in Puebla. Rosales immediately went to the institution and saw Oscar from a distance. At first she did not know what to say. Finally she asked him, "Do you want to come with me?" Apparently somebody had brought the child to the Salvation Army and registered him under the name of Ernesto Pérez Pacheco. In order for the parents to recover him, they had to show his birth certificate, and a number of family members and witnesses had to "recognize" the boy as their son. Rosales, overwhelmed with emotion, fainted. The next thing she remembered, Oscar was home with her.[79]

Dramatic events did not end when Rosales and Vega got their son back. The boy and his family faced a number of problems as a result of the nine years Oscar had been away. The boy had scarcely attended school, so he was illiterate. He had to start anew, and learning proved to be quite a challenge. According to Rosales, he spent nine important years of his life—from two and a half years old to eleven—under the supervision of a couple she claimed was paid by the state to take care of the child. For a few years this couple did not allow him outside, fearing someone might recognize him. By that time, Oscar did not remember his parents. His guardians abused him physically, and his body was covered with scars. He said the woman who took care of him was a drunk who beat him and threw hot objects at him, like the *comal* (the traditional Mexican flat griddle) where she heated tortillas.[80]

To add to their frustration and pain, the Vega Rosales family was unable to prove that the authorities had committed the kidnapping.[81] Officials continually denied any involvement in the child's disappearance. Worst of all, they began a defamation campaign against Vega and Rosales, spreading the rumor that the couple had staged their child's disappearance to instigate vendors against the authorities and that a family member was actually hiding the boy.[82] Such accusations made little sense.

CONCLUSION

Even before street vendors organized the UPVA, repression was at the core of their daily experience. Once the UPVA was created, all levels of the state tried to weaken it, lure union leaders to abandon their independence from the ruling party, and co-opt them. By 1977, when the UPVA leadership was imprisoned and Oscar Vega Rosales was missing, the UPVA was cooperating actively with a group of independent organizations fighting to defend the rights of their members. All these groups, the UPVA included, denounced state authoritarianism, corruption, and the blatant disregard of their demands. Authorities used repressive, cruel, and violent techniques against individuals who dared to organize ordinary people and challenge the status quo. In the case of the street vendors, the main and constant targets of violence were the UPVA leaders and the most active rank-and-file members—people like Teresa Rosales, Bulmaro Vega, and Simitrio. These people were victims of beatings, torture, and psychological damage inflicted by a state that sought to neutralize and depoliticize them and to punish those who were politically active.

Local and state police legally and illegally arrested and incarcerated vendors and their supporters. Some people vanished during this process and were later found at the infamous judicial police separos. Others, like Vega and El Polo, experienced torture at the hands of state thugs while in custody. The 1977 imprisonment of several UPVA leaders demonstrated all of the tactics that the PRI state used to weaken, divide, and extract financial resources from the UPVA.

The repression against street vendors during the Dirty War was possible thanks in part to the information that the state collected from the two secret intelligence agencies, the DFS and the DGIPS. Intelligence agents and their informants monitored and infiltrated the UPVA on an almost daily basis. This information was instrumental in identifying and punishing selected UPVA members. By repressing certain street vendors, their leaders, and their allies, the state had at least a couple of goals in mind. First, it intended to intimidate street vendors and create fear and divisions within the UPVA. Second, the state sought to divert vendors' attention from political acts and labor organizing, forcing them to engage in more narrow demands, such as freeing those in prison. Some people were able to channel their energies toward participating in national organizations such as the Comité Eureka. Their participation indirectly enabled street vendors to understand the extent of state repression across the nation in the late 1970s and early 1980s.

Local, state, and federal authorities were unable to destroy or co-opt the UPVA, despite all the violence and financial constraints they inflicted upon vendors. By the early 1980s, as the Mexican economy continued to decline, an increasing number of people sought to survive and make a living in the informal economy. More and more vendors joined the UPVA because it protected them and guaranteed them a spot in public spaces, mainly in Puebla's downtown. By the mid-1980s the organization claimed to have ten thousand members.

5 FROM LA VICTORIA TO WALMART

Located in the heart of downtown, Puebla's La Victoria market provided a variety of goods and services that chiefly benefited the lower classes. Thousands of marketers and street vendors made a living selling a wide variety of merchandise. Customers appreciated food at low prices, and for decades people could rent cheap apartments in the building that housed the market. Things changed in 1986, when Puebla's municipality, with the financial aid of the Mary Street Jenkins Foundation, began to renovate La Victoria. The municipality closed the market indefinitely, removing all street vendors and stall owners from the heart of downtown to the periphery of the city. This move was part of the application to include the city historic center on the UNESCO World Heritage List. Local and state authorities rapidly gentrified Puebla's downtown after the neoliberal turn, promoting large economic interests to the detriment of ordinary and working-class people.[1]

The closure of La Victoria market and the removal of street vendors from downtown occurred simultaneously with the federal government's selling or closing down state-led oil, railway, and steel enterprises.[2] Like thousands of industrial workers who lost their jobs after Mexico embraced neoliberal policies in the 1980s, vendors and marketers also lost access to their workplaces at the market and in the surrounding streets. By restricting or forbidding access to public spaces, local authorities hampered the economic activities of vendors and undermined their political activities. Indeed state authorities "have long known how to manipulate space for political purposes. . . . They plan and restructure roads, [and] neighborhoods . . . to challenge, control, or prevent potentially disruptive crowds."[3] Vendors found it increasingly difficult to carry out their meetings, pintas, study groups, and marches on downtown streets and street corners and in makeshift markets. Since the neoliberal turn, local and state governments have rapidly undercut forms of direct democracy. As the scholar Keally McBride succinctly puts it, "When we lose public space, we lose democracy."[4]

LA VICTORIA MARKET

The area located next to the Santo Domingo Convent in downtown Puebla had been a resource for vendors for over one hundred years. Sellers first used it as an open-air market before its transformation into an enclosed public market named La Victoria. Vendors sold right next to the convent until 1854, when Puebla's governor officially laid the first stone of the new market.[5] Hundreds of established marketers, street vendors, and their customers traded a wide variety of wares in and around the building. Situated only two blocks from the zócalo, La Victoria market was so important to the city's economic life that, from 1910 to 1913—at the very start of the Mexican Revolution—local authorities constructed a modern building to properly accommodate these merchants.[6] The construction was part of a larger trend during the Porfiriato (1876–1911), when authorities tried to modernize public spaces.[7] The agreement to build the enclosed public market was signed in December 1909 between the municipality and a financial company, the Compañía Bancaria de Fomento y Bienes y Raíces de México, and construction began in September 1910. The impressive two-story building that housed the market opened its doors in May 1913.[8]

La Victoria was the largest market in the city, with over seventeen thousand square meters and nine entries from four different streets, and became the commercial heart of Puebla. It served the needs of Puebla's residents and of people from towns in Tlaxcala, Veracruz, Morelos, and Oaxaca.[9] While the products available at La Victoria changed over time, customers regularly bought vegetables, fruit, flowers, meat, fish, tortillas,

FIG. 11. La Victoria market classroom. Courtesy of Archivo General Municipal de Puebla, 1963.

prepared food, clothes, fabrics, and live animals. One anthropologist described it as a "gigantic live museum."[10]

La Victoria market was more than a commercial center. It also provided the growing working-class community with a number of services. In the 1910s it was one of the first buildings with electricity. It had a laboratory for water testing, and people could rent cheap apartments on the second floor.[11] In the late 1940s the market provided beds, showers, and clothing for street children.[12] Marketers listened to their own radio station, AXA-Audio Victoria.[13] In the late 1950s there was a doctor's office and a classroom where women could learn how to sew.[14] In the 1960s the market housed a classroom where male children and teenagers learned basic reading and writing skills.[15]

La Victoria was instrumental in sustaining the livelihood of thousands of marketers and street vendors. Female marketers and street vendors performed reproductive labor while tending their business, feeding and watching after their children, teaching them the skills of the trade. The market became the second home for most market sellers and their families. Street vendors who traded outside the market used its public bathrooms, and some sent their children to its public day care center.[16] The most modest street vendors who came from small and remote rural towns utilized the market as an overnight warehouse for their merchandise. Some used it as a place to sleep; market administrators constantly complained about street vendors who spent the night inside the market.[17]

Outside the market hundreds and eventually thousands of street vendors set up rudimentary, semi-fixed, and even fixed stalls to display fruit, vegetables, pots, meat, live animals, flowers, and seasonal products. They sold these in small quantities and at low prices to a mostly poor and working-class clientele.[18] They set up their stalls on sidewalks, on street corners, outside stores, and sometimes right in the middle of the street. Although customers appreciated the street vendors' affordable and varied merchandise, their presence bothered some sectors of Puebla's society.

THE *DIGNIFICACIÓN* OF DOWNTOWN

As discussed in chapter 1, business owners, some local neighbors, and established marketers at La Victoria wrote letters to municipal officials complaining about the vendors. Established La Victoria marketers were among those who complained most frequently. In 1969, for instance, a group of wrote, "The whole city is becoming a market and this is a shame and an eyesore for Puebla's citizens and visitors. . . . Street vendors cause total anarchy around the market."[19] Using this language, marketers tried to appeal to the sensibilities of middle- and upper-class authorities who disdained the racial and class characteristics of street vendors and their clientele. In response city authorities temporarily removed vendors from downtown, but their efforts were ultimately unsuccessful.

After the early 1970s authorities and city boosters devised other plans—in addition to removals and physical violence—to expel vendors from the city center. Authors of urban planning proposals began calling for Puebla's downtown to be "dignified" and "rescued." Authorities, city boosters, market sellers, journalists, and others used the Spanish term

FIG. 12. A side street of La Victoria market. Courtesy of Archivo General Municipal de Puebla, image 146, Administración Municipal, 1975–78.

dignificación to describe the process of restoring the city's social and cultural value. Puebla, in their view, had "lost" that value, and now the city center was filled with urban and rural lower-class people of indigenous ancestry.[20] Although this supposed lost value offended and angered some Poblanos, they did not openly discuss the racial component of this perception. Instead they focused on "decentralizing" commercial activity.

One of the main problems the municipality emphasized was the concentration of formal and informal commercial activities. Most specialty stores, department stores, public markets, restaurants, and even bus depots were located in the heart of the city.[21] The busiest commercial areas downtown were those surrounding La Victoria market and the Cinco de Mayo market. The latter, located five blocks from La Victoria, was built in 1962 during the centennial celebrations of the famous battle against the French troops. The streets connecting these two markets were filled with mom-and-pop retail stores and thousands of street vendors.[22] But in the view of the city boosters the real problem was not established businesses but too many street vendors. In 1973 groups of architects, engineers, and representatives of small and medium-size business associations such as the Cámara de Comercio de Puebla and the Cámara de Comercio en Pequeño, the local chambers of commerce, proposed "to expedite Puebla's progress and decentralize commercial activities . . . [by] opening a large commercial area in the city's periphery where there would also be sport and housing facilities."[23] However, the relocation of vendors and their customers to the city's outskirts had to wait another decade.

Authorities also hoped to decentralize protests. The city center had become the hub of political activities for a number of unions and organizations. The zócalo and the state university were very close to the municipal palace, and many protests and marches took place in these downtown spaces. If vendors moved to the outskirts, there was a chance that the city center might be protected from the political activities of the common people. Removing street vendors would complement the partial relocation of students to Ciudad Universitaria, the second state university campus, which opened on the outskirts of the city in 1969 and was funded by the Mary Street Jenkins Foundation. MSJF president Manuel Espinosa Yglesias donated 60 million pesos of the foundation's money to the UAP to build this campus. Espinosa Yglesias was trying, in part, "to contain and counteract the communist activists of the UAP."[24] Removing some students from downtown would undercut their democratic practices.

The existence of La Victoria market also challenged business owners. Members of several business associations called the market an eyesore, a magnet for street vendors, and a source of traffic congestion. They wanted it closed down. At the end of 1973 the Cámara de Comercio en Pequeño insisted that La Victoria market "must disappear from downtown" because it had become a "nest of rats, a symbol of dirtiness." Claiming that the market "caused problems for traffic" and attracted street vendors, the group urged the city to "dignify" Puebla by building new markets that were strategically located.[25] These requests resembled those in previous decades to intervene on how public space should be used and by whom.

The idea of "dignifying" downtown became a common rhetorical strategy in urban planning projects, even if these proposals to decentralize commerce did not materialize in the 1970s.

At first, dignificación was an elusive idea. City boosters talked only vaguely about a mixed bag of imaginary attributes of the city center; for instance, they wanted Puebla's streets to "recuperate" their cleanliness and beauty.[26] By the late 1970s, however, the way to dignify Puebla's downtown became less vague. President José López Portillo decreed 6.99 square kilometers, most of it in downtown, a "historic monumental zone" in 1977. The zone consisted of 2,619 historic buildings (used as schools, churches, markets, hospitals, prison, and government offices) and twenty-seven plazas and gardens that were built between the sixteenth and nineteenth century. According to the decree, the monumental zone had an "exceptional value for Mexico's social and political history as well as for Mexican art." The state had to "protect this area and to pursue research, conservation, restoration, and recuperation of the monuments that constitute the cultural heritage of the nation."[27] The law and its accompanying regulations stated that changes to these buildings could be granted only by the Instituto Nacional de Antropología e Historia (National Institute of Anthropology and History, INAH).[28]

Puebla's authorities and private entities took seriously their role as protectors of the monumental zone and began to systematically renovate buildings, such as the Teatro Principal and the Santo Domingo Convent.[29] Emphasizing too that Puebla's downtown had official historical and artistic value, city boosters launched several plans to decentralize commercial activities; this was the essence of the dignificación process. The 1977 decree provided boosters' projects with official legitimacy. From then on it was a civic duty for self-selected groups to remove street vendors and established marketers from downtown and to push for the closure of La Victoria market. City planners conceived future projects in the name of preserving the historic heritage of the city.

Dignifying Puebla had clear class and racial components. Street vendors, some marketers, and their customers were mostly working-class and rural people who needed to be expelled from downtown in order to "revitalize" the historic center. Cultural and racial tensions also played a role in the "rescue" of downtown. As discussed in chapter 1, for many decades upper- and middle-class people had disdained street vendors and their commercial practices, food, products, and children. They believed downtown had to be cleansed of this kind of people, especially those of indigenous descent.[30] Even if people did not say so explicitly, they associated indigeneity with men in sandals (*huaraches*), women wearing rebozos on top of their braided hair, numerous children, a presumed lack of hygiene, and supposed backwardness and poverty.[31] The geographers Gareth Jones and Ann Varley likewise found that "gentrification in Puebla, as an expression of middle-class opposition to popular culture and livelihood strategies in the center, draws on unspoken racialized notions of difference."[32]

In the view of many Poblanos, vendors and marketers were not people who deserved the use of monumental buildings like La Victoria market. Elites valued these buildings more than the use of public space by ordinary people—indeed they valued the buildings over the people themselves.[33] They linked certain structures to the city's alleged European past through their Spanish or French architectural influence. As such, they dearly valued the buildings of the colonial era, the nineteenth century, and the early twentieth century. A tourist guidebook of the city, for instance, says nothing about La Victoria as the most important public market of raw and prepared food, only that the building belonged to the architecture of the Spanish Renaissance with a strong influence from Valencia.[34] Such omissions are not surprising: "low cultural capital rarely makes it into travel guides ... yet it is an important dimension of inner-city life."[35]

In 1980 city officials drafted the *Plan Global de Desarrollo 1980–1982*, which proposed building new markets in the periphery of the city.[36] It was revised in early 1984 by the city council, led by Mayor Jorge Murad Macluf, and renamed *Commercial Decentralization*. It now included two smaller plans: "Commercial Reordering" and "Historic Center Regeneration." *Commercial Decentralization* aimed to encourage businesses—meaning street vendors and established marketers at La Victoria—to move out in order to decentralize some of the commercial activity from downtown.

"Commercial Reordering" specified relocating sellers to markets the municipality would build on the outskirts of the city, and "Historic Center Regeneration" was a larger program that included dignifying the historic buildings in downtown.

Just as he had promised when he was a PRI candidate for mayor, Murad began testing these plans. In fact his 1983 political campaign was focused on the "revitalization" of the historic city center. Pressured by business associations and supported by Governor Guillermo Jiménez Morales (1981–87)—and eventually by the Mary Street Jenkins Foundation—his actions as mayor were quite successful.[37] One of his first measures was demanding that street vendors relocate to a large lot (23,755 square meters) in the northern part of the city. The municipality referred to this land as the Mercado Miguel Hidalgo y Costilla, one of the seven public markets on the periphery built by the municipality. Street vendors who agreed to move began calling it the Tianguis Popular 28 de Octubre. Technically speaking, the vendors—most of them UPVA members—were right: *tianguis*, a term with Nahuatl origins, means "open-air market." According to the vendors, the so-called market had only some electricity posts and a few water faucets.[38] This tianguis was a sour reminder of El Corralón, the makeshift market that authorities had granted the UPVA ten years earlier, which had been little more than four walls. At least El Corralón was located downtown; the Miguel Hidalgo market was far away, unreachable by public transportation, and vendors worried that few customers would make their way to it. This remote location also shattered vendors' ability to maintain political alliances and physical connections with other independent organizations. In short, removal translated into invisibility.

REMOVING THE STREET VENDORS

In the summer of 1986 authorities carried out the *Commercial Decentralization* plan. The first step was expelling thousands of street vendors from the forty to sixty downtown blocks they occupied, especially in and around La Victoria market. After months of negotiations between street vendors and municipal authorities, the UPVA leadership finally signed an agreement with Mayor Murad in August. The union committed to relocate voluntarily and peacefully all of its members to the new markets on the city's periphery.[39]

Why did such a militant vendors' union, which had long defended the right of sellers to work on downtown streets, agree to move to distant markets? What mechanisms did authorities employ to convince them? It is possible authorities bought or bribed the UPVA's main leadership, which was then headed by Simitrio. After all, this would not be the first time Puebla's government officials tried to buy or co-opt UPVA's non-charro leaders. Indeed observers at the time wondered if Simitrio had sold out. Six months after the agreement was signed, a journalist with a popular local political magazine asked him directly if the authorities had bribed him. Simitrio smiled and politely said, "When we were in negotiations, there were offers of money. It was said that 50 to 1,000 million pesos [would be offered] . . . but it was only gossip, just talk." The journalist wrote that the leader still lived in a modest apartment, very close to one of Puebla's downtown markets, took his meals at market stalls, and did not own any properties.[40] The conclusion was that Simitrio had not compromised the organization's integrity. Rank-and-file members also believed that Simitrio was honest; they described him wearing simple clothes made out of a cheap cotton fabric called *manta*.[41] Rosa Martínez recalled that Simitrio "wasn't pretentious. He always wore a *guayabera* (traditional Mexican shirt) and sandals. He never wore a suit, not even to parties. He didn't have cars. People gave him rides. He didn't carry guns."[42]

The UPVA's acceptance of the removal had to do with the rather generous terms of the agreement, which seemed politically and economically beneficial for both the municipal government and the UPVA. In return for the UPVA's promise to move, the municipality committed to help vendors relocate and promote their commerce. Local authorities would also help them acquire products from wholesalers, transport merchandise, and publicize the new markets. The municipality granted the UPVA large subsidies for the acquisition of stalls in the markets and agreed to provide legal advice to the union, and vendors were allowed to sell on downtown streets during three commercial high seasons: Todos Santos

(October 28 to November 2), Christmas (December 16–24 and 30–31), and Reyes (January 4–5).[43]

The city council's dream finally became a reality on August 3, 1986, when vendors left the streets. The removal helped strengthen Murad's political position and facilitated the election of the next priísta mayor.[44] Murad's campaign had been a difficult one for the PRI. In the early 1980s the ruling party's candidate did not have the support of the middle and upper classes, who had been disillusioned by President López Portillo's 1982 nationalization of the banking industry. Puebla's elite—among them the Consejo Coordinador Empresarial (Business Coordinating Council), a group of several employer associations—supported the PAN candidate, the right-wing textile industrialist Ricardo Villa Escalera.[45] Unsurprisingly the election was fraudulent and the priísta Murad became Puebla's mayor.[46] While he did not have the support and trust of important business leaders like Manuel Espinosa Yglesias during his first years in office, his government counted on the financial support of the MSJF president by the beginning of 1986.[47] The removal of vendors in August only solidified Espinosa Yglesias's support of Puebla's officials.

Simitrio could argue that the generous terms of the agreement ended years of vendors' struggle, that the membership would finally get the markets they always wanted at reasonable prices. Moreover they could have peace of mind, as the police would not harass them. Even if the markets were far from the city's core, vendors would have the full support of the mayor to ensure that their commercial activities prospered. This contrasted greatly with the agreements between La Victoria marketers and the municipality a couple of months later, despite the affiliation of the market sellers' unions with the PRI.

Unfortunately for everyone concerned, the agreement between the city and the vendors was not to last. Murad died in a car crash on August 9, 1986, just one week after signing the agreement and after the street vendors had left downtown.[48] The new interim mayor, Amado Camarillo Sánchez, and subsequent administrations refused to comply with the original agreement, causing friction between the disgruntled vendors and authorities for years to come.

As soon as the vendors were removed, local authorities sent eight hundred public employees to clean and fix the streets. Firefighters hosed sidewalks, and, according to *El Sol de Puebla*, street sweepers allegedly removed five hundred tons of trash. Municipal workers fixed the pavement on the streets surrounding the market where vendors had installed their semi-fixed stalls.[49] All of this activity occurred while hordes of local police guarded downtown to keep vendors from taking back the streets around La Victoria. The authorities were trying to protect downtown Puebla from the masses.

Removing the vendors and hosing down the streets was not enough. *El Sol de Puebla* did not miss the opportunity to badmouth UPVA members. The newspaper editors suggested that organized street vendors were criminals who had endangered the safety of pedestrians and Puebla's citizens in general. They insisted that the removal of vendors made the streets of Puebla much safer. According to the widely circulated newspaper, police found almost one hundred Molotov cocktails, along with weapons, gunpowder, and marijuana, at the UPVA's headquarters.[50]

El Sol de Puebla also devoted numerous pages in early August 1986 to the end of street vending. The editors carefully selected for print letters from Puebla's inhabitants that sided with the mayor's measure "to clean the city." A female student simply stated that before removal she was "afraid of walking on the streets of downtown." A middle-class housewife predicted that street traffic would be simplified and the danger of walking on the streets would end. Another woman stated that she had been afraid of getting close to vendors' stalls because of their smell and because she feared being denigrated and offended by the vendors.[51] Editors drew from middle-class and gender anxieties about having to share public spaces with the masses in order to justify the vendor removal.

At the end of the summer shopkeepers and some members of the elite were excited that the authorities had finally "dignified" the city center and restored its historic value. A political magazine reported that shopkeepers especially were happy that vendors were gone. They lauded Mayor Murad as the best politician the city ever had; their sales were up, and the city was cleaner, more modern, and prettier.[52] Others applauded city authorities and declared that national and international tourists would finally have a good impression of Puebla's citizens.[53] José Rodoreda, a staunch enemy of street vendors, a member of the Consejo Coordinador Empresarial, and the president of the local Cámara Nacional de Comercio (National Chamber of Commerce), described the removal of sellers as "a fabulous measure because it would promote tourism."[54]

Health officials also congratulated the mayor for altering the urban landscape. They claimed that his efforts would improve public health among Poblanos because "the food that street vendors sold was contaminated with feces because vendors lacked access to running water and could not wash their hands." Puebla's chief of public health, Carlos Galindo, thought the mayor's policies placed Puebla next to other modern cities, falsely claiming that in "advanced countries there is no street food." He naïvely believed vendors would have fixed stalls in the new markets, with potable water and bathrooms.[55]

Not everyone was as satisfied as the media and officials suggested. Referencing the commercial synergy of the streets surrounding La Victoria before removal, a small business owner recalled that the street vendors had attracted customers to the area: "There were lots of people walking on the streets, buying from vendors, and a lot of these people had a look at the clothes in my shop windows, and came in to my store, and bought from me. After street vendors left, the streets were empty and my sales decreased."[56] Eventually pedestrians returned to the streets, but they were not the working-class, rural migrants that used to shop at her store.

NEOLIBERALISM: *EL DESPOJO DEL SIGLO*

Right after the street vendors left downtown, La Victoria marketers requested meetings with the mayor about the future of the market. Perhaps fearing they would experience the same fate as the street vendors, the established marketers wanted to engage in a joint effort with authorities to renovate the market.[57] However, authorities used La Victoria's allegedly unsanitary conditions as evidence that the market was a danger and an eyesore. The removal of the street vendors was not enough; the second step in the so-called rescue of downtown was the relocation of approximately two thousand stall owners in La Victoria—in total about fifteen thousand people: owners, their family members, and their employees who depended economically on the market.[58]

In mid-October 1986 the interim mayor, Amado Camarillo Sánchez, announced the immediate end to market activities and the temporary relocation of these sellers.[59] The city council convinced the leaders of the various marketers' unions—all of them affiliated with the PRI—to relocate by assuring them they could return to La Victoria once the market was renovated. Against their will and against their economic interests, marketers had to move to the periphery, where the former street vendors had been relocated.[60] Ironically authorities did not do much to accommodate these marketers; they experienced almost the same treatment as the union members had.[61]

How was it possible that authorities dismissed the marketers who were members of official unions and had loyally supported them in the removal of street vendors? Scholars argue that by the mid-1980s the relationship between official unions and the state had changed. After neoliberal reforms began, the state did not compromise with its old political clients as it once did. It did not have the resources to do so. An "exclusionary state" had displaced the "populist state" of earlier decades.[62] Indeed the economic crisis was so severe that "it was no longer peasants, workers, and radicalized students that the party needed to impress but multilateral agencies, foreign lenders, and government officials—all of whom needed to be mobilized to help bail Mexico out."[63] To top it off, the PRI governor Mariano Piña Olaya was a political outsider who was not interested in forging alliances or building political clients among the local population.

Based on the 1977 decree on the monumental zone, INAH considered La Victoria market a "monument" in the "historic downtown" that needed urgent renovations and "needed to be dignified." Municipal health officials claimed the market posed sanitary, environmental, and structural risks: it was infested with rats, and the drainage system and electric connections were in terrible shape.[64]

State agencies made it sound like markets and their marketers were the antithesis of modernity and cleanliness. They suggested that La Victoria's terrible condition was largely due to marketers' commercial activities. Municipal documents, however, prove otherwise; they show that marketers constantly petitioned municipal authorities to help them clean the market and renovate the building. Most of these requests were ignored, but sometimes the city council carried out extermination campaigns, called *campañas de desratización*, at marketers' requests; fifty thousand rats were reportedly killed in 1971 alone.[65] In addition marketers themselves cleaned the building on occasion, with the help of firefighters. They even closed the market while they cleaned because they wanted to show their customers that La Victoria was as clean as the supermarkets.[66]

The city council and the marketers could resolve La Victoria's deficiencies, but Puebla's downtown dignification project had a bigger problem: La Victoria served the needs of working-class people, of rural folks of indigenous background who did little to "dignify" the historic center. Blue-collar workers' wives and children were the usual clientele, along with maids and country people. Middle- and upper-class people preferred to shop at the spacious modern supermarkets that had been built since the late 1960s, such as Comercial Mexicana.[67] Though more expensive than the public markets, the supermarkets provided free parking, shopping carts, bright lights, and a sense of order and cleanliness that contrasted with the boisterous and disorderly nature of La Victoria.

If elites did not interact directly with the masses, why did they still want to get rid of the market and gentrify downtown? La Victoria was the only large "monument" in downtown prime space that housed thousands of lower-class people. The economic activities happening inside and outside the Porfirian building, and all the people involved in these transactions, were an eyesore to elites and a challenge to larger economic objectives. City boosters, such as a group of local architects, argued that La Victoria did not attract tourists. They wanted to transform it into a "folkloric market" with small restaurants, ice-cream shops, sandal stores, and flower shops.[68] Obviously these men had their own definition of *folkloric*.

Established marketers immediately opposed the project that sought to remove them. They formed La Victoria Market Defense Committee to defend marketers' right to stay in La Victoria. Some two thousand marketers claimed that the market was their workplace (*centro de trabajo*) and an important institution in Puebla's history. In a letter to the president of Mexico they stated that they had been working in the market for at least fifty years.[69] The group carried out a series of protests, among other initiatives. They employed revolutionary slogans during their marches, carrying banners declaiming, "The market belongs to those who work it," an echo of Emiliano Zapata's famous phrase "The land belongs to those who work it."[70] Marketers tried to gain the support of Puebla's residents and aired their plight on radio stations. They even had the backing of other market people in town who sent letters to the governor protesting the mayor's plan to close La Victoria.[71]

But marketers' efforts were useless. After months of negotiations, their charro leaders agreed to move. On October 20, 1986, Germán Méndez Silva—the leader of the Unión de Locatarios (Union of Stall Owners) and a union affiliated with CNOP and PRI, Comerciantes en Pequeño y Ambulantes del Mercado La Victoria (Small Vendors of La Victoria Market)—signed an agreement with Mayor Camarillo Sánchez to voluntarily vacate the market.[72]

Authorities did not hesitate to use force and intimidation, employing armed police, dogs, and firefighters, to make sure that every market seller left the facility.[73] Immediately after the last seller left the building, city workers began destroying all the cement stalls and closing all the doors to prevent anyone from returning.[74] These were the saddest days for the marketers; some had spent most of their lives in the building, as their parents had started the business. The removal of marketers whose unions were affiliated with CNOP unions signified a new relationship indeed between old allies and the state.

The relocation of La Victoria marketers also delivered a heavy blow to their economic survival. Their leadership forced them to share street vendors' hardships in the unfinished markets on the periphery of the city.[75] The timing was especially unfortunate as the country was experiencing an economic crisis, the so-called lost decade. Between 1983 and 1988 the GDP grew 0.2 percent, inflation reached 86.7 percent annually, and real wages went down by 40 percent.[76] Former La Victoria sellers and street vendors had many reasons to be upset and disillusioned with authorities. The seven markets the municipality built in the mid-1980s lacked roofs, water, lights, sewage, janitors, security guards, telephones, and access to public transportation.[77] Vendors complained that the streets that surrounded the markets were unpaved, making it difficult for cars to reach them.[78] Yet authorities chose heroic names for these markets: Héroes de Puebla, Ignacio Zaragoza, Francisco I. Madero, Independencia, Miguel Hidalgo y Costilla, José María Morelos y Pavón, and Emiliano Zapata.

Adding insult to injury, these new markets were poorly designed. Authorities never met with vendors to consider their needs before planning the construction and location of the markets.[79] Despite vendors' desire to be consulted, authorities simply refused to take their opinions into account.[80] As a result architects who had no idea about vendors' business practices designed the markets inadequately. In meetings between the municipality and the UPVA that took place after the markets were built, vendors expressed their dissatisfaction with the terribly designed stalls that would not allow them to display their merchandise effectively. This prevented them from making profits in an economy already in deep crisis.

UNESCO WORLD HERITAGE SITE

While street vendors and marketers faced numerous challenges in the new unfinished markets, municipal authorities and boosters were devising another project. A group of officials and state institutions had already asked UNESCO to include Puebla's downtown on its World Heritage List. In the 1986 nomination proposal, state officials claimed that Puebla's historical zone was "a living witness that represents the different historical stages that have determined the city's and the nation's development throughout the colonial, independence, reform, and revolutionary periods." The officials made sure to include the urban changes that the government had recently carried out to "preserve and conserve" historical monuments. Among these changes, authorities prided themselves on the fact that they had been working to relocate street vendors and to "safeguard La Victoria Market" since the early 1980s.[81] UNESCO was convinced of the value of the historic center and on December 11, 1987, designated Puebla's downtown a World Heritage Site.[82] This recognition reinforced the authority of political and city boosters to determine which buildings would perform which functions, which ones would be renovated, which agencies would be in charge of preserving them, and ultimately who could use and enjoy the historic city center.

David Harvey writes, "Increasingly, we see the right to the city falling into the hands of private or quasi-private interests."[83] And indeed the municipality increasingly relied on private funds. This reliance on private capital was part of a trend occurring in other Latin American World Heritage Sites where neoliberal government officials did not consider urban preservation an important concern. In addition the UNESCO title did not come with a lot of money.[84] For these reasons local authorities eagerly sought private money to finance their projects. In Puebla's case the main investor was the Mary Street Jenkins Foundation (MSJF), a U.S.-style philanthropic organization in Mexico founded in 1954 by William O. Jenkins (1878–1963). Jenkins was born in Shelbyville, Tennessee, moved to Monterrey in 1901, and relocated to Puebla in 1906. The highly controversial Jenkins became the wealthiest entrepreneur in Mexico at the time, and his charitable foundation mainly supported projects that fostered sport and educational activities in Puebla.[85]

Once La Victoria Market was vacated, the MSJF invested in the building and its surrounding streets. Nicolás Vázquez Arreola, the MSJF spokesperson, announced the investment of 1 billion pesos to renovate the market and sixty-two surrounding blocks.[86] The MSJF's interest in renewing historic buildings—or investing in public works, for that matter—was not new. The foundation's money had served as "a coffer into which Puebla's governors and mayors could dip—once they convinced Jenkins of the worth of their projects."[87]

In the early 1990s the municipality complained that the ongoing renovation had become too costly. So after six years of the market's closure, and while marketers were still waiting, authorities decided on another approach: to sign an agreement to lend the building to the Amparo Foundation, another philanthropic organization presided over by Manuel Espinosa Yglesias (1909–2000), one of the leading Mexican businessmen and the "the brains of the Jenkins organization."[88] An acute entrepreneur most famously known as Bancomer's CEO, he worked hand-in-hand with Jenkins for decades and learned much from the American's philanthropic activities. In fact Espinosa Yglesias's own organization shared some similarities with Jenkins's. Espinosa Yglesias named it in honor of his wife, Amparo Rugarcía de Espinosa Yglesias, just as Jenkins had honored his late wife, Mary Street. The Amparo Foundation too supported educational activities in addition to "social development, arts, and the preservation of Mexican cultural heritage."[89] Though on a much more modest scale compared to Jenkins, Espinosa Yglesias supported state projects in Puebla, especially those he thought were beneficial to maintaining his own fortune.[90]

In 1992 authorities declared that La Victoria was an "integral part of Puebla's historical center" and "needed to be architecturally preserved while at the same time, its use should benefit the collectivity."[91] They had determined that no entity other than the Amparo Foundation could be entrusted with the responsibility of preserving the building. Represented by Mayor Marco Antonio Rojas Flores, the municipality therefore "lent" La Victoria market to the Amparo Foundation for a span of ninety-nine years through a legal mechanism called a *commodatum*. This gratuitous bailment was a legal contract between the municipality (the bailor) and the Amparo Foundation (the bailee) in which the latter was required to "preserve the market as an authentic heritage of the state" while "ensuring that it fulfilled the social objectives to which it was first built."[92] Unlike renting a property, using a commodatum meant the municipality did not receive any material compensation for this agreement. In other words, the Amparo Foundation did not pay the city of Puebla for using the building.

Why did authorities agree to this contract? Just as previous administrations made deals with the Jenkins Foundation, it is possible that municipal authorities wanted to continue securing private funds from these philanthropic organizations—especially during the neoliberal years, when the state barely funded these projects. Internal discussions during April 1992, prior to the signing of the commodatum, revealed local officials' intentions. Some council members wanted to ensure that Espinosa Yglesias would continue investing in other projects to "dignify Puebla." Others added that his foundation's funds would relieve the municipality from the burden of paying for the renovation and maintenance of the building. One council member claimed that governments in other countries used private funds to restore monuments. Another stated that the terms of the commodatum should not look like a mechanism for Espinosa Yglesias to make more money; instead the commodatum should be presented to Puebla's citizens as a nonprofit contract for the Fundación Amparo and should emphasize the benefits of such a contract to the people.[93]

The terms of the agreement were vague. The Amparo Foundation was to use the market for commercial and artisanal purposes and for "activities that the Amparo Foundation decides would be socially and culturally beneficial." There was no indication of what kind of activities the municipality had in mind when it drafted the agreement. Accordingly all the income the foundation received for the use of the building would be intended mainly for the "restoration, preservation, adaptation, and maintenance of the building" and to promote cultural activities that "directly benefit the city's and state's communities." At least in theory the commodatum emphasized that the agreement benefited the collectivity, but the collectivity definitely did not include street vendors and marketers.

The entrepreneurial ideas of Espinosa Yglesias matched the neoliberal project of the state. When he first approached authorities, he argued that the state did not always have the capacity to carry out and fund cultural projects. He emphasized the role of private investment and private enterprise in cultural and educational activities. His philanthropic organizations had participated in major renovation works, such as the Templo Mayor in Mexico City's downtown; therefore, he had the clout to propose what to do with certain buildings in Puebla's historical center. He wanted Puebla to reclaim its status as one of Mexico's major cities.

In his view, one way to do so was through the development of tourism. To this end he wanted to transform La Victoria from a public market to a modern tourist attraction. Taking advantage of Puebla's inclusion on the UNESCO World Heritage List, he proposed the market could become a tourist attraction if it were properly restored and maintained by his foundation and used as a private commercial facility. The revenue obtained from the commercial use of La Victoria—which, in his view, was "descuidado y desaprovechado" (not well taken care of and misused)—could help his organization maintain the building and sustain a museum complex located elsewhere. He also proposed using 20 percent of La Victoria market as a parking lot.[94]

This was not the first time Espinosa Yglesias tried to use a historic building. Back in 1969, as head of the MSJF, he had requested the use of El Carolino, the former Jesuit convent, from the state university. In exchange he would provide further economic aid to the university. The administration refused.[95] The Autonomous University of Puebla would later become one of the main advocates—along with the MSJF, the Amparo Foundation, and the state—for preserving and restoring historical buildings in downtown.[96]

When word of the deal between the municipality and Espinosa Yglesias leaked to a group of former La Victoria marketers, they requested that the municipality sign a commodatum with them instead. In an ambitious but futile effort, this group wrote several times to municipal officials; officials filed the requests without responding to the group. The use and potential preservation of La Victoria by marketers themselves was out of the question during the neoliberal turn.

THE WALMART RETAILERS

In 1994, two years after the signing of the commodatum, the Amparo Foundation reopened the La Victoria building as a shopping mall called Centro Comercial La Victoria. It contained the department store Suburbia, a restaurant called Vips, and other stores. Most people did not know that both Suburbia and Vips belonged to CIFRA, Mexico's top retail company.[97] Even fewer people knew that, in 1991, three years before the reopening of La Victoria, Walmart began operations in Mexico by taking a 50 percent share of CIFRA. The change in ownership was not widely known because one of Walmart's many strategies in its global expansion was to maintain the name of retailers that had been operating in their home country for many years. The clearest example of this strategy was keeping the name Aurrera, which was the leading supermarket of the CIFRA group.[98] The only two stores that Walmart launched in Mexico with their American names were Walmart Supercenter and Sam's Club.[99]

Former marketers and the street vendors who used to sell in and around the market were tremendously upset about the opening of the Centro Comercial La Victoria. It excluded them and put an end to the possibility of making a living there. Even two months before Suburbia and Vips opened, former La Victoria marketers were still writing to the municipality through their organizations to find out when they could go back to selling in the market. An official responded to these inquiries by stating that they could return to the market and continue their commercial activities once renovations were finished. Either this official was unaware of the now two-year-old commodatum, or he was simply lying to them.[100]

In November 1994, when the Centro Comercial La Victoria was inaugurated, hundreds of UPVA sellers and former marketers protested.[101] They marched through downtown streets, carrying huge banners demanding "Suburbia Out of La Victoria Market." They closed down the main entrances to the building and glued banners across them. Police were deployed around La Victoria while the Espinosa family, Mayor Rafael Cañedo Benítez, and Puebla's governor Manuel Bartlett Díaz, along with journalists and a selected group of Puebla's elite, attended the private inauguration ceremony. In a speech in which she tried to legitimize the Amparo Foundation's takeover, Angeles Espinosa Rugarcía, the daughter of Espinosa Yglesias and the foundation's new president, emphasized that La Victoria's renovation had been carried out under the supervision of the INAH and the state government. She added, "The rescue of the La Victoria market shows that these kinds of buildings can be adapted to Puebla's modern life."[102] For the foundation's representative, modernity meant the establishment of global capital in Puebla's historic center at the expense of thousands of working-class people who made a living in that market. The centuries-old practice of selling herbs, food, flowers, and local prepared food disappeared from the space, along with a long-established sense of community.

La Victoria market experienced what Sylke Nissen calls "the hybridization of public space," in which there was "semi-privatization of public space by a transfer of rights of use and maintenance tasks on private subjects [and the] temporary exclusion through opening hours."[103] What used to be the largest enclosed public market in town, with a rich history that dated back to the nineteenth century, was now a shopping mall regulated by the schedule of private retailers. Worse, as Margaret Crawford notes for other locations, La Victoria went through a "spontaneous malling," that is, "a process by which urban spaces are transformed into malls without new buildings or developers."[104] It seemed like a relatively seamless transition, and it almost gave the impression that La Victoria was still a public place. But it was not. Vendors could not use it as they did in the past: as a warehouse to keep their merchandise safe and as a political space to post propaganda and to hold meetings.

Evidently the commodatum and the opening of these two retail stores—and mom-and-pop stores later on—did nothing to maintain the original objectives of La Victoria; it did not offer cultural activities and it did not become a magnet for tourists. Today the former La Victoria market is a low-end shopping center of small shops that sell clothes, leather bags, underwear, jewelry, Chinese-made trinkets, cell phones, and beauty products. There are two hair salons, an ice-cream shop, an arcade in the center of the plaza, and a train for children to ride that runs inside the building. The second floor features an unpopular food court with seven small food stands selling hamburgers, fries, nachos, chips, and hotdogs.

La Victoria market was one of the many sites that were restored and "rescued" during the 1980s and 1990s. Perhaps anticipating the request to UNESCO for World Heritage designation, Puebla's government and other entities repaired façades in what some have described as *fachadismo*, and they restored and "rescued" historic monuments and gardens.[105] The renovation of these so-called monuments brought a change in function in some cases, but the buildings continued to be used by the public. For instance, Puebla State Prison—a former Jesuit convent—was restored and in 1985 became Puebla's Cultural Institute. Until very recently the Institute housed a newspaper repository and Puebla's state historical archive.[106] The Saint Domingo atrium next to La Victoria market was restored between 1985 and 1986 without being repurposed. The Paseo Bravo's street vendors and fair were relocated between 1986 and 1987, but it continued as a public park. The old train station was converted into the Railroad Museum in 1988.[107]

The "rescue" of La Victoria market was the first time in Puebla's recent history that a private organization was able to use a public historic monument for commercial activities linked to the global expansion of a U.S. retailer. It set the precedent for future projects of this sort in the eastern area of downtown, across what used to be the San Francisco River in the late 1990s. It also set the precedent for the rapid gentrification around the portales that surround the main plaza, which began at the turn of the twenty-first century. The opening of the Centro Comercial La Victoria was part of a larger trend of the "reconquest" of the city center, ushering in a wave of urban gentrification in other cities in Mexico and Latin America.[108] In the case of the Paseo de San Francisco, in the old barrios of the city, authorities and the private sector carried out the construction of a convention center, gardens, movie theaters, a large parking lot, and hotels, which were inaugurated in 1998. According to the anthropologist Nancy Churchill, these facilities too were built at the expense of thousands of low-income people who lived in the tenements of these barrios. Authorities forcefully evicted these residents and demolished their homes. Puebla's officials carried out a profitable project that disregarded the interests of low-income families who had resided, worked, and forged their identities in that old area of town.[109]

CONCLUSION

Thousands of small and medium-size sellers made their living in and outside of La Victoria during the more than seven decades the market functioned in the twentieth century. At the same time, the building served the needs of countless customers from mostly working-class backgrounds. Beginning in the 1970s authorities and city boosters began launching projects to eliminate vendors in the name of dignifying the downtown area. They based their arguments on the 1977 presidential decree making Puebla a monumental zone. As such the area needed to be protected and preserved. In essence the Porfirian, neoclassical building that housed La Victoria required elite protection from the ordinary people who had been using it for decades. It was not until the mid-1980s, however, that authorities and city boosters formally launched specific projects to decentralize commercial activities. By the end of 1986 they had succeeded in expelling vendors and marketers and closing down La Victoria market. UNESCO included Puebla on the list of World Heritage Sites, which provided further justification for the final removal of all sellers.

A turning point in urban renewal policies in Puebla occurred in 1986, at the dawn of Mexico's embrace of neoliberalism. The historic downtown began to gentrify and to welcome large companies connected to the global economy. In their efforts to rescue the historic center, authorities continued making use of private funds—especially from the Mary Street Jenkins and Amparo foundations—to renovate and revitalize certain downtown buildings. In 1992, however, local authorities followed a different path by lending La Victoria to the Amparo Foundation, which in turn rented part of the building to the two Walmart-owned retailers and other shops.[110]

The supporters of the neoliberal turn won the battle over the use of prime public space. The urban projects that began in the mid-1980s displaced street vendors, marketers, and their most loyal customers from the very heart of the city. The building that once served the needs of the urban poor and working class came to an end in the fall of 1986. After Puebla's downtown gained the title of UNESCO World Heritage Site, the urban working class did not fit in the neoliberal city center. The local government eagerly cooperated in driving thousands of people away from their traditional workplaces. These policies officially "dignified" Puebla's downtown, remaking it according to elite notions of beauty and modernization: purifying it of its indigenous people, turning it into a shopping mall, and welcoming Walmart-owned retailers. Certainly "our world is one in which the neoliberal ethic of intense possessive individualism, and its cognate of political withdrawal from collective forms of action, becomes the template for human socialization."[111]

Beyond economics, vendors lost access to their symbolic and highly visible political stage. The neoliberal limitations on the use of public space thus damaged democratic principles. Vendors could not use the market and its surrounding spaces to carry out meetings, study circles, and mítines relámpago. This is a political cost that, along with the loss of workplaces, often goes unacknowledged when scholars study the effects of neoliberalism on people engaged in the informal economy. In short, the changes brought by the neoliberal turn left Puebla's vendors dispossessed of their prime political and work sites. Under these conditions and against the backdrop of an increasingly authoritarian regime, UPVA members had to remake their commercial and political activities.

According to observers, the UPVA's identity and strength depended significantly on this downtown location, as it allowed vendors a certain degree of spatial cohesiveness. Yet the UPVA continued to exist despite its geographical dislocation.[112] The Amparo Foundation and Walmart de México made out well in the arrangement. Suburbia and Vips emerged in prime locations, and the Amparo Foundation secured its ability to use its profits to preserve the Porfirian building that was once La Victoria market.

6 THE STRUGGLE CONTINUES

Rita Amador has led the UPVA since the 1990s. Prison guards knew her as the wife of the *preso cantor*, the singing prisoner.[1] In an attempt to remain sane during twelve long years, some of them spent in solitary confinement, he used to sing. Amador visited her husband, Simitrio, in several high-security Mexican prisons during this time. Sometimes she took her children with her, including the youngest, Tonatiuh, to see their dad: "All I remember is [a cell] with a window covered by a metallic sheet and a gate with three locks. I think I was two or three years old."[2] Simitrio went to prison in 1989, when officials in the administrations of President Carlos Salinas de Gortari and Governor Mariano Piña Olaya attempted to decapitate the street vendors' union. Simitrio achieved his conditional and temporary freedom in 2001.[3] His imprisonment was just one of the tactics the state and federal governments used to undermine the UPVA after the vendors' removal from downtown.

Mexico's adoption of neoliberal economic policies in the 1980s created a dramatic change in the relationship between the state and the unions. The state began to dismantle its clientelistic structure, as politicians no longer deemed it necessary to negotiate with the unions or to provide them with benefits.[4] According to scholars, in this new political context, independent unions had a potential advantage, since they had always been financially and politically autonomous from the state, and their political legitimacy came from below.[5] I argue, however, that the UPVA was also a target of the state's attempts to dismantle all forms of organized labor.

The imprisonment of the UPVA's most charismatic and powerful leader must be understood as part of the state's fight against all unions, whether charro or independent.

In this chapter I discuss the problems UPVA members faced as a result of their displacement from downtown streets in the summer of 1986 and the strategies they devised to survive their relocation. I explore the oppression and violent attacks Puebla's governors Mariano Piña Olaya (1987–93) and Manuel Bartlett Díaz (1993–99) carried out against the UPVA.

THE AFTERMATH OF THE 1986 REMOVAL

City and state authorities believed that removing street vendors from downtown would achieve two goals: the "dignification" and rescue of the historic center and the weakening and eventual destruction of the UPVA. They achieved the first goal, but not the second. The authorities, and even some scholars, thought that relocating UPVA sellers to seven different public markets on the outskirts of the city would destroy the geographical cohesiveness attached to the city center that had brought them together.[6] The UPVA, however, did not disappear. Vendors created new organizational strategies, recruited more members, and reconfigured their union despite the more repressive state regimes that began when Governor Piña Olaya took office in 1987.

One of the main problems the union faced after its downtown removal was the loss of about half of its members. Before the removal the UPVA claimed to have ten thousand members; after the summer of 1986 there were only five thousand.[7] Not all street vendors had the means to move to the new markets. Some could not afford the fixed stalls. Others, especially the very old, had little energy to move and start anew, and many were deterred by the markets' distance from downtown. The ones who relocated were extremely frustrated with the facilities, which lacked basic services such as running water, a roof, electricity, a phone, and bathrooms. The municipality called them markets, but the vendors found still unfinished buildings. At the end of 1988, two years after the removal, even the urban design and architecture department at the state university claimed that all but one of the markets lacked adequate infrastructure, equipment, and services.[8]

Vendors also complained about low sales during their first few years in their new location. In addition to the severe economic crisis that Mexico was experiencing, very few customers could reach the new facilities because there was no public transportation to the markets. Some vendors went back to the streets to protest; others went back to sell. UPVA vendors demanded that the municipal government comply with the August 1986 agreement, not only to help vendors relocate but to support and promote their commerce. The municipality had also agreed to help vendors acquire products directly from wholesalers and to promote and publicize the new markets. This promotion was supposed to include fifty minibuses to the new markets.[9] The problem rested on the fact that the interim mayor, Amado Camarillo Sánchez, and his successors, did not comply with the agreement. Vendors spent endless hours protesting to no avail.

THE MIGUEL HIDALGO MARKET

Fortunately for the UPVA most of its members relocated to a single spot, the Miguel Hidalgo market, at more than twenty-three thousand square meters the largest of the seven new markets. Located in the northern part of the city and not far from the new bus station, the Central de Autobuses de Puebla (CAPU), the market eventually housed thousands of merchants who sold fruit, vegetables, tortillas, fish, chicken, herbs, prepared food, pots, candles, piñatas, cleaning products, toys, handcrafts, knickknacks, clothes, flowers, live animals, and, at the close of the twentieth century, all types of pirated merchandise, such as music CDs. Later the market expanded across the street, where vendors sold electronics. The size of stalls at the Hidalgo market varied. Former established market vendors from La Victoria, who had access to more capital, bought large stalls in prime areas. Others set up mats on the floor; some walked up and down the halls selling their products.

Ultimately the market's proximity to the CAPU bus station provided certain advantages to the Hidalgo Market sellers.[10] Hundreds of buses, carrying about fifty thousand people, arrived there each day, all year long, from Mexico City and thirty other cities and small towns in states such as Veracruz, Tlaxcala, Oaxaca, and Morelos. Eventually dozens of local public transportation vehicles passed in front of the market on their way to and from the bus station.

Along with its commercial function, the Miguel Hidalgo market also replaced the downtown streets as the vendors' political spaces. In the early 1990s the UPVA built modest offices and a room for meetings in this market. It became a link for smaller markets where UPVA members sold and a space for meetings and general assemblies. Leaders of diverse independent organizations met with UPVA members there. In short, the Hidalgo Market became the new "radical democratic space" for the vendors, the "political [site] outside of the state where the disenfranchised generated power." It was here the union celebrated anniversaries by organizing parties, hiring musicians, and offering food and wrestling matches. At the Hidalgo Market UPVA members met to march, to meet with other organizations, and to discuss ideas in study circles. As Margaret Kohn writes, "Physical places that bring people together to experience, celebrate, and reinforce their unity are of outmost political importance."[11] Eventually local and state authorities realized the political importance of the Miguel Hidalgo market and targeted it in yet another effort to repress the vendors.

EXPANDING THE MEMBERSHIP

As a first step, the former street vendors sought to recruit new UPVA members to counter the number lost during the move to the new markets.[12] A wide variety of merchants, including former La Victoria sellers and people in the informal service industry, now joined the union, and about a thousand disgruntled marketers also became members of the UPVA after their charro leaders forced them to leave the market and municipal authorities refused to allow them to go back and sell downtown.[13] Usually these former marketers from La Victoria had more capital at their disposal and acquired one or more permanent stalls in the Miguel Hidalgo market.

Another set of vendors also joined the UPVA. In mid-November 1988 the UPVA opened a new market called La Cuchilla in front of the Miguel

Hidalgo market, where vendors sold shoes, clothing, and electronics.[14] In the past these vendors were called *fayuqueros*, the ones who sold merchandise from the U.S.-Mexico border illegally. After 1986, when Mexico joined the General Agreement on Tariffs and Trade, the number of *fayuca* smugglers declined and vendors began selling the now legal merchandise.

UPVA leaders in the smaller new markets also invited people from surrounding neighborhoods, especially housewives, to buy stalls and join the union. As incentives the union kept entry costs low and allowed the newcomers to sell vegetables, fruit, chili peppers, grains, and other staples from their kitchens. That way, if they were unable to sell everything, they could still use these products to feed their families.[15] In theory it was a win-win situation.

Rosa Martínez was a housewife in a working-class family who accepted the offer. She opened a stall in the Francisco I. Madero market, located a few blocks from her house. She was attracted by the fact that she could earn her own money and become financially independent from her abusive husband. In her case, simply leaving the house for part of the day was an attractive idea. With seven children to feed, it was not too difficult to convince her that selling at the market could contribute to her family's survival. In the 1980s, the so-called lost decade, it was easy to persuade anyone that a bit of extra money would come in handy.

In an unexpected turn the UPVA also began recruiting public transportation drivers. Before the vendors' removal from downtown, when the UPVA was negotiating the terms of their relocation with Mayor Murad, the leadership was also negotiating the management of some public transportation service. The UPVA negotiators took advantage of two basic problems that affected both the users and the employees of Puebla's public transportation system: the limited number of buses that served the city and the drivers' poor working conditions.

Puebla's transportation system depended on buses that were owned by a few companies. Employers organized the Alianza de Camioneros (Alliance of Bus Operators) to lobby the state for government subsidies. Employers invested hardly any money in maintaining the buses or acquiring more vehicles, which created many inconveniences for the largely working-class commuters; such a small fleet of old and overcrowded buses was a problem for and a danger to riders. While the population of the city continued to increase, the number of buses did not; at peak hours they were packed; unable to get on the bus, people often clung to the outside of the door and the back of the bus. Drivers earned low wages and worked long hours, and many quit after three or four years. They belonged to PRI-affiliated unions that did little to improve labor conditions and raise their wages.[16]

The UPVA started recruiting drivers who could operate taxis and *combis* (short for the Kombinationskraftwagen van made by Volkswagen). Combis filled a gap in the public transportation system; they reached areas of town where there were not enough public buses to satisfy increasing demand and provided access to the markets. The UPVA hoped to manage five routes that were originally negotiated between union leadership and the municipality in the August 1986 Agreement.[17] The union also recruited about three hundred taxi drivers.[18] Puebla's authorities did not expect this kind of membership expansion.

The UPVA's strategy directly challenged the monopoly on the public transportation system held by the Alianza de Camioneros and the PRI-affiliated Consejo Taxista del Estado de Puebla (Council of Taxi Operators of the State of Puebla), the organization to which taxi drivers in the city had to belong.[19] Unsurprisingly local and state authorities began attacking the UPVA's "transportation sector" by preventing these vehicles from circulating on the streets. State officials in the Dirección de Tránsito (Transit Department, the equivalent of the Motor Vehicles Department in the United States) refused to grant permits for these vehicles. This did not deter UPVA combis and taxi drivers from offering their services. The transit police regularly fined UPVA drivers or impounded their vehicles. At the end of 1988 the transit police had removed over fifty "pirate" vehicles.[20]

The UPVA used these vehicles politically, as tools of protest. On at least two occasions members drove thirty combis to the front of Puebla's Attorney General's Office to protest the police seizure of fifteen UPVA-affiliated vehicles.[21] The following month more vehicles blocked Reforma Avenue, one of the city's main downtown streets. Instead of using hijacked buses, as they had done in the past, UPVA vendors set up loudspeakers on the roof of combis and marched through the streets. Likewise, instead of buses they used combis to transport members and as protective barriers in front of marchers.[22]

Governor Piña Olaya had zero tolerance for UPVA taxis and combis. He ordered the Dirección de Tránsito to send these vehicles to the state transit depot. If drivers wanted to retrieve them, they had to prove they owned the vehicle and pay prohibitive fines that ranged from 50 to 100,000 pesos.[23] Alternatively Piña Olaya ordered that vehicles not be returned unless their owner joined the PRI-affiliated Consejo Taxista.[24]

The government also began a media campaign against UPVA vehicles. It called the UPVA-affiliated vehicles "pirate taxis" because the drivers lacked permits. UPVA-affiliated drivers did not spurn the term; they painted their vehicles, usually Volkswagen Beetles, in black and yellow, the official colors of city taxis, and dubbed themselves "the Base Corsario," a fitting name, as they indeed were pirates. Another term authorities used for these cars was "chocolate," which meant they had been stolen and then put to work as taxis.[25] The state government tried to undermine the reputation of these drivers and their vehicles by telling riders their safety was in peril. Who would want to ride in these pirate cars, the state asked? In fact many people did. UPVA combis and taxis, especially those that dropped off riders at the new markets, provided customers with a service that local officials did not. By offering these options, vendors tried to boost their commercial activities in markets; politically the UPVA sought to challenge the transportation monopoly.

The UPVA also tried to gain new allies. Leaders offered free legal services to the so-called *inquilinos*, those who rented rooms in old tenements, or *vecindades*. The lawyers who advised these renters were affiliated with the state university. In fact law students had been quite involved with the plight of the inquilinos since 1964.[26] Renters experienced harsh conditions in tenements. Entire families shared public bathrooms and *lavaderos* (washing boards) located on the buildings' patios. Landlords paid little attention to the poor condition of their buildings. While rents were low, so was the quality of life. In the late 1980s the UPVA provided assistance to people in around one hundred vecindades. Although the inquilinos did not join the UPVA, they became supporters of the union and began to follow its organizational model. According to a former lawyer from the state university's legal office who had been a student organizer, inquilinos had one representative per tenement and began to organize against rising rent and threats of removal.[27]

In addition to supporting renters in tenements, the UPVA leadership established the Coordinadora de Colonias Independientes (Association of Independent Neighborhoods, CCI), which organized ten poor neighborhoods. The newest of these was the Barranca Honda neighborhood, which had been created after a group of people occupied sixty hectares to build about 1,600 modest homes. The CCI protested the increase in taxes on household water consumption and property; CCI leaders called for a tax increase on industries only, not on ordinary people whose water consumption fee was equivalent to three days of work. The CCI had other demands: that the city organize workshops to teach citizens how to treat rainwater; that industries have their own water treatment systems; and that schools be built in some of the new neighborhoods.[28]

Thus the CCI highlighted the conditions in which poor people lived and offered specific solutions to their problems, which, to be sure, often fell on deaf ears. Nevertheless, in guiding the CCI the UPVA continued to broaden its alliances and support. UPVA members were ideal allies. Since the early 1970s vendors had fused home-based and work-based demands; they understood inquilinos' problems trying to improve their living conditions for they themselves were trying to combine urban demands with their own work-related demands, realizing the potential of "the collective right to the city."[29]

THE STATE'S RESPONSE

Even after vendors' removal from downtown and their relocation to different markets, the UPVA survived because of new membership that counterbalanced its loss in 1986. This development was not what the state expected. To counteract the union's power Governor Piña Olaya went after its most charismatic leader.

Guided by his teachers at the Prepa Zapata, Simitrio read Marxist texts, which, according to intelligence reports, explains his militancy. But his activism came not only from reading left-wing literature; he came from a working-class family and was fully aware of vendors' hardships. In the mid-1970s he married a chicken seller; years later, when he remarried, it was to another street vendor. Vendors saw him as one of their own.

Political divisions within the UPVA had emerged since the detention and subsequent incarceration of the union's leaders in 1977. After that conflict a group of vendors accused Bulmaro Vega of mismanaging vendors' fees and mishandling negotiations with authorities over Simitrio's release from prison.[30] The group believed Simitrio was an honest person and had "learned a lot during his time in prison."[31] In June 1979 these members expelled Vega and proposed that Simitrio, still in his twenties, become the UPVA's new leader. Five months later vendors reelected Simitrio, along with Lorenzo Hernández Becerra, his former teacher at the Prepa Zapata.[32] On June 18, 1980, vendors elected Simitrio once again, this time for a six-month term as the new director of the executive committee. Rank-and-file members continued to reelect him through the 1980s.

Why did Simitrio remain in power from 1979 to 1989 if one of the UPVA's objectives was to avoid long-lasting leaders? Why did vendors allow it? Did he become a "petty cacique" or a "street-corner" cacique?[33] As the vendors tell it, they had many reasons for choosing him to lead the organization. He was a natural leader, a man with an excellent memory for detail, and seemed to care about the rank and file. He was able to remember vendors' names and the details of their lives—their family, children, and past experiences. Until 1986 his office was located at El Corralón, the makeshift market downtown. From intelligence reports we know he spent countless hours there, meeting with individuals, leaders, and members of organizations from Puebla and neighboring states. He met with the vendors in their stalls, on street corners (especially during the mítines relámpago), in assemblies, and during marches. When UPVA vendors were relocated to the periphery markets, Simitrio walked up and down the aisles to speak with the people, which they appreciated. His actions, his modest background, and the time he spent in prison gave him credibility, power, and respect from the UPVA members.[34]

Authorities and members of the UPVA agreed that Simitrio was a modest person. Unlike many charro leaders, he did not make any display of wealth, despite the fact that he had access to union fees. He wore very simple clothing made of *manta*, a cheap thick cotton cloth, along with blue jeans, sandals, and a palm hat; he had long hair and a beard.[35] One vendor described him as a wise person; another said he was the most honest leader the UPVA ever had.[36]

Simitrio's relationship with the state was complicated. He was imprisoned from 1977 to 1979 for his alleged participation in the killing of a thief. He then enjoyed years of relative calm, between 1979 and 1989, a period that may be considered his political apex, all the while operating outside the PRI and independently of any other political party. Simitrio had been on the radar of the federal intelligence police since at least 1976. Authorities described him as a *líder antigobiernista*, an antigovernment leader. The local government was also attentive to his political activities. A police report noted that he "was an active participant in the organization of [social] movements, and in street assemblies. He is combative and charismatic in the eyes of street vendors."[37] All the information on him, especially his prison record, came in handy for the Piña Olaya administration, which portrayed him as a criminal and sent him back to prison in 1989.[38]

Scholars have concluded that during the Piña Olaya and Bartlett Díaz administrations independent organizations confronted considerable levels of institutional violence, including the assassination of their leaders, the beating of rank-and-file members, and the imprisonment of Simitrio. According to Jaime Castillo Palma and Elsa Patiño, there was a quasi-formulaic procedure against Puebla's independent leaders that always involved the "fabrication" of crimes to inculpate leaders. First, officials refused to talk or negotiate with these organizations, which resulted in protests and marches. Second, officials incited brawls and confrontations with the protestors in order to accuse their leaders of crimes. Third, the police arrested the leaders, preferably during marches or public events.

Fourth, officials imprisoned the leaders. Thus authorities transformed legal social protests into criminal acts and in this way institutionalized violence.[39] However, Castillo Palma and Patiño's analysis of officials' usual procedures falls short in describing what happened to the UPVA.

By the end of the 1980s Simitrio had become a high-profile, powerful, and charismatic UPVA leader who operated outside the PRI state system and had connections with several regional independent organizations. Governor Piña Olaya needed an excuse to send him to prison for as long as possible. This opportunity came in the summer of 1989, when Rodolfo Kiesslich, an engineer and entrepreneur of German descent and the owner of Pozos y Bombas, a well and water systems company, went missing in Puebla.[40] Local authorities claimed Kiesslich had had a conflict with a UPVA member over the ownership of some machinery; the two men could not resolve the problem, so UPVA members kidnapped Kiesslich, beat him, and forced him to give them 100 million pesos. The UPVA declared that the organization had nothing to do with the kidnapping; however, the leadership admitted that one of their members had participated in the crime, in connivance with a man named Elías Pérez.[41]

How does one make sense of this kidnapping? Was the UPVA leadership complicit? As mentioned earlier, the union had established a modest legal office where lawyers volunteered to provide free legal assistance to the general public. Union members usually asked the lawyers for advice not related to vending, such as problems with their landlord. Elías Pérez, who was not a member of UPVA, asked the legal office for advice on resolving a conflict with Kiesslich. Since the problem was not resolved, Pérez and his friend Jaime Contreras, a UPVA member, decided to kidnap Kiesslich.[42]

Immediately after the kidnapping, the police, in yet another rare instance of efficiency and speed, rescued Kiesslich from his captors. Local authorities and a number of organizations accused Simitrio of the kidnapping. Business organizations such as the Consejo Coordinador Empresarial accused the UPVA leadership and its members of seeking to break the rule of law (*estado de derecho*) and threatening the social order.[43] The Cámara Textil de Puebla y Tlaxcala (Puebla and Tlaxcala Chamber of Textile Industry), another business organization, urged authorities to make "courageous" decisions in Simitrio's case in order to preserve the rule of law.[44]

The UPVA leadership remained relatively calm but alert. *El Heraldo de México en Puebla* even published a picture of Simitrio on May 18, 1989, during a press conference at a local restaurant, with a caption describing him as "smiling, calm, and showing no worries." Yet, the reporter added, about two dozen vendors waited outside the restaurant to protect their leader in case he was arrested. Indeed vendors and their leaders had many reasons to be wary, and the government's next actions proved they were justified. With no evidence of the UPVA's involvement in the kidnapping of Kiesslich, on June 16, 1989, under the command of Public Safety Secretary José Ventura Rodríguez Verdín, 225 local and federal police plus police dogs entered the UPVA's offices in El Corralón in what authorities called a "surprise operation."[45]

According to UPVA members, the police planted arms and drugs at the headquarters. A few hours later additional police officers arrived and "discovered" propaganda items, forty-nine Molotov cocktails hidden in two empty fruit cases, one kilogram of marijuana divided into two packages, dynamite, rifles, and long-range guns. Cars and trucks that UPVA members had allegedly stolen were also found. Seventeen vendors were arrested.[46]

The newspaper *El Heraldo de México en Puebla* asserted that the union intended to use these items to promote violence. Because of the enormous amount of illicit activities carried out by the UPVA "most of the population" believed the state should punish the organization. "Workers and peasants" were concerned about the "arsenal" and the damage vendors inflicted on the city and its inhabitants as a result of UPVA's pintas, marches, and occupation of public space. The photographs that accompanied the article showed hardly anything more than five old rifles, two guns, and two small bags that allegedly contained marijuana.[47]

Of the seventeen vendors detained, five were UPVA leaders: Guillermo Herrera, who, according to authorities, faced twelve criminal accusations and had occupied the CAPU bus station, along with José Maldonado

Reyes, Ramón Alcalá Salinas, Raúl Ronquillo Hernández, and Felipe Jesús Tovar Cano. They were charged with crimes against public health (for possession of marijuana) and the crime of stockpiling arms.[48]

The press reported that the detainees had admitted their crimes under the supervision of special agents of the Attorney General's Office (the Procuraduría General de la República) and narcotics "special agents."[49] The detainees told the press that these agents beat them during interrogation so they would plead guilty. Their fellow street vendors supported them, but *El Heraldo de México en Puebla* dismissed the accusation, reporting that "doctors' statements showed absolutely no sign of violence" on the detainees' bodies.[50] As discussed in chapter 4, it was common practice for doctors to submit false reports denying that detainees had been abused.[51]

In order to legitimize the "surprise operation," *El Sol de Puebla* published photographs of the empty streets where UPVA vendors used to sell without permits. The newspaper lauded Rodríguez Verdín as a man "of firm actions [who] sought to establish social equilibrium"—*firm* being a euphemism for *repressive*.[52] The press was relentless against the vendors. *El Sol de Puebla* pointed out that now the streets were filled only with "garbage, waste, and nauseous smells," all products of the street vendors who continued to sell in these spaces illegally.[53] One reporter called UPVA members delinquents and "dangerous people" and emphasized that some had criminal records.[54] *El Heraldo de México en Puebla* also made sure to publish photographs of the union leaders in handcuffs.[55]

During the "surprise operation" Simitrio and other leaders had escaped, but authorities soon caught them. On July 4, 1989, Simitrio was arrested in Mexico City outside his doctor's office. According to Attorney General Humberto Fernández de Lara, Simitrio was carrying a gun that only army officers were authorized to carry, along with a "certain amount of drugs."[56]

The details of Simitrio's 1989 arrest, verdict, and imprisonment reflect the injustice, corruption, dirty tricks, and human rights violations the state carried out against important leaders of social organizations. Simitrio later claimed that he had been illegally detained in Mexico City by more than thirty of Puebla's judicial police officers. These men transported him to Puebla, where they kept him blindfolded and restrained for eight hours in a clandestine cell while agents fired their guns (*cortaban cartucho*) to terrorize him. That night, as they drove him back to Mexico City, officers put a plastic bag over his head several times, threatening to asphyxiate him. He was kept in Mexico City for two days at the Attorney General's Office, then, at dawn on July 7, the police took him to Puebla's state penitentiary, Centro de Readaptación Social San Miguel. That morning state authorities publicly announced that Simitrio had been incarcerated. For two days his family and UPVA members had not known of his whereabouts.[57]

Simitrio was found guilty of stockpiling arms, rebellion, possession of marijuana, kidnapping, theft, and many other crimes.[58] Judges sentenced him to 116 years in prison, although his sentence was later reduced to 67 years.[59] Many years later, looking back at what happened in 1989, Simitrio declared, "My sin was to refuse to work for Carlos Salinas de Gortari, by not allowing UPVA members to affiliate with the PRI. That was the problem."[60] He was partially right.

After four years in Puebla's state penitentiary, Simitrio was transferred to a high-security federal prison, the Penal de Seguridad No. 2 in Puente Grande, El Salto, Jalisco, for four years, and then to a maximum-security federal prison, Centro de Readaptación Federal No. 1 de Almoloya de Juárez in the state of Mexico, for five more.[61] Almoloya de Juárez hosted Mexico's most wanted criminals, including Mario Aburto, who assassinated the 1994 PRI presidential candidate, Luis Donaldo Colosio, and Raúl Caro Quintero, the famous drug lord and founder of the Guadalajara Cartel, who allegedly killed U.S. Drug Enforcement Administration Special Agent Enrique Camarena in 1981.[62] Last but not least, Almoloya also held Raúl Salinas de Gortari, the "uncomfortable brother" of the former president, who had been convicted for the assassination of PRI's general secretary José Francisco Ruíz Massieu and for money laundering on a massive scale.[63]

Street vendors wondered why their leader shared the same roof with Mexico's most wanted criminals. In fact the answer was simple: the state sought to destroy the independent and militant UPVA in its larger fight against unions during the neoliberal years. The imprisonment of militant leaders was not uncommon in Mexican history. At the beginning of 1989, just as President Salinas began his term, the military and the federal police arrested the tremendously powerful leader of the national petroleum workers union, Joaquín Hernández Galicia (aka La Quina) for allegedly trafficking arms and committing homicide. The PEMEX union had opposed changes in the labor contract and the privatization of some of the petrochemical giant's activities. The Salinas administration removed La Quina and replaced him with a more compliant leader.[64] At the local level there were at least two cases besides Simitrio's during the Piña Olaya administration. One was the assassination of Martín Melchi Lira, head of the independent Organización de Acción Campesina Independiente (Independent Organization of Peasant Action), which fought for land in northern Puebla. According to a 1987 Amnesty International report, he was detained "on charges of murder and robbery" on June 5, 1985, and police tortured the people who incriminated him to make them confess.[65] Melchi was "mysteriously" assassinated a few months later.[66] The other case was the assassination of Gumaro Amaro, the leader of a housewives' organization and the independent garment union Sindicato Único de Trabajadoras de la Industria de la Confección; he was shot outside his home in front of his children on February 18, 1989.[67]

Unlike the special treatment that some influential inmates, like Raúl Salinas de Gortari, received, political prisoners and common criminals like Simitrio were subjected to human rights violations. Street vendors accused Rodríguez Verdín and Fernández de Lara of mistreating union members and their leader in Puebla's jail.[68] A deputy in the Party of the Democratic Revolution (Partido de la Revolución Democrática) stated that prison authorities did not allow Simitrio to talk with other inmates and denied him other basic human rights.[69] In multiple interviews Simitrio granted to the media after 2011—ten years after his conditional and temporary release—he talked of enduring solitary confinement and singing to avoid losing his mind and his ability to talk.[70] Prison authorities even put roaches and worms in his food as an additional form of punishment.[71]

Unintentionally, the state actually increased the fame and charisma of the UPVA leader. Union members began to idolize him as a representative of victimization, injustice, and repression and as the crucial element that held them together as they organized marches and protests for his release. Vendors printed Simitrio's face on T-shirts and banners, and at least one person produced artwork featuring the leader's image. Three years after the vendors' removal, the UPVA had not perished. Rather it was steadily strengthening its base of support.

Although vendors continued selling in the markets and holding meetings and assemblies with various organizations in and outside of Puebla, Simitrio's imprisonment represented a political and financial blow to their union. Yolanda Bejarano said one of the state's achievements was that "people lost training, preparation, and guidance while Simitrio was incarcerated."[72] Some UPVA members felt frustrated that, despite organizing dozens upon dozens of marches in Puebla and in Mexico City, they had not been able to secure his release. They were certain that Simitrio's imprisonment was unjust and a prime example of state authoritarianism, but they also had to make a living. Attending marches and participating on the negotiation and propaganda commissions took time away from selling. Rosa Martínez had mixed feelings about her political participation. On one hand, she felt empowered when she traveled to Mexico City and saw new places and met new people; on the other, she believed all those years Simitrio spent in jail represented a failure for the organization, and for all vendors, who spent countless hours away from their stalls and suffered tremendous material losses in the process.[73]

Using a combination of different techniques, including a defamation campaign, the state tried to discredit the UPVA. Prior to Simitrio's imprisonment, Puebla's media attacked all UPVA members in articles in the crime section (*nota roja*). Journalists, especially those writing for *El Sol de Puebla*, were contemptuous of vendors and portrayed them as lacking political agency, unable to organize independently of the country's dominant institutions, and manipulated by their leaders. Editorials referred to the leaders as "pseudo-leaders," "troublemakers," and "outsiders." One writer contrasted the leaders with the vendors, demonizing the former and labeling the latter as naïve, "simple people [*gente sencilla*] who were controlled by the manipulative leaders." The journalist ended by saying, "Let's not allow [the leaders] to continue exploiting [vendors'] innocence and good faith."[74] Criticism continued over the years. In February 1993, in an effort to attack vendors' respectability, an article accused UPVA leaders of allowing their members to set up brothels in markets, disguising them as seafood restaurants.[75]

The municipal government played its part in the defamation campaign, portraying vendors as hooligans. Council members claimed that Puebla's citizens and shopkeepers constantly complained about the behavior of UPVA's members. Marching vendors were blamed for stealing shopkeepers' merchandise, damaging their stores, and verbally or physically injuring people. On top of this, there were complaints that the UPVA disrupted public order and tranquility when its members engaged in marches, sit-ins, and protests. According to Mayor Rafael Cañedo Benítez (1993–96), shopkeepers had to close their stores during UPVA marches out of fear. Moreover the UPVA frequently obstructed traffic.[76] Apparently "different sectors of Puebla's society" were angry because vendors occupied sidewalks and streets during these protests. Worst of all, they argued, street vending by those who refused to sell in the city's periphery caused "gang activity and the propensity to drug addiction."[77] The use of public space by the lower classes was considered a criminal offense and an affront to established shopkeepers and the rest of respectable Pueblan society.

In 1995, in an act of selective democracy, Mayor Cañedo Benítez organized a popular forum, the Foro de Consulta Popular, in which diverse groups evaluated and analyzed all of the problems the UPVA caused in Puebla.[78] In their ostensible role as defenders of order and democratic values, authorities invited "all sectors of Puebla's society" to vent their dissatisfactions with the UPVA.[79] For three days in February shopkeepers, political parties, municipal employees, business associations, PRI-affiliated unions, and city residents participated in the forum. According to the UPVA and its allies, authorities sought to appear neutral toward the union and to act democratically.[80] In reality, however, the mayor had organized the Foro de Consulta to have a legitimate excuse to discipline and punish UPVA members. At the end of the forum the city council made public the results of the discussion: everybody agreed that the UPVA was a real problem for Puebla and that it was necessary to correct the organization's behavior by reinforcing standards of public safety in the markets.[81]

Unlike other types of union workers, such as doctors, teachers, miners, and automobile workers, vendors were easier for the state to demonize because they were poor, often illiterate people of rural or indigenous background who caused a number of urban complications for other citizens. When vendors used downtown public space to protest, authorities portrayed them as criminals and gang members.

While the forum took place at the municipal level, punishment for the UPVA came from all levels of government. Backed by the alleged support of Puebla's residents, Governor Bartlett Díaz struck. At the break of dawn on March 8, 1995, two thousand federal police with their dogs, as well as firefighters and municipal inspectors, broke into the Miguel Hidalgo market. Police arrested approximately seventy-eight UPVA members, destroying thousands of products and setting between 1,000 and 1,400 stalls on fire.[82] Witnesses said the arrested vendors (men and women alike) were held at the Procuraduría General del Estado (Puebla's Attorney General's Office), where they were beaten by the police.[83] On March 20 the police engaged in a similar action against UPVA vendors in a smaller market, the Emiliano Zapata, destroying stalls and tons of merchandise. Approximately five thousand vendors were affected by the two attacks, which resulted in "the loss of 2,000 jobs."[84] Officials justified their actions by saying that Puebla's markets needed "to be secured" and "non-UPVA marketers and consumers needed protection."[85]

Without a doubt vendors experienced hard times during the governorships of Piña Olaya and his successor, Bartlett Díaz, another priísta. Bartlett was a highly educated man who studied law at the UNAM and obtained a PhD there after studying in Manchester and Paris.[86] "A leading national politician," he had a history of repressing social movements and carrying out other political tricks.[87] He had been secretary of the interior from 1982 to 1988 during Miguel de la Madrid's administration and was the intellectual author of the electoral fraud in 1988 that brought victory to Salinas after the famous computer crash. Some groups in the United States have suggested Bartlett was involved in the 1985 assassination of DEA agent Enrique Camarena.[88] He was secretary of education during the 1989 teachers' strikes and accused them of harming their students by temporarily stopping their education.[89] In Puebla Bartlett was an authoritarian governor who spent most of his energy and intellectual talent in suppressing democratic and independent organizations.

As a response to the repression and aware that the Bartlett administration portrayed UPVA members as criminals, vendors organized the Marcha Nacional de Protesta Pacífica de la UPVA, a peaceful protest against state violence. Ironically, when the demonstration took place on March 22, 1995, five hundred riot policemen attacked it using clubs, biting dogs, and tear gas. The state police took pictures and a video of the protestors in order to keep track of the so-called troublemakers, and a police spy wrote a report identifying the UPVA leaders. The government claimed that the protestors had damaged the municipal building in front of the zócalo.[90] Immediately after the march was dissolved, the government apprehended eighty vendors who were politically active.[91] That summer vendors bitterly complained that the police had violently arrested Heraclio Juárez Cordero, Simeón Amaro Mora, Crescencia Alcantarilla Orea, Ramón Herrera, and Antonio Vidal Pérez.[92] I interviewed the wife of one of the detainees, who remembered that day clearly. Her husband was taken away and tortured while an officer drove her and one of her daughters in an undercover police vehicle through the city in the dark and intimidated them for hours.[93]

In addition to physical violence, police used verbal abuse and harassment. For instance, officers intimidated vendors by threatening to demolish the organization's office, bathrooms, and one of the Hidalgo Market's chapels, where vendors venerated the Virgin Mary. Police also threatened vendors themselves, saying that if they did not join the PRI, their lives would be more than miserable.[94] Such threats caused a great deal of anxiety for vendors. Though they no longer faced removal from the streets, they now had much more to lose, for they had become established market vendors who had invested capital to buy their stalls and keep their markets open. They were protecting their property, their markets, their right to make a living, and their union's independence.

Another tactic the state government used to punish vendors was to destroy their merchandise. When UPVA vendors refused to pay their electricity bills, insisting the electrical system was in such terrible shape it put their markets in danger, the state-owned electricity company, Comisión Federal de Electricidad, cut power to the markets. Without refrigeration thousands of perishable products rotted. On one occasion municipal firefighters refused to extinguish a fire at the Emiliano Zapata market caused by the poor electrical system.[95] The blaze reduced dozens of stalls and hundreds of products to ashes in a couple of hours. It was a kind of low-intensity war against this independent organization, punishment for refusing to join the PRI.

Vendors used their political connections and contacted human rights organizations, the Chamber of Deputies, and even President Ernesto Zedillo Ponce de León (1994–2000), the last PRI president of the twentieth century. In addition to exposing the violence carried out under the command of Governor Bartlett Díaz and Mayor Cañedo Benítez, vendors accused police officers of using drugs, which made them more aggressive.[96] Vendors also asserted that some of their colleagues were not in prison or hospitals, as the government claimed, but had been disappeared. One of these was Juan Tapia. According to witnesses, in June 1995 federal police took him away in a white car without license plates.[97] Vendors did not know what happened to him.

While vendors lacked information about some of their colleagues' whereabouts, the state kept detailed files on the UPVA's most active militants. In 1996 the Jesuit priest David Fernández Dávalos, the director of the Centro de Derechos Humanos Miguel Agustín Pro (Miguel Agustín Human Rights Center), told the press he had received an anonymous eighteen-page document in 1995; it was a list of organizations and members whom the army and the secret police were spying on and infiltrating. The UPVA and some of its leaders appeared on that list.[98] For street vendors the Dirty War continued.

CONCLUSION

The UPVA declined in strength immediately after the 1986 removal of vendors from downtown, losing about half of its membership and prime commercial and political spaces. In order to reemerge from a weakened position, it found ways to recruit new members and re-create political sites. The UPVA extended its membership successfully to former market vendors from La Victoria and to public transportation drivers, and it gained allies among tenement dwellers and people living in working-class neighborhoods. By 1989 the UPVA was growing stronger again, emphasizing the many problems that the urban poor faced in Puebla. In addition the Miguel Hidalgo market emerged as a new radical democratic space. Here vendors and members of diverse organizations could meet, discuss, and plan.

The UPVA's political reemergence led authorities to oppose it with renewed strength. Using coercion, intimidation, and legal mechanisms, Puebla's government simultaneously attacked the UPVA from the top down and from the bottom up. In 1989 the state government of Governor Piña Olaya incarcerated the UPVA's main leader once again. Although there were legal irregularities in Simitrio's trial, he spent years in high-security federal prisons. In this way the state sought to behead the UPVA in hopes of destroying the independent organization.

Simitrio's imprisonment was part of a fierce antiunion fight. Beginning with the Salinas administration, the federal government had aimed to weaken both official and independent unions, especially those that resisted the neoliberal changes occurring across the country. Some protested the privatization and closure of state-led enterprises, and vendors opposed their removal from downtown and their relocation to unfinished markets. They also continued their political and material support to independent unions of workers, peasants, and inquilinos. The UPVA kept growing as an organization that could effectively mobilize other organizations.

When the federal government failed to destroy the UPVA, local and state authorities began attacking the rank and file in every way possible: recurring intimidation, detentions, defamation campaigns, and merchandise raids. In this the state was successful in demoralizing and exhausting rank-and-file members. The dozens of marches the UPVA had organized over the years when Simitrio was imprisoned had a sharply negative impact on vendors' ability to make a living. In short, the state became more authoritarian as Mexico embraced neoliberalism.

Scholars have concluded that during the neoliberal turn, independent unions or those whose legitimacy and power came from rank-and-file members fared better than their charro counterparts. One reason was that these unions "proved most effective at formulating innovative strategies to address the multiple challenges they face in the workplace and beyond."[99] The vendor union remade itself successfully due its political and material independence from the ruling party. But the fact that the UPVA survived does not excuse the official repression that organized vendors and their allies confronted. Using torture, disappearances, and physical violence and twisting legal mechanisms to suit them, the federal and state governments carried out a Dirty War against those who refused to cooperate with the ruling party, the state, and the neoliberal turn. Still the vendors remained resilient and the struggle continued.

CONCLUSION

In October 2013 Puebla's street vendors celebrated the fortieth anniversary of the UPVA with a march from the Hidalgo market to the zócalo. Men, women, and children carried banners criticizing the neoliberal labor, educational, and energy reforms embraced by the Ernesto Peña Nieto administration (2012–), among them "We repudiate international financial institutions that are responsible for the misery and hunger of countries" and "Labor reforms oppress and exploit the working class."[1] After the march participants met with representatives of independent organizations from other Mexican cities who had come to Puebla to show their solidarity with the UPVA. The celebrations ended with a *baile*, a dance party.

A couple of days later, as part of these commemorations, Puebla's state university invited Simitrio to give a talk on the history of the UPVA. Wearing a red shirt—the organization's color—and a heavy-duty jacket associated with working-class men, the UPVA leader read from his laptop. Dozens of people, including university students and longtime friends and supporters of the vendors' union, heard him speak. Despite the state university's disengagement with left-wing activism, the UPVA sustains a connection with certain members of the university.[2] This alliance, if now tenuous, reflects the student origin of the vendors' union; after all, Simitrio and several of the founding members were former students at the university-affiliated Prepa Zapata and together experienced the last stage of university reform, acquiring their left-wing ideology from progressive teachers. The vendors' union had also learned several political strategies from the student movement during the long 1960s. At the end of the commemorative event organizers spoke on behalf of the Humanities and Social Sciences Institute and the PhD program in political economy. They recognized the four-decades-long political struggle of the UPVA and granted the leader a diploma for contributing to Puebla's fight for democracy.[3]

Simitrio looked quite different from the man he was two decades earlier, before he spent twelve years in high-security prisons. He no longer had the long hair or the *barbudo* look so characteristic of his youth. He seemed softer, shy, and his voice had mellowed. Without a doubt his incarceration had taken a toll, but his message had not changed. He focused on the institutional history of the UPVA and emphasized the role of the leadership. He did not mention female vendors and their role in shaping the union. This omission was not surprising; the democratic political practices of the UPVA suffered from serious gender-related problems, and few women held high-level leadership positions. At least half—if not more—of the street-vending population were women, but they did not rise above treasurers, street representatives, or members of commissions. In this sense the UPVA replicated the patriarchal structure of the Poblano student movement.

Simitrio provided a brief political context for the UPVA's emergence. He reminded the audience that street vendors were the product of a corrupt postwar world system in which both the United States and the Soviet Union had become "imperialist superpowers." The former openly embraced capitalism and the latter followed a disguised form of it. Both, however, oppressed weaker nations within their spheres of influence, and Mexico was one of those countries under the yoke of U.S. imperialism. Informed by his Maoist background, Simitrio lauded the Chinese Cultural Revolution, in which the masses fought against oppression. Alluding to the repression the UPVA faced, he stated that in Mexico the Dirty War was an outgrowth of the Cold War.[4]

Simitrio described the most important features of the UPVA: "a class-based, democratic, independent, and militant organization [*organización* de lucha]." It is "a class-based union because street vendors see themselves as part of the Mexican working class; it is independent because it does not depend on the government, political parties, business associations, or the church to survive." The UPVA "does not receive money from any of these entities. Members only rely on their own economic resources and on the support that they receive from the people [el pueblo]." He proudly stated that the union was democratic because it "makes decisions from the bottom up and listens to vendors' proposals and criticisms. Members debate and decide what to do." Finally, he said, "it is an organization de lucha because members do not beg anyone or wait for miracles to occur. They are active participants who embrace their rights and responsibilities to act and to achieve their goals." Indeed for four decades organized street vendors have been politically active, trying to maintain and redefine union democracy under adverse conditions. Emerging during the new labor insurgency of the 1970s, street vendors have survived repression and economic crises and have created new strategies to face the increasing neoliberal authoritarianism of the Mexican state.

The UPVA still gives approximately nine thousand recent migrants and urban dwellers an opportunity to survive economically. Organized vendors constantly fight to defend their historical and constitutional right to make a living. This independent union continues to protect vendors' spaces in markets and other public spaces outside downtown. This is a major achievement, especially as Puebla's neoliberal officials have restricted the use of prime urban space for the rich. Vendors still provide a wide range of products to a mainly working-class clientele. The markets where vendors labor continue to be places where communities resist the neoliberal world of processed food, standardized shopping malls, and what the Oaxaca-based painter Francisco Toledo calls the "savage commercialization," the "reckless disregard for the unique and irreplaceable."[5] UPVA markets are still the spaces where vendors refuse to give up their legitimate and traditional ways of making a living. It is the street vendors, who identify with the working class, who have waged a fight for the right of the city over the past forty years.[6]

UPVA vendors have found it essential to forge and sustain a political space for ordinary people to exercise forms of direct democracy in a country where authoritarianism has been steadily on the increase. Vendors have made themselves visible by marching and protesting on Puebla's main streets. Despite restrictions on the use of public space, vendors continue to use it as a political stage. According to a *Proceso* journalist, the UPVA rank and file make up the largest number of protesters against the governor's authoritarian policies. In fact the Tribunal Permanente de los Pueblos (Permanent Peoples' Tribunal) maintains that the UPVA is "the spinal cord" of Puebla's social movement.[7]

As they have done for four decades, and thanks to their political independence from the ruling party, the vendors' leaders seek alliances with independent organizations to challenge the status quo. Recently these groups have protested Puebla's Bullet Law, which allows police officers to shoot protestors who supposedly represent a threat to the "preservation of social order." On May 19, 2014, Puebla's state congress passed this law (32–5) under the initiative of Governor Rafael Moreno Valle Rosas.[8] Without a doubt the former PRI politician turned PAN official Moreno Valle Rosas (whose grandfather was an avilacamachista governor) is trying to instill fear among the population and dissuade people from protesting or marching in the streets. Organizations like the UPVA have protested the authoritarian character of the law, insisting it is unconstitutional.[9] In an outrageous and tragic event the state government implemented the Bullet Law against a group of demonstrators in San Bernardino Chalchihuapan who objected to the relocation of Civil Registry Offices. State police shot into the crowd with rubber bullets, severely injuring the activists and shattering the skull of thirteen-year-old José Alberto Tehuatlie Tamayo.[10] The boy died eleven days later, on July 20, 2014. The UPVA has demanded that authorities be held accountable.

One of the UPVA's most recent experience with state authoritarianism occurred on December 19, 2014, when some fifteen police officers violently accosted and detained Simitrio without a warrant as he was about to meet with the city's attorney general. Three days later twenty armed men in Mexico City detained one of Simitrio's sons, Atl Rubén Sarabia Reyna, an active UPVA leader, after a march protesting the disappeared students in Ayotzinapa. Prior to Sarabia Reyna's detention, police and their dogs allegedly entered his home and planted small bags of drugs and forcefully detained his mother and sister. The judge sentenced Simitrio to forty years in prison; this was less than a month before his term of conditional freedom was to end.[11] He and his son remain in prison, convicted of homicide, *narcomenudeo* (small-scale drug trafficking), and several other charges.[12] Social organizations have joined the UPVA in protests in Puebla and Mexico City to fight for the liberation of Simitrio and Sarabia Reyna, whom the UPVA considers to be political prisoners. According to Simitrio, "Governor Rafael Moreno Valle wants to demonstrate to investors that he is paving the path so that no organization or union challenges investors' economic interests. To do so, the governor can do anything, legally or illegally."[13]

A few months later about thirty armed agents of the Ministerio Público apprehended the eldest of Simitrio's sons, Xihuel Sarabia Reyna, who was attending the first communion of his goddaughter. A shocking amateur video taken inside the church of San Antonio Abad in Puebla shows young children, women, and men screaming and running behind Sarabia Reyna. Agents prevent people from leaving the church, and one pushes a woman. Puebla's Procuraduría General de Justicia (Attorney General's Office) claimed that Sarabia Reyna distributed drugs for sale at the Mercado Hidalgo.[14] Simitrio was right again: Puebla's state government will do anything to destroy unions and militant organizations.

Vendors have paid a high price over the years for their political independence. Federal secret agents and informants have monitored the vendors' union since its earliest days. Puebla's governors used this information to identify and punish the union's leaders and most active members. Local, state, and federal authorities have engaged in numerous campaigns to weaken and destroy the union, using physical violence, torture, kidnapping, removal, and imprisonment. Street vendors, especially the most politically active among them, did not escape state violence during Mexico's Dirty War. Vendors were dual targets, in a sense: they felt the special hardship of making a living in difficult economic conditions, while confronting state authoritarianism.

UPVA members have refused to forget and be silent. Since the late 1970s they have denounced the disappearance of hundreds of people all over Mexico and have fought for the liberation of political prisoners. Some joined the organizations of family members of the disappeared, such as the Comité Eureka. Recently vendors joined thousands of people protesting the disappearance of forty-three students from Ayotzinapa, Guerrero. For the UPVA as well as other social organizations, these kinds of atrocious events are nothing new.

The street vendors' union has changed dramatically since its inception. It has tapped into the world of social media to disseminate information and seek support from other unions, social organizations, and young people, reaching an online audience the 1973 cultural commission could have never imagined. The UPVA has a website and at least two Facebook accounts, and some of its leaders have Twitter accounts. Social media has complemented and slowly replaced the mitines relámpago, the brief meetings vendors carried out on street corners or at makeshift markets to spread messages to their members and other groups. Social media has also allowed the organization to tell its history, and, perhaps unintentionally, it has created an archive of documents and photographs. Although this informal archive is still very limited in scope, it is available to a broad audience, and its electronic format has the potential to survive police burnings and the seemingly ever-changing rules of the Ministry of the Interior's archivists. In this way vendors continue to challenge the state's control over information. In the absence of a free media, street vendors have used several tools to convey their demands, from theater to Twitter.

Another major change is vendors' geographical location. As I explained in chapter 5, in 1986 municipal authorities, aided by the private sector, removed vendors from dozens of downtown streets and relocated them to new enclosed markets on the outskirts of the city. Most UPVA members landed in the Miguel Hidalgo market, which for the first few years was very hard to reach because of its distance from downtown and the absence of public transportation. Puebla has grown, however, and today the market no longer sits on the city's desolate fringes.

Still the fight continues against the invisible hand of the market. National and international supermarket chains such as Walmart, Sam's Club, and Soriana are located just a couple of blocks away from the Miguel Hidalgo market. Competition has become increasingly fierce since these supermarkets offer many of the same products that vendors sell and most customers can easily qualify for credit cards. To counteract the chains, the UPVA suggested that municipal and state authorities build small markets close to the many housing projects and new neighborhoods that have sprung up all over the city. According to Rita Amador, vendors could help design a distribution system to bring fresh and affordable food and other products to people in these areas. The UPVA leadership worries that the state government's plan to construct a new toll highway, the Distribuidor Vial Santa Ana, will make it difficult for customers to reach the Hidalgo market.[15] Fearing that the Hidalgo market will become unreachable again, the UPVA has even planned to relocate it close to the Volkswagen plant in San Francisco Ocotlán.

UPVA members have other reasons to be anxious. Recent urban changes have resulted in the gentrification of several areas of the city center, and these changes have negatively affected street vendors. Puebla began to exclude the urban poor and the working class in favor of welcoming large investors. Gentrification, started in the mid-1980s with the removal of vendors from downtown and the conversion of La Victoria market into a shopping mall, has accelerated in the past two decades. Large local and international retailers have opened stores at the heart of the city in the portales, including McDonald's, Domino's Pizza, the Italian Coffee Company, and Telcel. Puebla's neoliberal downtown is increasingly a place where the popular classes have fewer opportunities to labor—and to consume. Their presence and work have been highly regulated, taxed, monitored, policed, and ultimately excluded.

Amid these increasingly difficult circumstances vendors continue to be resilient. The street vendors who still manage to sell their wares downtown have done so by being as discreet as possible. They have found ways to occupy little space and maximize the number of articles they display by hanging merchandise from their neck, back, head, wrists, and arms. Some walk through the streets displaying bags, caps, hats, and aprons. Others, especially in the gentrified area of downtown, conceal their products in bags hanging from their shoulders, surreptitiously offering their merchandise in soft voices. These vendors do not have fixed or semi-fixed stalls. One vendor of yellow handmade Minions (the characters from the animated film *Despicable Me*) put one puppet on each of her hands and hung a bag across her chest announcing "Minions for your children." When she spotted a municipal inspector, she quickly put the puppets in the bag and disappeared in the flow of pedestrians. Street vendors must be constantly alert to the presence of undercover police officers and municipal inspectors who can prevent them from selling in the historic center.

Against many odds the UPVA has survived the state's and large businesses' countless attempts to weaken it, co-opt it, and destroy it. The organization still represents a refuge for the working class, and it is highly likely that membership will continue to grow. According to a UPVA spokesperson, Alberto Hernández, around twenty people arrive daily at the union's main office to inquire about selling at the market. There are simply no jobs, and these people urgently need an income. They hope to sell food, toys, clothes, or any other merchandise that will help them provide for their family.[16] These people seek the aid and guidance of the only organization of vendors in Puebla that can help them make a living regardless of which political party is in office. As long as the rich and powerful continue to repress the poor and dispossessed, the UPVA will remain a powerful voice.

NOTES

ABBREVIATIONS

AGN   Archivo General de la Nación, Mexico City

AGPJ   Archivo General del Poder Judicial, Puebla

AHMP   Archivo Histórico Municipal de Puebla

AHU, BUAP   Archivo Histórico Universitario, Benemérita Universidad Autónoma de Puebla

DFS   Dirección Federal de Seguridad

DGIPS   Dirección General de Investigaciones Políticas y Sociales

EM   Expedientes de Mercados

exp.   *expediente*, file

h., hs.   *hoja(s)*, page(s)

INAH   Instituto Nacional de Antropología e Historia

leg.   *legajo*, a bundle of sheets

UAP   Universidad Autónoma de Puebla

INTRODUCTION

1. Castillo Palma, "El movimiento urbano popular en Puebla," 261; Jones and Varley, "The Contest for the City Centre," 32.

2. Condés Lara, *Represión y rebelión en México*, 3:99; Rothwell, *Transpacific Revolutionaries*, 24.

3. Bensusán and Middlebrook, *Organized Labour and Politics in Mexico*, 19–20. On how the end of the Mexican Miracle affected the middle classes, see Walker, *Waking from the Dream*.

4. Bensusán and Middlebrook, *Organized Labour and Politics in Mexico*, 21–22. For the neoliberal "new labor culture," see Snodgrass, "New Rules for the Unions," 81–103.

5. Zolov, "Expanding Our Conceptual Horizons," 49, 51, 55.

6. For independent unions in the formal economy, see Roxborough, *Unions and Politics in Mexico*; Snodgrass, "How Can We Speak of Democracy in Mexico?"

7. Scholars have acknowledged the active political roles of vendors and others in the informal economy. In his pioneering work on street vendors in Mexico City, the sociologist John C. Cross argues that street vendors were political actors who took advantage of the state's clientelism and formed organizations in order to gain favors from authorities in exchange for vendors' political support. See Cross, *Informal Politics*. See also Gordon, "Peddlers, Pesos, and Power"; Vanderbush, "Independent Organizing in Puebla, Mexico"; Fernández-Kelly and Shefner, *Out of the Shadows*. Focusing on market vendors in the country's capital, Ingrid Bleynat sees them as active participants of state formation who helped create the midcentury PRI ("Trading with Power," 248).

8. See, among others, Padilla, *Rural Resistance in the Land of Zapata*; Gauss, *Made in Mexico*; Alegre, *Railroad Radicals in Cold War Mexico*; Pensado, *Rebel Mexico*; Aviña, *Specters of Revolution*; Walker, *Waking from the Dream*; Gillingham and Smith, *Dictablanda*; Rubin, *Decentering the Regime*.

9. Jaime Pensado has correctly emphasized that the PRI regime did not have a monopoly on violence. Other groups (i.e., right-wing organizations) and other political parties also used agents to inflict violence on their enemies (*Rebel Mexico*, 6, 11).

10. In *The Logic of Compromise in Mexico* the historian Gladys McCormick argues that in Morelos's countryside the PRI was able to forge a real base of support.

11. President Cárdenas created it in 1938. Rath, *Myths of Demilitarization in Post-Revolutionary Mexico*, 38–39, 50; Hellman, *Mexico in Crisis*, 46–47.

12. Hellman, *Mexico in Crisis*, 47–49; Walker, *Waking from the Dream*, 7; Middlebrook, *The Paradox of Revolution*, 93.

13. Rath, *Myths of Demilitarization in Post-Revolutionary Mexico*, 50; Middlebrook, *The Paradox of Revolution*, 361n86.

14. For the power that union leaders gained for hiring, firing, and disciplining factory workers at the end of the Mexican Revolution, see Bortz, "Authority Reseated."

15. In Mexico City this was the case for the leaders Celia Torres and Sergio Jiménez Barrios (Alba, "Local Politics and Globalization from Below," 214). For a colorful description of vendors' *jefes* (leaders) and how they could help vendors while supporting the party, see Hellman, *Mexican Lives*, 33–42. John C. Cross argues that these leaders were savvy in negotiating with PRI *camarillas* (*Informal Politics*, chapter 5).

16. Usually some union statutes contained a provision that affiliated them with the PRI (Middlebrook, *The Paradox of Revolution*, 143).

17. The term arose after the leader of the National Railroad Union (Sindicato de Trabajadores Ferrocarrileros de México), Jesús Díaz de León, gained the nickname of El Charro because he enjoyed rodeos (*charrerías*) and wore rodeo gear (Alegre, *Railroad Radicals in Cold War Mexico*, 57).

18. For a reconsideration of *charrismo* that gives more credit to charros in defending the rank-and-file members' interests, see Snodgrass, "The Golden Age of Charrismo." For student charrismo, see Pensado, *Rebel Mexico*.

19. For democratization efforts among railroad workers, see Alegre, *Railroad Radicals in Cold War Mexico*. For the teachers' fight for a democratic leadership, see Cook, *Organizing Dissent*.

20. In *Unions and Politics in Mexico* Ian Roxborough cautions that not all independent unions were democratic; some official unions had democratic and militant characteristics, and their leaders negotiated decent gains for the membership.

21. La Botz, *Mask of Democracy*, 33–34, 42; Carrillo, "Women and Independent Unionism in the Garment Industry," 215.

22. Middlebrook, *The Paradox of Revolution*, 77–78, 92; Lear, *Workers, Neighbors, and Citizens*, 350.

23. Middlebrook, *The Paradox of Revolution*, 85–86, 89–95.

24. Gauss, *Made in Mexico*, 143.

25. Snodgrass, "How Can We Speak of Democracy in Mexico?," 165–66.

26. Snodgrass, "The Golden Age of Charrismo" and "How Can We Speak of Democracy in Mexico?," 166–67.

27. Roxborough, *Unions and Politics in Mexico*, 32.

28. De la Garza Toledo, "Independent Trade Unionism in Mexico," 155.

29. Roxborough, *Unions and Politics in Mexico*, 33.

30. For independent unions in the automobile industry, see Roxborough, *Unions and Politics in Mexico*; for the garment industry, see Carrillo, "Women and Independent Unionism in the Garment Industry," 213–33. For the controversial case of electrical workers, see Gómez Tagle and Miquet, "Integración o democracia sindical."

31. For the Authentic Labor Front, see Hathaway, *Allies across the Border*. For the existence of the two incarnations of the Central Campesina Independiente (Independent Peasant Organization), see Montes de Oca, "The State and the Peasants," 56; Henderson, "Rural Unrest and Political Control."

32. Roxborough, *Unions and Politics in Mexico*, 32.

33. La Botz, *Mask of Democracy*; Hathaway, *Allies across Borders*.

34. Snodgrass, "The Golden Age of Charrismo," 191.

35. For the collapse of the avilacamachistas, see Pansters, *Política y poder en Puebla*, chapter 7.

36. For street protests and their impact on policymaking, see Irazábal, "Citizenship, Democracy, and Public Space in Latin America," 12.

37. Avritzer, *Democracy and the Public Space in Latin America*, 5.

38. For the definition and practice of *acarreo* and *acarreados*, see Lettieri, "A Model Dinosaur," especially 307, 318, 333.

39. Vanderbush, "Assessing Democracy in Puebla," 8.

40. Reyna, "Redefining the Authoritarian Regime," 161; La Botz, *Mask of Democracy*, 65.

41. Padilla, *Rural Resistance in the Land of Zapata*; Walker, *Waking from the Dream*.

42. Castillo Palma, "El movimiento urbano popular en Puebla," 233–34.

43. Middlebrook, *The Paradox of Revolution*, 95–105.

44. Harvey, "The Right to the City," 33.

45. These state agencies include the Secretaría de Educación Pública (Ministry of Public Education), the Instituto Nacional de Antropología e Historia (National Institute of Anthropology and History), and the Secretaría de Desarrollo Urbano y Ecología (Ministry of Urban Development and the Environment). See "Expediente Técnico de Postulación a la Lista del Patrimonio Mundial de la UNESCO del sitio 'Centro Histórico de Puebla,'" Dirección de Patrimonio Mundial, INAH.

46. Jones and Varley, "The Reconquest of the Historic Centre."

47. Harvey, "The Right to the City," 38. For the philosopher Henri Lefebvre *the right to the city* is as important and essential as "the right to work, to culture, to rest, to health, [and] to housing" (*Writings on Cities*, 157). For David Harvey the right to the city is "one of the most precious yet most neglected of our human rights" ("The Right to the City," 23).

48. Kohn, *Radical Space*, 16.

49. This plight was not new, as Christina Jiménez has shown; it goes back to the nineteenth century when the urban poor began making claims of citizenship and rights based on liberal ideas linked to the 1857 Constitution. See Jiménez, "Making the City Their Own."

50. On the underappreciated broadness of labor history, see Pearson, "From the Labour Question to the Labour History Question." In his award-winning work, *El trabajo en las calles*, the historian Mario Barbosa Cruz has situated street vendors as "workers of the streets" who carried out independent and often unskilled labor (13, 14, 18).

51. Denning, "Wageless Life," 85–86. Denning has proposed a need to "decenter wage labor in our conception of life under capitalism" (80).

52. Harvey, *Rebel Cities*, 139.

53. Kohn, *Radical Space*, 64.

54. Florence Babb points out that market women's work should be considered productive labor as they add value to the goods they sell, especially prepared food (*Between the Field and the Cooking Pot*, 180).

55. For a list of many other dishes that Puebla offered, see Cordero y Torres, *Guía Turística de Puebla*, 22–23. For an analysis of the displacement of local food in

favor of large food chains since 1986, see Mendiola García, "Food Gentrification in Downtown Puebla," 59–76.

56. Paula Javier, interview by author, January 25, 2007, Puebla, México.

57. Paula Javier interview, January 25, 2007.

58. Kohn, *Radical Space*, 16.

59. Article 4, 1917 Mexican Constitution.

60. Harvey, *Rebel Cities*, 128–29.

61. LaFrance, *Revolution in Mexico's Heartland*, 90, 115.

62. Jones and Varley, "The Reconquest of the Historic Centre," 1549.

63. Guerra and Lempérière, *Los espacios públicos en Iberoamérica*, 30.

64. Many UPVA street vendors became market vendors after the summer of 1986, when they moved to the new public markets. From that moment on, I refer to them as former street vendors, UPVA members, or simply sellers.

65. I use "marketers" or "market sellers" to refer to those who owned or rented stalls inside enclosed markets. They had more capital and were better off than street vendors. Marketers became some of the staunchest enemies of street vendors because the latter represented their main competitors. Interestingly most market sellers belonged to official unions.

66. From 1960 to 1970 about one-fourth of the inhabitants of the city of Puebla came from other states and cities (Nolasco Armas, *Cuatro Ciudades*, 144–45, 151).

67. Niblo, *Mexico in the 1940s*, 188; Henderson, "Rural Unrest and Political Control," 3–4; Padilla, *Rural Resistance in the Land of Zapata*, 9.

68. Gauss, *Made in Mexico*, 5fn13.

69. Another alternative, especially for men, during this time was to migrate to the United States; see, for instance, Cohen, *Braceros*.

70. Census, Secretaría del Trabajo y Previsión Social, Departamento de Registro de Asociaciones, 1969, box 42, file 319, AHMP.

71. Iragorri, *Diagnóstico del ambulantismo en la ciudad de Puebla*, 55.

72. Municipal archival photographs were not intended to record vendors' presence. They were commissioned by city officials to keep a visual record of certain streets, scenes of markets, and mayors' political activities. The municipality published some of these pictures in "Informes de Gobierno," the mayors' yearly reports. Biblioteca, AHMP.

73. The youngest ones were two sisters, Cristina and Marcela Guzmán, twelve and thirteen, respectively. Census, Secretaria del Trabajo y Previsión Social, Departamento de Registro de Asociaciones, 1969, box 42, file 319, AHMP.

74. Elaine Carey has shown that Mexico City's female street vendors were involved in the sale of drugs on the streets and close to La Merced market in the 1920s

and 1930s (*Women Drug Traffickers*, 74–75, 93). I did not find any archival reference to vendors selling drugs, although in the twenty-first century local authorities have accused UPVA vendors of drug trafficking.

75. Teresa Rosales, interview by author, July 16, 2010, Puebla, México.

76. Alba, "Local Politics and Globalization from Below," 205. For pirate products sold in makeshift markets all over Mexico, see Aguiar, "'They Come from China'"; Cross, "Pirates in the High Streets."

77. Estrada Urroz, *Del telar a la cadena de montaje*, 39; Gilbert and Varley, *Landlord and Tenant*, 64.

78. Estrada Urroz, *Del telar a la cadena de montaje*, 36–37.

79. The owners of these textile industries were for the most part families of Spanish descent; after World War II they were joined by Lebanese families. For Spanish industrialists, see Gamboa Ojeda, *Los empresarios de ayer*. For Lebanese entrepreneurs, see Palacios Alonso, *Los libaneses*; Alfaro-Velcamp, *So Far from Allah*. The literature on Puebla's textile industry is extensive. For two relatively recent works that address the industry from a labor and business perspective, respectively, see Bortz, *Revolution within the Revolution*; Gauss, *Made in Mexico*.

80. "Continúan en huelga 40 fábricas textiles," *El Sol de Puebla*, July 7, 1974.

81. Melé, *Puebla*, 82.

82. Escobar Latapí and González de la Rocha, introduction, 2, n1.

83. Tirado Villegas, *La otra historia*, 28–29. According to Susan Gauss, between 1945 and 1965 women made up only 3 percent of workers in this industry ("Masculine Bonds and Modern Mothers," 64).

84. Gauss, "Working-Class Masculinity and the Rationalized Sex," 190.

85. Garza Villarreal, *La urbanización de México*, 45.

86. The city of Puebla had 513,237 inhabitants in 1970; 835,759 in 1980; and 1,057,000 in 1990 (Melé, *La producción del patrimonio urbano*, 18).

87. Gilbert and Varley, *Landlord and Tenant*, 72–73.

88. Estrada Urroz, *Del telar a la cadena de montaje*, 236–38.

89. Gilbert and Varley, *Landlord and Tenant*, 72. For a discussion of the privileged geographical position of Puebla between the port of Veracruz and Mexico City, see Melé, *Puebla*, 15–16.

90. In 1970, 36.7 percent of the economically active population in Puebla was employed in the industrial sector, 6.8 percent in agriculture, and 50.6 percent in commerce and manufacturing (Gilbert and Varley, *Landlord and Tenant*, 64).

91. Quoted in Bhowmik, *Street Vendors in the Global Urban Economy*, 4.

92. Census, Secretaría del Trabajo y Previsión Social, Departamento de Registro de Asociaciones, 1969, box 42, file 319, AHMP.

93. "Información de Puebla," October 30 and November 1, 1973, box 1511-A, exp. 4, pp. 295, 313, DGIPS, AGN.

94. "Acuerdo conjunto de organismos oficiales y de vendedores para resolver el problema," *La Opinión*, February 28, 1977. According to local studies, in 1977 there were between 2,067 and 2,500 street vendors in forty-one blocks (Castillo Palma, "El movimiento urbano popular en Puebla," 242).

95. Castillo Palma, "El movimiento urbano popular en Puebla," 221. Castillo Palma notes that by 1983 there were around ten thousand street vendors in Puebla (221).

96. Currently street vendors have employers and sell products from large companies such as Telcel and Coca-Cola. These vendors lack contracts and benefits.

97. Gabina Rodríguez, interview by author, January 20, 2007, Puebla, México; Paula Javier interview, January 25, 2007; Juana Sánchez Maldonado, interview by author, August 30, 2007; Rosa Martínez, interview by author, January 14, 2007, Puebla, México.

98. Alan G. Gilbert uses this term to denote housing built by "'informal' processes and on land initially lacking titles, deeds and services" ("Self-Help Housing during Recession," 221n1). In 1980 nonowners made up 52 percent in Puebla (235).

99. See, for example, "Pese a las numerosas denuncias," *El Sol de Puebla*, May 13, 1973; "Evita circulación de peatones y vehículos," *El Sol de Puebla*, May 23, 1973; "La invasion de las banquetas," *El Sol de Puebla*, September 7, 1973; "Un peligro para automovilistas y peatones," *El Sol de Puebla*, February 15, 1977.

100. Aguayo Quezada, *La Charola* is the most comprehensive Spanish account of the government's secret police in Mexico. See also Navarro, *Political Intelligence and the Creation of Modern Mexico*; Padilla and Walker, "In the Archives."

101. Padilla, *Rural Resistance in the Land of Zapata*, 17. For the Soviet case, see Velikanova, *Popular Perceptions of Soviet Politics in the 1920s*, 17.

102. In her study of female market and street vendors during the Porfiriato, Susie Porter notes that they used the streets "to work . . . sleep, eat, socialize, make love, raise children, and fight" (*Working Women of Mexico City*, 148).

103. In one report a police officer refers to a female vendor and organizer as "the lover of Bulmaro Vega" ("Mercado Popular 28 de Octubre," September 20, 1977, exp. 100-19-1-77, leg. 59, h. 42, DFS, AGN).

104. Véliz and O'Neill, "Privatization of Public Space," 97.

1. PRELUDE TO INDEPENDENT ORGANIZING

1. Letters from María del Carmen Teyssier to city authorities, August 12, 1946, vol. 1141, file 93, p. 121, and August 6, 1945, vol. 1114, file 102, p. 300, EM, AHMP.

2. Letter from Ernesto Espinosa Yglesias, June 10, 1946, book 1141, file 93, p. 133, EM, AHMP.

3. Pansters, *Política y poder en Puebla*, 108–9. For a comprehensive biography of Maximino Ávila Camacho and the origins and weakening of the avilacamachista cacicazgo, see Quintana, *Maximino Ávila Camacho and the One-Party State*. For a discussion of the role military officers played in creating and sustaining the avilacamachista machine, see Rath, *Myths of Demilitarization in Post-Revolutionary Mexico*, chapter 4.

4. Henderson and LaFrance, "Maximino Avila Camacho," 157, 165.

5. For Maximino's interest in bullfighting and the analysis of a popular protest against him, see Gillingham, "Maximino's Bulls," 175–211.

6. Henderson and LaFrance, "Maximino Avila Camacho," 164–67; Manjárrez, *Puebla*, 93–94.

7. Pansters, *Política y poder en Puebla*, 69, 114; Henderson and LaFrance, "Maximino Avila Camacho," 163.

8. Manjárrez, *Puebla*, 123.

9. Pansters, *Política y poder en Puebla*, 117, 132.

10. Manjárrez, *Puebla*, 109, 123.

11. For a thorough study of these entrepreneurs during the first decades of the twentieth century, see Gamboa Ojeda, *Los empresarios de ayer*.

12. Pansters, *Política y poder en Puebla*, 127–28; Henderson and LaFrance, "Maximino Avila Camacho," 165. On places of origin, see Gamboa Ojeda, *Los empresarios de ayer*, 159–64.

13. Gamboa Ojeada, *Los empresarios de ayer*, 118, 154–56, 201–28.

14. Susan Gauss explains that Puebla's industrialists sometimes had a difficult time negotiating economic favors with the federal government, especially with the Miguel Alemán administration (*Made in Mexico*, chapter 4).

15. Pansters, *Política y poder en Puebla*, 127; Gamboa Ojeda, *Los empresarios de ayer*, 118, 164–77; Alfaro-Velcamp, *So Far from Allah*.

16. While some upper-class Poblanos lived downtown, some left the area and built their homes in the periphery (Jones and Varley, "The Contest for the City Centre," 29).

17. In 1956 it was renamed Universidad Autónoma de Puebla, having gained its autonomy (Lara y Parra, *La lucha universitaria en Puebla*, 64).

18. Pansters, *Política y poder en Puebla*, 136–37.

19. Lara y Parra, *La lucha universitaria en Puebla*, 47, 58n15.

20. Tirado Villegas, *Vientos de la Democracia*, 77, 11–12.

21. For Octaviano Márquez y Toriz, see Manjárrez, *Puebla*, 174, 187. For the creation of the Frente Universitario Anti-comunista (Anticommunist University

Front) in 1954, see Lara y Parra, *La lucha universitaria*, 104n15. For the local and national activities of the Movimiento Universitario de Renovadora Orientación (University Movement of Renovating Orientation), see González Ruiz, *Muro*; Pensado "To Assault with the Truth," 493–94, 496–97.

22. Cordero y Torres, *Guía Turística de Puebla*, 76–84.
23. Leicht, *Las Calles de Puebla*, 470–71.
24. Leicht, *Las Calles de Puebla*, 341, 338. For a through history of the portales from the colonial era to the 1930s, see 317–41.
25. The Expedientes de Mercados (Market Files) at the AHMP contain letters and petitions in which vendors or their foes specified the products vendors offered and where and how they were sold.
26. Piccato, "Urbanistas, Ambulantes and Mendigos," 113–48; Porter, *Working Women of Mexico City*; Jiménez, "Making the City Their Own"; Jiménez, "Performing Their Right to the City"; Jiménez, "From the Lettered City to the Sellers' City"; Barbosa Cruz, *El trabajo en las calles* and "Trabajadores en las calles de la ciudad de México"; Bleynat, "Trading with Power."
27. Barbosa Cruz, *El trabajo en las calles*, 193, 209, 218.
28. Letter from Enrique Belague to municipal authorities, June 13, 1919, book 630, file 318, EM, AHMP.
29. Gamboa Ojeada, *Los empresarios de ayer*, 184–86.
30. Letter from Hijos de Ángel Díaz Rubín to H. Ayuntamiento de la ciudad, April 2, 1921, book 691, exp. 481, Comisión del Síndico Municipal, EM, AHMP. The Díaz Rubíns were an elite family that for generations owned textile factories, including La Covadonga (Gamboa Ojeda, *Los empresarios de ayer*, 123–27).
31. Letter from Carrie Purdy to the Municipality, August 16, 1911, book 511, file 14B, p. 280, Comisión de Mercados, EM, AHMP. Porter mentions that *el pueblo* means "the common people or the popular classes" (*Working Women of Mexico City*, 140).
32. Letter from Coronel de Infantería Fernando P. Dávila to Presidente Municipal, June 16, 1947, vol. 1160, file 94, p. 78, EM, AHMP.
33. Letter from Sindicato Único de Tortilleras y Similares de la Ciudad de Puebla to Ayuntamiento de la Ciudad, June 17, 1936, book 975, file 228, EM, AHMP.
34. "Reglamentos," July 29, 1929, vol. 34, file 112–13, and August 4, 1936, vol. 975, file 325, AHMP.
35. Street vendors wrote letters complaining about abusive fee collectors and the lack of clarity on the amount of fees they should pay to the municipality. Established marketers also witnessed fee collectors' abuses.
36. The general market inspector earned 5 pesos daily; inspectors 4.5 pesos, night watchers 3.5, and the sweepers 2.50 pesos each (Market Report, 1947, vol. 1157, p. 17, EM, AHMP).

37. For example, see letter from Mariano Tlapanco and Macario Apanco to Presidente Municipal, January 23, 1918, book 608, file 186; letter from Lucrecia Torres to Presidente Municipal, March 13, 1947, vol. 1157, file 49, p. 235; letter from Antonia Mendoza to León García, Jefe de la Oficina de Quejas de la Presidencia de la República, Palacio Nacional, June 12, 1962, box 42, file 99, AHMP.

38. Gabina Reyes, interview by author, January 28, 2007, Puebla, Mexico.

39. "Información de Puebla," June 9, 1970, box 1511A, exp. 4, pp. 420–23, DGIPS, AGN.

40. Yolanda Bejarano, interview by author, March 17, 2007, Puebla, México.

41. Teresa Rosales, interview by author, March 8, 2007, Puebla, México. A number of vendors who were removed by authorities from the streets defended themselves legally through amparos. Unfortunately vendors commonly lost their cases against authorities. "Niegan más Amparos a ambulantes," *El Sol de Puebla*, February 2, 1971.

42. Paula Javier interview, January 25, 2007.

43. Yolanda Bejarano interview, March 17, 2007.

44. Letter to Carlos Arruti from Comisión de Vendedores Ambulantes, June 8 1970, box 42, file 5, EM, AHMP.

45. Blanca Pastrana, interview by author, April 12, 2007, Puebla, Mexico.

46. "Operan agitadores," *El Sol de Puebla*, 28 February 1971.

47. Yolanda Bejarano interview, March 17, 2007; Yolanda Bejarano, interview by author, July 27, 2010, Puebla, México.

48. "Información de Puebla," November 30, 1973, box 1511A, exp. 4, p. 709, DGIPS, AGN.

49. Porter describes officials' sexual harassment of vendors in Mexico City during the Porfiriato (*Working Women of Mexico City*, 149).

50. Lear, *Workers, Neighbors, and Citizens*, 81.

51. Gauss, "Working-Class Masculinity and the Rationalized Sex."

52. Tirado Villegas, *La otra historia*, 29, 30, 37.

53. On their right to make an "honest" living, see Jiménez, "Making the City Their Own," chapter 6.

54. See, for instance, Porter, *Working Women of Mexico City*, chapter 6; Jiménez, "From the Lettered City to the Sellers' City"; Marti, "Nineteenth-Century Views of Women's Participation in Mexico's Markets"; Barbosa Cruz, *El trabajo en las calles*.

55. Jiménez, "From the Lettered City to the Sellers' City," 215.

56. Barbosa Cruz, *El trabajo en las calles*, 248–49, 263.

57. Jiménez, "Performing Their Right to the City," 448. For a discussion of the meanings of *vecino*, see 448–50.

58. Porter, *Working Women of Mexico City*, chapter 6, especially 148.

59. Marti, "Nineteenth-Century Views of Women's Participation in Mexico's Markets," 29, 37.

60. Letter from Bernarda Aguilar to municipality, December 17, 1913, book 544, exp. 8, letter C, p. 86; letter from Aurelia López to municipality, August 18, 1947, vol. 1160, exp. 98, p. 206, E M, A H M P; letter from Sra. Socorro Torres Huerta to municipality, November 5, 1947, vol. 1160, exp. 98, p. 239, E M, A H M P. In their letters to authorities throughout the twentieth century women vendors often emphasized the fact that they were mothers and *mujeres solas*. In 1919 a woman wanted to sell food on the street because it was an honest activity appropriate to "mujeres solas y desvalidas" (letter from four female vendors to municipality, January 29, 1919, book 630, file 345, p. 550, E M, A H M P). In 1987 a woman asks permission to sell candy because she has four daughters and her husband is an "irresponsible man" (letter from Dolores Arévalo to Governor Mariano Piña Olaya, September 18, 1987, box 42, file 9, A H M P). In 1955 Margarita Cortes said that instead of begging on the streets, she sold candy outside the Templo de las Capuchinas. She asked authorities not to relocate her because it was hard for her to be under the direct sunlight (letter from Margarita Cortés to Mayor, May 4, 1955, box 42, file 2861, A H M P). At the beginning of the 1950s authorities banned vendors outside churches ("Primer Informe de Gobierno," Mayor Nicolás Vázquez, February 14, 1952, A H M P).

61. Letter from Teresa Nava Mendoza to Mayor, April 17, 1946, vol. 1141, file 93, p. 106, A H M P; Amparo promovido por Carmen Molina, vol. 1128, file 315, p. 141, A H M P; letter from Rita Zarate to Mayor, July 21, 1945, vol. 114, file 107, p. 506, A H M P; letter from Gregorio García to Mayor, August 2, 1946, vol. 1141, file 97, p. 256, A H M P; letter from Rubén Ramírez to Mayor, January 9, 1947, vol. 1141, file 97, p. 293, A H M P; letter from Francisco Canaliso to Mayor, August 17, 1946, vol. 1141, file 97, p. 263, A H M P.

62. In her study of Mexico and Guadalajara vendors, Judith Marti found that "good will, mercy, and compassion are standard endings to the requests for both men and women" ("Nineteenth-Century Views of Women's Participation in Mexico's Markets," 39).

63. Jiménez, "Making the City Their Own," 14, 275, 567.

64. Article 4, chapter 1, title 1, 1917 Mexican Constitution. Jiménez notes that vendors in Morelia went back to using this constitutional rhetoric after 1917 ("Making the City Their Own," 419–26).

65. After a few months the vendors were able to continue their trade (letter from vendors to Comisión de Fomento, September 3, 1921, book 674, file 335, E M, A H M P).

66. Letter from La Victoria marketers to Municipality, August 21, 1921, book 674, file 80, pp. 303–4. In 1921 authorities canceled the fee ("Cancelación de alcabala," book 688, file 223, p. 773, EM, AHMP).

67. Letter from Luz Andrade to Municipal Authorities, June 25, 1948, vol. 1377, file 7, p. 93, AHMP.

68. Letter from Raquel Herrera, Filiberto Ramírez, and Tamy González to Presidente Municipal, March 8, 1950, vol. 1375, p. 372, AHMP.

69. In Puebla targets of complaints were members of the Lebanese community. For a history of Middle Eastern migration to the country, see Alfaro-Velcamp, *So Far from Allah*. Ingrid Bleynat found instances of xenophobic acts by both market vendors and authorities in Mexico City in 1931 ("Trading with Power," 161).

70. Letter from María Moreno to Presidente Municipal, March 17, 1947, vol. 1160, file 94, p. 71, EM, AHMP.

71. Letter to the Mayor from vendor Antonia Mendoza, June 22, 1962, box 42, file 99, EM, AHMP.

72. This political calculation is what Jiménez calls a "balanced containment" ("Making the City Their Own," 21, 382–83, 400).

73. Cross, *Informal Politics*; Marti, "Subsistence and the State"; Jiménez, "Performing Their Right to the City"; Fernández-Kelly and Shefner, *Out of the Shadows*.

74. Bleynat, "Trading with Power," chapter 1.

75. Marti, "Subsistence and the State," 319–22.

76. Jiménez, "Making the City Their Own," 21, 382–83, 400.

77. Letter from Juan Blanco Segura, Secretario de la Federación de Ligas del Sector Popular del Estado de Puebla to Presidente Municipal, June 5, 1945, vol. 1114, file 102, p. 325; letter from Municipality to Nicolas Bravo marketers, June 19, 1945, vol. 1114, file 102, p. 329, AHMP.

78. Letter from Nicolas Bravo marketers to Municipality, July 17, 1945, vol. 1114, file 102, p. 333, AHMP.

79. Marti, "Subsistence and the State," 315, 318, 322.

80. Health authorities obviously were concerned about these sorts of practices because they said that vendors also sold rotten food in addition to the ripe fruits and vegetables ("Reporte de Médico Director to Crecencia Bonilla," August 23 and November 14, 1922, book 685, file 108, pp. 547, 573 EM, AHMP).

81. Castillo Palma, "El movimiento urbano popular en Puebla," 222, 225.

82. Letters from Directiva de la Colonia Obrera Lázaro Cárdenas to Presidente Municipal, Lic. Nicolás Vázquez, and Arcadio Medel Marín, May 31, 1951, and August 1966, exp. year 1948, vol. 1355, file 223J, pp. 306–95, AHMP; letter from Junta to Colonos de la Colonia Obrera Lázaro Cárdenas, November 7, 1968, vol. 1355, file 233J, p. 372, AHMP.

83. Letter from Colonos de la Colonia Héroes de Nacozari to Presidente Municipal, vol. 1356, no date, pp. 186–88; letter from Francisco Ubaldo, Juez de Paz de la Colonia "Santa Cruz Los Angeles," to Honorable Ayuntamiento Municipal, January 23, 1950, vol. 1358, p. 87, AHMP.

84. As I show in chapter 5, it was not until the mid-1980s that, based on elites' proposals, the municipality began building markets in places people could not access.

85. Owensby, *Empire of Law*, chapter 3. For a classic work on the amparo suit, see Lira González, *El amparo colonial y el juicio de amparo mexicano*.

86. Sausi Garavito, "Las primeras tres décadas del juicio de amparo," 123. For a comparative study in Latin America of the modern amparo, see Ferrer Mac-Gregor, "El amparo iberoamericano."

87. The first group of common people who began using amparo suits were merchants and mothers who wanted to recover their children who had been drafted for the war (Sausi Garavito, "Las primeras tres décadas del juicio de amparo," 138–39).

88. Letter from Faustina Cerón to the Municipality, June 22, 1913, Comisión de Mercados, exp. 8C, AHMP.

89. Juicio de amparo 97/952, March 15, 1952, Juana Torres y Coagraviadas vs. Presidente Municipal Constitucional, Secretario General del Ayuntamiento, y Jefe de Impuestos y Reglamentos, Poder Judicial, AGPJ.

90. Juicio de amparo 97/952.

91. Juicio de amparo 97/952.

92. "Tercer Informe de Gobierno," Rafael Artasánchez, 1960, Sección "Administración General de Mercados," Biblioteca, AHMP.

93. Letter from Secretario General del Ayuntamiento to Director General de Tránsito, March 4, 1969, box 42, file 319, AHMP; "List of Amparos," June 10, 1970, box 42, file 5, AHMP.

94. Letter by Agrupación de Locatarios Libres del Estado de Puebla, Benito Juárez, June 3, 1970, AHMP.

95. Barbosa Cruz, *El trabajo en las calles*, 258.

96. Jiménez, "Making the City Their Own," 427–28.

97. Jiménez, "Making the City Their Own," 22. Jiménez has demonstrated "the importance of voluntary associations as channels through which popular groups could gain access to the state and its resources" (22–23).

98. It is interesting to note that despite the fact that vendors were not workers in the traditional sense, state-sponsored organizations such as the CROM and FROC incorporated vendors into their ranks.

99. Letter to Mayor Francisco Pacheco from Unión de Comerciantes e Industriales en pequeño de la cd. de Puebla, May 31, 1960, box 42, file 3, AHMP.

100. Castillo Palma, "El movimiento urbano popular en Puebla," 228.

101. A charro is a state-appointed union leader who does not represent his membership and who is violent and corrupt. The term was first used after authorities appointed Jesús Díaz de León as the general secretary of the rail workers' union, the Sindicato de Trabajadores Ferrocarrileros de la República Mexicana, in 1948 (La Botz, *Mask of Democracy*, 66–67). For similar definitions of *charrismo* and *sindicalismo charro*, see De la Garza Toledo, "Independent Trade Unionism in Mexico," 153.

102. Castillo Palma, "El movimiento urbano popular en Puebla," 228, 230–31.

103. Letter to Mayor from FROC-CROC representatives, December 5, 1969, box 42, file 319, AHMP.

104. Letter to Director de Tránsito from Unión de Vendedores, September 15, 1955, box 42, file 286-1, AHMP.

105. "Mercado Popular 28 de Octubre," October 28, 1977, exp. 100-19-1-77, leg. 59, p. 268, DFS, AGN.

106. Castillo Palma, "El movimiento urbano popular en Puebla," 241. For Mexico City's acarreados, see Lettieri, "A Model Dinosaur," especially 307, 318, 333.

107. See, for example, the photograph of *acarreados* (those dragged to PRI political rallies) above the caption that begins "El Gobernador del Estado Guillermo Morales Blumenkron" in *El Sol de Puebla*, October 22, 1973.

108. Gordon, "Peddlers, Pesos, and Power," 127.

109. Knight and Pansters, *Caciquismo in Twentieth-Century Mexico*, 17n69.

110. La Botz, *Mask of Democracy*, 42.

2. VENDORS AND STUDENTS IN THE 1970S

1. The Dirección Federal de Seguridad kept track of Vega's political activities. His file contains information that goes back to 1966. For his activities in 1968, see "Embajada Cubana," exp. 100-4-1970, leg. 112, hs. 93–94, DFS, AGN.

2. For the student-worker connections, see the case of university students in Monterrey who supported miners in the 1930s and 1940s in Snodgrass, *Deference and Defiance in Monterrey*, 225–26, 292. For teacher-student organizing with peasants, see Blacker, "Cold War in the Countryside." For urban guerrillas, see Herrera Calderón, "From Books to Bullets"; Padilla, *Rural Resistance in the Land of Zapata*; and more recently Aviña, *Specters of Revolution*.

3. By "the long 1960s in Mexico," I am referring to the historian Jaime Pensado's periodization of the student movement, approximately 1956 to 1971 (*Rebel Mexico*, 3).

4. Pansters situates this broader alliance through the Frente Obrero Campesino Estudiantil Popular that Puebla's state university articulated (*Política y poder en Puebla*, chapter 7, especially 241–42, 260–65).

5. For a discussion of the several factors that resulted in the collapse of the avila-camachistas, see Pansters, *Política y poder en Puebla*, chapter 7.

6. Pansters, *Política y poder en Puebla*, 265.

7. For Echeverría's policies toward the student movement, see Walker, *Waking from the Dream*, chapter 1. For labor policies during the democratic opening, see Middlebrook, *The Paradox of Revolution*, 160, 224.

8. José Luis Díaz, interview by author, July 6, 2010, Puebla, México; Omar Castro, interview by author, December 27, 2011, Puebla, México; Huberto Juárez, interview by author, December 2011, Puebla, México.

9. "Información de Puebla," February 14, 1975, box 1510, exp. A/1, p. 43, DGIPS, AGN.

10. Tirado Villegas, *La otra historia*, 72.

11. Jeffrey Gould discusses the participation of high school students in 1968 throughout Latin America in "Solidarity under Siege," 364.

12. Vallejo and Ramírez Ramírez, "Escuela Preparatoria Popular Emiliano Zapata," 117, 115.

13. Márquez Carrillo and Diéguez Delgadillo, "Política, universidad y sociedad en Puebla," 117–18, 121.

14. Seventy-four of these eighty-eight teachers were college students, and fourteen of them had a BA degree (Vallejo and Ramírez Ramírez, "Escuela Preparatoria Popular Emiliano Zapata," 115–17).

15. José Luis Díaz interview, July 6, 2010.

16. Omar Castro interview, December 27, 2011, and summer 2011, Puebla, México.

17. These dangers were part of what Pansters refers to as a "moral panic" (*Política y poder en Puebla*, 248–60).

18. Flier, box, 4, file 62, n.d., "Vida Universitaria," AHU, BUAP.

19. Vallejo and Ramírez Ramírez, "Escuela Preparatoria Popular Emiliano Zapata," 116.

20. Vallejo and Ramírez Ramírez, "Escuela Preparatoria Popular Emiliano Zapata," 115, 117, 114.

21. Pensado, *Rebel Mexico*, 51.

22. Vallejo and Ramírez Ramírez, "Ecuela Preparatoria Popular Emiliano Zapata," 116–17. Pensado describes the various political meanings of other novatadas in Mexico City in the 1940s and 1950s (*Rebel Mexico*, 51–58).

23. Vallejo and Ramírez Ramírez, "Escuela Preparatoria Popular Emiliano Zapata," 119.

24. Berguiss, María Luisa, Omar Castro, et al., interview by author, August 2007, Puebla, México.

25. Tirado Villegas, *La otra historia*, 18, 45, 62–63.

26. Flier, box, 4, file 62, n.d., "Vida Universitaria," AHU, BUAP.

27. Pansters, *Política y poder en Puebla*, 248–60.

28. Pensando, *Rebel Mexico*, 11.

29. Pansters, *Política y poder en Puebla*, 241.

30. See a summary of Joel Arriaga's activities in Alberto Domingo, "La muerte llegó como heraldo de traición y de terror: Joel Arriaga, la víctima seleccionada por quienes anhelan devolvernos a las épocas del fascio, de la intolerancia y del culto a la violencia desatada," *Revista Siempre!*, August 9, 1972, 18–19. See also Heberto Castillo, "Sin hablar de culpables no podrá detenerse la violencia," *Revista Siempre!*, August 8, 1972, 22–23; Pansters, *Politics and Power in Puebla*, 130.

31. Part of the democratic opening consisted of freeing political prisoners (Middlebrook, *The Paradox of Revolution*, 224).

32. "Escalada de la violencia: Márquez y Toriz y el clima de la violencia en Puebla," Vida Pública, *Revista Siempre!*, August 2, 1972, 8; Pansters, *Política y poder en Puebla*, 240–41. For coverage of Arriaga's murder, see "Novedades," *Diario de la Tarde*, July 21, 1972.

33. Pansters, *Política y poder en Puebla*, 242, 256.

34. Bautista O'Farrill declared that the dead students were a lesson for other students who protest. See Sotelo, "La reforma universitaria y el movimiento popular de 1973," 128.

35. Arnaldo Córdova, "Gobierno a la Mexicana: Matar de un tiro," in Benemérita Universidad Autónoma de Puebla, *Sucesos universitarios*, 134–36.

36. Worst of all, the governor and his allies were never penalized for these murders. In October 2003 the Fiscalía Especial para Movimientos Sociales y Políticos del Pasado accused Bautista O'Farrill of being the intellectual author of the killing of students on May 1, 1973. See David Carrizales, "Posponen la comparecencia de Bautista O'Farrill ante la Femosp," *La Jornada*, October 10, 2003.

37. Photograph of Governor Bautista O'Farrill as Hitler in Garmendia, *Los sucesos del 10. de mayo en Puebla*.

38. *La Opinión*, August 30, 1972.

39. Some have questioned the Echeverría administration's involvement in the student repression in Puebla during that May 1971. See Hellman, *Mexico in Crisis*, 202, 208. See also the interview with Alejandro Gallardo Arroyo in Tirado Villegas, *Vientos de la Democracia*, 209–13.

40. Hernández Rodríguez, *El centro dividido*, 85–86. Rafael Moreno Valle and Gonzalo Bautista O'Farrill were two of the six governors removed from their posts by President Echeverría. In Puebla's history the federal executive removed a total of three governors. The first one was Antonio Nava Castillo in 1964

under Adolfo López Mateos. Nava Castillo and Bautista O'Farrill were deposed because of their repressive tactics.

41. Pansters, *Política y poder en Puebla*, 268, 269. Two years before removing Bautista O'Farrill, Echeverría had deposed Alfonso Martínez Domínguez, Mexico City's executive (*jefe del Distrito Federal*), and his political foe within the PRI, in the aftermath of the June 10, 1971, massacre of students. On that day a group of one thousand paramilitary soldiers, known as Los Halcones, killed fifty students in Mexico City during a peaceful demonstration. For an overview of the *halconazo*, see Walker, *Waking from the Dream*, 27–29.

42. "Reporte de Gobernación," February 24, 1971, box 1511A, exp. 4, p. 1, DGIPS, AGN.

43. "La Palabra de Dios es lo más Explosivo que Existe," *La Opinión*, August 18, 1970.

44. "Habla de Ideas de Mao Para la Liberación de Puebla," *El Sol de Puebla*, June 12, 1971.

45. Mackin, "Becoming the Red Bishop of Cuernavaca," 504–5; Pensado, *Rebel Mexico*, 222.

46. The attack was mainly carried out in newspaper articles, although members of CTM began a lawsuit against Méndez Arceo for violating the Constitution, which prohibited members of the Church from being involved in political activities (Pansters, *Política y poder en Puebla*, 253). For attacks by the ultraconservative right in Mexico City, see Pensado, *Rebel Mexico*, 220–22.

47. Pensado, "To Assault with the Truth," 491.

48. Flier, July 1970, Jornada Nacional de Solidaridad con la UAP, "Vida Universitaria," box 4, file 58, AHU, BUAP. For specific activities of comités de lucha in Mexico City, including their formation, see Carey, *Plaza of Sacrifices*; Pensado, *Rebel Mexico*; Walker, *Waking from the Dream*.

49. "Padre LEA," flier, "Vida Universitaria," box 8, file 66, n.d., AHU, BUAP.

50. "Homenaje al Che Guevara en la Preparatoria," *El Sol de Puebla*, October 9, 1970.

51. "Reporte de Gobernación," February 24, 1971, box 1511A, exp. 4, p. 4, DGIPS, AGN.

52. "Manifestación de la UAP y Sectores Populares," *El Sol de Puebla*, September 11, 1974.

53. Tirado Villegas, *Vientos de la Democracia*, 117–18. A new generation of historians has investigated these events. See Padilla, *Rural Resistance in the Land of Zapata*; Alegre, *Railroad Radicals in Cold War Mexico* and "Las Rieleras"; Pensado, *Rebel Mexico*; Soto Laveaga, "Shadowing the Professional Class." For a thorough study of Guerrero's peasants, see Aviña, *Specters of Revolution*.

54. Arturo Rodríguez, "La Prisión como escarmiento," *Proceso*, October 21, 2015.

55. During this student strike that began in April 1956, approximately twenty-five thousand students demanded the dismissal of several administrators at the Instituto Politécnico Nacional (National Polytechnic Institute) and autonomy and student participation in the institution's affairs (Pensado, *Rebel Mexico*, 85).

56. Pensado, *Rebel Mexico*, 89–93, 99.

57. See photographs of buses painted with slogans in "Vida Universitaria" collection, box 3, AHU, BUAP. Samuel Salazar, interview by author, August 2007, Puebla, México.

58. A classic work on Tlatelolco is Poniatowska, *Massacre in Mexico*. For an analysis of the movement that emphasizes gender, see Carey, *Plaza of Sacrifices*.

59. Pensado, *Rebel Mexico*.

60. Tirado Villegas, *La otra historia*, 121–38, 18, 25.

61. Herrera Calderón, "From Books to Bullets," 108. Pensado notes that U.S. surveillance of students had occurred since the early 1960s (*Rebel Mexico*, 225–26).

62. His children remember that Vega did not sleep on many nights; he preferred reading and studying. He went on for days without eating properly while he was immersed in his studies. Close friends say Vega did not go to any trainings in China, as did some of the Maoist intellectuals that Matthew Rothwell explores in "Transpacific Revolutionaries," 107.

63. José Luis Díaz, interview by author, June 2013, Puebla, México.

64. Rothwell, *Transpacific Revolutionaries*, 29, 35, 34, 37–38, 24. In the 1960s authorities were concerned about the literature and the material assistance that the Chinese could have provided to Mexican political activists. Indeed the secretary of the interior closely followed members of the Sociedad. According to Enrique Condés Lara, this paranoia decreased in 1973, after President Echeverría traveled to Beijing and the Chinese promised they would not support any Mexican social movement or armed guerrillas. Nevertheless this Maoist group continued distributing Chinese propaganda (*Represión y rebelión en México*, 3:99, 103–35).

65. Tirado Villegas, *Vientos de la Democracia*, 50.

66. For the domestication of Maoism in Mexico, see Rothwell, *Transpacific Revolutionaries*, chapter 2.

67. "Bulmaro Vega," exp. 100-19-1-73, leg. 31, h. 434, DFS, AGN.

68. For paid students, see Bennett, "Orígenes del movimiento urbano popular mexicano," 92. For becoming proletarian, see Walker, *Waking from the Dream*, 25. For orthodox left students, see Pensado, *Rebel Mexico*, 161.

69. Vanderbush, "Independent Organizing in Puebla, Mexico," 147.

70. Rothwell, *Transpacific Revolutionaries*, 18.

71. Carr, *Marxism and Communism in Twentieth-Century Mexico*, 225–38.

72. Pensado, *Rebel Mexico*, 4–5, 152–53.

73. Lara y Parra, *La lucha universitaria en Puebla*, 234–35, 236.

74. Pansters, *Política y poder en Puebla*, 221

75. Their *pintas*, as students called them, said "Fuera el Gobierno!" and "Nava Castillo Out!" (Samuel Salazar interview, August 2007).

76. Pansters, *Política y poder en Puebla*, 229.

77. Tirado Villegas, *Vientos de la Democracia*, 30–31.

78. Unlike students in Mexico City, who could count on support from at least one of the two main public higher education institutions of their time, the UNAM and the Instituto Politécnico Nacional, students in Puebla were isolated.

79. Pansters, *Política y poder en Puebla*, 233, 265. The CCI was founded on January 6, 1963. It was an independent union composed of agricultural workers and landless peasants. See Carr, *Marxism and Communism in Twentieth-Century Mexico*, 227–28. The CCI had had strong links with students since the mid-1960s. It was also part of the Frente Obrero Campesino Estudiantil Popular (Pansters, *Politics and Power in Puebla*, 126, 139).

80. Pensado, "To Assault with the Truth," 497.

81. Juana Sánchez Maldonado interview, August 30, 2007.

82. "Información de Puebla," June 9, 1970, box 1511A, exp. 4, pp. 420–23, DGIPS, AGN.

83. "Grave División en la UAP," *El Sol de Puebla*, February 11, 1971.

84. María Luisa, interview by author, August 2007, Puebla, México; Berguiss, María Luisa, Omar Castro et al. interview, August 2007; Yolanda Bejarano, interview by author, August 2007, Puebla, México. When the police chased them, the vendors also hid in the university.

85. "Información de Puebla," November 7, 1974, box 1510, exp. A1, DGIPS, AGN.

86. Yolanda Bejarano interview, March 17, 2007; Paula Javier interview, January 25, 2007; Vanderbush, "Independent Organizing in Puebla, Mexico," 234.

87. Yolanda Bejarano interview, July 27, 2010.

88. Yolanda Bejarano interview, July 27, 2010; Paula Javier interview, January 25, 2007. For the number of vendors, see "Información de Puebla," October 30 and November 1, 1973, box 1511-A, exp. 4, pp. 295, 313, DGIPS, AGN.

89. Mendiola García, "Vendors, Mothers, and Revolutionaries."

90. "Mercado Popular 28 de Octubre," exp. 100-19-1-79, leg. 71, h. 19, DFS, AGN.

91. After the mid-1980s the name changed again when vendors added an "and," Unión Popular de Vendedores *y* Ambulantes, to denote that their organization now included established market vendors and peddlers.

92. "Información de Puebla," October 14, 1974, box 1510A, exp. 1, hh. 46–47, DGIPS, AGN.

93. "Culpables las Autoridades si hay Actos Violentos, Dijeron," *La Opinión*, January 8, 1975.

94. Teresa Rosales interview, March 8, 2007; Rosa Martínez interview, January 14, 2007.

95. José Luis Díaz, interview by author, March 8, 2007, Puebla, México.

96. "Mercado Popular 28 de Octubre," August 5, 1977, exp. 100-19-1-77, leg. 58, h. 110; June 22, 1976, leg. 53, h. 73; April 23, 1979, and September 5, 1980, leg. 72, h. 114, DFS, AGN.

97. Pensado, *Rebel Mexico*, 6, 132–38.

98. Yolanda Bejarano interview, July 27, 2010.

99. "Rubén Sarabia Hernández [*sic*]," July 19, 1979, exp. 021-056-002, leg. l, h. 6, DFS, AGN.

100. Yolanda Bejarano interview, July 27, 2010. UPVA members and leaders produced documents that reflected the theories and language they learned in the study groups. Jaime Castillo Palma consulted UPVA documents that used Marxist language: "La Lucha de clases en los vendedores ambulantes" and "Planes y proyectos del gobierno y la burguesía contra los vendedores ambulantes," cited in "El movimiento urbano popular en Puebla," 245, 254.

101. José Luis Díaz interview, January 16, 2007. Ten years later, in 1983, when the UPVA was organizing poor tenants, leaders insisted that people should know Mao's ideology and Marxist-Leninist thought in order to understand that *colonos* and other marginalized people should always engage in revolutionary activities ("Mercado Popular 28 de Octubre," September 1983, exp. 021-056-002, leg. 21, AGN). In practical terms Mao's *Little Red Book* was easily available and free thanks to organizations such as the Sociedad de Amistad México-China and the Chinese embassy that distributed this kind of literature.

102. Yolanda Bejarano interview, July 27, 2010. In 1979 the leader of the UPVA, Simitrio, sought to reintroduce the reading of Mao's *Little Red Book* into vendors' study circles, which took place on Fridays ("Mercado Popular 28 de Octubre," September 13, 1979, exp. 021-056-002, leg. 52, DFS, AGN).

103. Yolanda Bejarano interview, July 27, 2010; Rosa Martínez interview, January 14, 2007.

104. Rosa Martínez interview, January 14, 2007.

105. Rosa Martínez, interview by author, February 6, 2006, Puebla, México.

106. Yolanda Bejarano interview, July 27, 2010.

107. "Mercado Popular 28 de Octubre," March 22, 1978, exp. 100-19-1-78, leg. 62, h. 216; exp. 100-19-1-77, leg. 58, h. 138, DFS, AGN.

108. "Mercado Popular 28 de Octubre," February 9, 1978, exp. 100-19-1-78, leg. 61, h. 288; November 11, 1980, exp. 021-056-002, leg. 1; exp. 100-9-1-78, leg. 67, h. 27; August 16, 1982, exp. 021-056-002, leg. 1, DFS, AGN.

109. "Cuando todas las posibilidades pacíficas están agotadas, la iglesia admite la insurrección." See "Mercado Popular 28 de Octubre," October 28, 1981, exp. 021-056-002, h. 108, DFS, AGN.

110. "Mercado Popular 28 de Octubre," October 28, 1981, exp. 021-056-002, h. 108, DFS, AGN.

111. "Información de Cholula," February 13, 1975, box 1510A, exp. 2, p. 31, DGIPS, AGN.

112. For specific material, political, and legal benefits of PRI-affiliated unions, see Middlebrook, *The Paradox of Revolution*, 82, 95–105.

113. Yolanda Bejarano interview, July 27, 2010.

114. "600 ambulantes serán acomodados en el corralón de Santa Rosa," *El Sol de Puebla*, May 3, 1974.

115. "Los del 28 de Octubre proponen lugar para dar acomodo a todos los vendedores ambulantes," *La Opinión*, January 24, 1977.

116. "Predios se destinarán a ambulantes," photograph, *El Sol de Puebla*, May 20, 1974.

117. "Varios Predios se Destinarán a Ambulantes," *El Sol de Puebla*, May 23, 1974.

118. "Información de Puebla," October 17, 1974, and February 20, 1975, box 1510A, exps. 1 and 2, pp. 190, 82–84, DGIPS, AGN.

119. "Mañana inician obras en el mercado de la 14 Pte.," *El Sol de Puebla*, March 2, 1975.

120. Kohn, *Radical Space*, 7.

3. STAGING DEMOCRACY AT HOME AND ABROAD

1. Huerta, *Chicano Theater*, 2.

2. Shank, "A Return to Aztec and Mayan Roots," 56–57.

3. Shank, "A Return to Aztec and Mayan Roots," 67–69.

4. Habermas, *The Structural Transformation of the Public Sphere*.

5. Viya, *Puebla Ayer*, 110–11.

6. José Luis Díaz, interview by author, January 25, 2007, Puebla, México. Also see fliers students produced to publicize their plays ("Vida Universitaria," AHU, BUAP).

7. Omar Castro, interview by author, August 2, 2007, Puebla, México.

8. Tirado Villegas, *Vientos de la Democracia*, 48–49.

9. Zolov, "Expanding our Conceptual Horizons," 62.

10. Huerta, *Chicano Theater*, 2–3, 14, 16, 15.

11. Valdez, *Actos*, 6, quoted in Huerta, *Chicano Theater*, 16.

12. See Huerta, *Chicano Theater* and *Chicano Drama*.

13. Shank, "A Return to Aztec and Mayan Roots," 68.

14. Excerpts of the play were recorded in *Los Vendedores Ambulantes*, short film, produced by Arturo Garmendia, Filmoteca de la Universidad Nacional Autónoma de México, 1974. Previous and subsequent references are to this recording.

15. Paula Javier interview, January 25, 2007.

16. Shank, "A Return to Aztec and Mayan Roots," 67.

17. Porter claims that Mexico City's sellers were defending their sexual morality when they petitioned authorities (*Working Women of Mexico City*, chapter 6).

18. "If the Raza [the people] will not come to the theater, then the theater must go to the Raza" (Valdez, *Actos*, 4, quoted in Huerta, *Chicano Drama*, 4).

19. José Luis Díaz, interview by author, January 16, 2007, Puebla, México.

20. Paula Javier interview, January 25, 2007.

21. Paula Javier interview, January 25, 2007.

22. Paula Javier interview, January 25, 2007.

23. In 1978, when authorities imprisoned several street vendors, some of the vendors' leaders wanted to create another play to show the conditions in which prisoners lived. But the play was never written ("Mercado 28 de Octubre," May 4, 1978, exp. 100-19-1-78, leg. H125-L64, DFS, AGN.

24. Arturo Garmendia, interview by author, March 20, 2007, Mexico City.

25. Arturo Garmendia interview, March 20, 2007.

26. Years later Olga Corona and Arturo Garmendia got married (Arturo Garmendia interview, March 20, 2007).

27. Jorge Ayala Blanco, "Contra el tianguis de la sociedad clasista," originally published in *La Cultura en México, Revista Siempre!*, Imagenmedica, August 14, 1974, accessed June 21, 2016, http://www.imagenmedica.com.mx/data/tag /contra-el-tianguis-de-la-sociedad-clasista/.

28. Arturo Garmendia interview, March 20, 2007.

29. Yolanda Bejarano interview, July 27, 2010. Copies of these newspapers have mysteriously disappeared from the major newspaper repositories in Puebla and Mexico City.

30. *Los Vendedores Ambulantes*, Filmoteca; electronic correspondence with Sandy Norwing, Archiv der Internationalen Kurzfilmtage Oberhausen, Germany, February 2007.

31. In 1975 a group of street vendors accused Paula Javier and her in-laws of stealing the money; others accused the state university of Puebla of having kept the prize; still others blamed the producer (letter to Ciudadano Procurador General de Justicia del Estado, Dr. Alfredo Toxqui Fernández de Lara from several street vendors, April 2, 1975, box 58, file 10, AHMP).

32. Paula Javier interview, January 25, 2007.

33. Pérez, *There Was a Woman*, 2.

34. Kearny, "La Llorona as a Social Symbol," 199–206; Pérez, *There Was a Woman*, 23.
35. Pérez, *There Was a Woman*, footnote 15, 215–16. For a discussion of how people, especially Chicanas, have used La Llorona as a figure of resistance, see Pérez's chapter 3.
36. This is the only reference of vendors as communists that I encountered, although in the 1970s the Mexican government feared and punished communists.
37. Vanderbush, "Independent Organizing in Puebla, Mexico," 67.
38. Vendors sometimes used interior walls. For instance, they painted one wall of their makeshift UPVA market with the slogan "Le pese a quien le pese, le guste a quien le guste, Lucio Cabañas es su mero, mero" ("Like it or not, Lucio Cabañas is the best"; untitled photograph, Eduardo Cué Merlo administration, fototeca, AHMP).
39. Rosa Martínez interview, February 6, 2006.
40. "Información de Puebla," July 3, 1970, box 1511A, exp. 4, p. 508, DGIPS, AGN.
41. "Información de Puebla," April 30, 1974, box 1510D, exp. 15, p. 328, DGIPS, AGN.
42. Although Leonardo Avritzer's ideas of the public sphere and space in Mexico and other parts of Latin America are useful, he overemphasizes the novelty of social movements in the 1980s when Latin America allegedly transitioned toward more democratic systems (*Democracy and the Public in Latin America*; the section on expression is 81–82).
43. Irazábal, "Citizenship, Democracy, and Public Space in Latin America," 15.
44. After 1986 most marches began at the Hidalgo market, the UPVA-dominated municipal market in the northern part of the city.
45. Tamayo and Cruz-Guzmán, "Political Appropriation of Public Space," 36.
46. María de los Angeles, aka María Quesos, private photographic collection.
47. Secret police records at the AGN usually contain details of these marches and vendors' related activities, including exact times, approximate number of participants, and trajectories.
48. "Mercado Popular 28 de Octubre," April 21, 1977, exp. 100-19-1-77, h. 112, DFS, AGN. Lucio Cabañas and Genaro Vázquez led armed struggles for the rights of rural people in Guerrero. For the movements they headed, see Aviña, *Specters of Revolution*.
49. "Información de Puebla," October 17, 1974, box 1511A, exp. 4, p. 32, DGIPS, AGN.
50. The demands of the street vendors changed over time. From 1977 to 1979 UPVA members protested the incarceration of UPVA leaders. In 1979 and 1980 these marches protested the implementation of the newly created sales tax, the Impuesto al Valor Agregado ("Rubén Sarabia Hernández [*sic*]," January 9,

1980, exp. 021-056-002; for the increase in the cost of transportation, February 9, 1980, exp. 021-056-002, DFS, AGN). On March 2, 1980, the UPVA protested a suggestion by the Secretaría de Educación Pública (Ministry of Public Education) to close down the Prepa Zapata ("Rubén Sarabia Hernández [sic]," March 2, 1980, exp. 021-056-002, DFS, AGN).

51. "Información de Puebla," December 28, 1978, box 1411B, exp. 8, pp. 231–32, DGIPS, AGN.

52. Pensado, *Rebel Mexico*, 91–92.

53. "Información de Puebla," February 24, 1971, box 1511A, exp. 4, pp. 131–32; "Información de Puebla," April 18, 1974, box 1510D, exp. 15, pp. 284–85; "Información de Puebla," December 28, 1978, box 1511B, exp. 8, pp. 231–32, DGIPS, AGN.

54. Paula Maldonado, interview by author, January 23, 2007, Puebla, México.

55. On different occasions women kept UPVA compañeros in San Juan Prison in Puebla well fed. According to a former prison gatekeeper, when some street vendors' leaders were in jail (1977–78), dozens of women brought boxes of fruit (interview by author, 2007, Puebla, México). For female students providing food for their male counterparts during the 1968 student movement in Mexico City, see Frazier and Cohen, "Defining the Space of Mexico '68," 640, 649. Politécnicas in the 1950s also prepared food and organized paperwork (Pensado, *Rebel Mexico*, 90). For women in Guerrero transforming their cooking or the sale of food as a political activity, see Aviña, *Specters of Revolution*, 63–64.

56. Rosa Martínez interview, January 14, 2007, and February 6, 2006.

57. Lettieri, "A Model Dinosaur," 318.

58. Rosa Martínez interview, February 6, 2006.

59. Teresa Rosales interview, July 16, 2010.

60. "Información de Puebla," May 16, 1974, box 1511A, exp. 4, pp. 11–12, DGIPS, AGN.

61. For a thorough analysis of the television coverage of the Tlatelolco Massacre, see Bustamante, *Muy Buenas Noches*, chapter 6, especially 150–76.

62. Carpenter, "The Echo of Tlatelolco in Contemporary Mexican Protest Poetry," 496, 501. Carpenter claims the state intimidated journalists, editors, and newspapers alike.

63. Molly Moore, "Unveiling a Hidden Massacre: Mexico Sets Honors for 300 Slain in '68," *Washington Post*, October 2, 1998. In an act of protest, Octavio Paz quit his post as Mexico's ambassador to India some days after the massacre (Brewster, "The Student Movement of 1968 and the Mexican Press," 156, 183–84).

64. "Rubén Sarabia Hernández [sic]," October 2, 1979, exp. 021-022-001, DFS, AGN.

65. In the early 1960s Rubén Jaramillo, the militant agrarian leader of Morelos, spoke to workers on how the government had co-opted this celebration (Padilla, *Rural Resistance in the Land of Zapata*, 204).

66. Kaplan, *Red City*, 25. In Italy it was also celebrated in 1890, but industrial workers were mostly absent. Kohn, *Radical Space*, 57.

67. Lomnitz, *The Return of Comrade Ricardo Flores Magón*, 403.

68. Lear, *Workers, Neighbors, and Citizens*, 234–38.

69. Porter, *Working Women of Mexico City*, 104, 114–15.

70. "Información sobre Puebla," May 1, 1976, box 1510-A, exp. 3, pp. 221–23, DGIPS, AGN.

71. "Información sobre Puebla," April 21, 1978, box 1511-B, exp. 8, pp. 93, 94; April 28, 1975, box 1511-A, exp. 4, pp. 78–79, DGIPS, AGN.

72. "Rubén Sarabia Hernández [*sic*]," April 23, 1981, exp. 021-056-002, DFS, AGN.

73. Lear, *Workers, Neighbors, and Citizens*, 239.

74. The political scientist Walter Vanderbush, who studied the UPVA in its early years, suggested that the union was not democratic because vendors sometimes did not even vote in their union elections ("Independent Organizing in Puebla, Mexico").

75. In the mid-1980s Jaime Castillo Palma wrote that the cultural dimension of the UPVA was a success during that time ("El movimiento urbano popular en Puebla," 236).

4. THE DIRTY WAR ON STREET VENDORS

1. "El Niño Oscar Vega continúa extraviado," *La Opinión*, October 11, 1977.

2. "Información de Puebla," October 5, 1977, box 1511-B, exp. 8, pp. 133, 134, DGIPS, AGN.

3. "Mercado Popular 28 de Octubre," exp. 100-9-1-77, leg. 59, h. 19, DFS, AGN.

4. "Mercado Popular 28 de Octubre," October 22, 1977, exp. 100-19-1-77, leg. 58, h. 232, DFS, AGN.

5. Teresa Rosales interview, March 8, 2007.

6. See, among others, Padilla, *Rural Resistance in the Land of Zapata*; Aviña, *Specters of Revolution*; Castellanos, *México Armado*; Condés Lara, *Represión y rebelión en México*; Aguayo Quezada, *La Charola*; Herrera Calderón and Cedillo, *Challenging Authoritarianism*; and the official report created during the Vicente Fox administration, Special Prosecutor, *Informe Histórico a la Sociedad Mexicana 2006*, National Security Archive Electronic Briefing, Book no. 209, posted November 21, 2006, http://nsarchive.gwu.edu/NSAEBB /NSAEBB209/#informe.

7. Muñoz, "State Spying on the State," 66.

8. Aguayo Quezada, *La Charola*; Doyle, "'Forgetting Is Not Justice,'" 61–72; Padilla and Walker, "In the Archives."

9. See the special issue edited by Padilla and Walker, *Journal of Iberian and Latin American Research* 19, no. 1 (2013).

10. Aviña, *Specters of Revolution*, 14.

11. Padilla and Walker, "In the Archives," 1–2.

12. Aguayo Quezada, *1968 Los Archivos de la Violencia*, 30–31.

13. Iber, "Managing Mexico's Cold War," 15; Castellanos, *México Armado*, 43.

14. María Quesos, interview by author, July 30, 2010, Puebla, México.

15. "Información de Puebla," February 8, 1971, box 1511A, exp. 4, n.p., DGIPS, AGN.

16. "Mercado Popular 28 de Octubre," February 21, 1976, exp. 100-19-1-76, leg. 47, h. 346, DFS, AGN.

17. Shank, "A Return to Aztec and Mayan Roots," 68.

18. Also in 1975 the Federal Security Department opened a file in which the agency carefully traced all the activities of the UPVA street vendors. Researchers could consult the file up to 1985. The DFS also had a file on the leader of the UPVA, Rubén Sarabia Sánchez, under the name Rubén Sarabia Hernández [*sic*], exp. 021-056-002, which starts in 1976. In November 1979 he was a UPVA leader of street coordinators.

19. "Mercado Popular 28 de Octubre," November 19, 1979, exp. 100-19-1-79, leg. 71, hh. 18–22, DFS, AGN.

20. "Información de Puebla," February 8, 1971, box 1511A, exp. 4, n.p., DGIPS, AGN.

21. "Mercado Popular 28 de Octubre," September 20, 1977, exp. 100-19-1-77, leg. 59, h. 42, DFS, AGN.

22. "Información de Puebla," February 23, 1977, box 1511B, exp. 8, p. 31, DGIPS, AGN.

23. Teresa Rosales interview, March 8, 2007.

24. "Investigación," exp. 100-19-1-79, leg. 71, h. 19, DFS, AGN.

25. "Información de Puebla," February 18, 1977, box 1511B, exp. 8, pp. 27–28, DGIPS, AGN.

26. "Información de Puebla," February 23, 1977, box 1511B, exp. 8, p. 31, DGIPS, AGN.

27. "Información de Puebla," August 24, 1977, box 1511B, exp. 8, p. 95, DGIPS, AGN; "Interrogation Report," August 1977, box 4, exp. 33, "Vida Universitaria," AHU, BUAP.

28. "Información de Puebla," August 24, 1977, box 1511B, exp. 8, p. 95, DGIPS, AGN.

29. "Dicen que son presos políticos tres líderes acusados del asesinato," *La Opinión*, August 25, 1977.

30. "No aparece el Profesor Bulmaro Vega León," *La Opinión*, August 24, 1977.

31. Teresa Rosales interview, March 8, 2007.

32. "Rubén Sarabia (a) 'El Simitrio' Junto con Otros Están Acusados de Homicidio: Están en la Cárcel," *La Opinión*, August 24, 1977.

33. "Interrogation Report," August 1977, box 4, exp. 33, "Vida Universitaria," AHU, BUAP.

34. Amnesty International, *Mexico: Torture with Impunity*, 6, 9, 5–11.

35. Martínez de Murguía, *La policía en México*, 107, 108.

36. "Información de Puebla," September 14, 1977, box 1511B, exp. 8, p. 110, DGIPS, AGN.

37. "Dicen que son Presos Políticos 3 Líderes Acusados de Homicidio," *La Opinión*, August 25, 1977.

38. Yolanda Bejarano interview, July 27, 2010, and March 17, 2007.

39. Castellanos, *México Armado*, 127.

40. "Insisten en la ilegalidad de la detención de 4 dirirgentes y confirman que han sido torturados," *La Opinión*, August 28, 1977.

41. "Dicen que son Presos Políticos 3 Líderes Acusados de Homicidio," *La Opinión*, August 25, 1977.

42. Martínez de Murguía, *La policía en México*, 112.

43. Amnesty International, *Out of Control*, 10.

44. "Información de Puebla," February 23, 1977, box 1511B, exp. 8, p. 31, DGIPS, AGN. After all, "divide and rule" was a strategy the PRI commonly utilized (McCormick, *The Logic of Compromise*).

45. "No Aparece el Profesor Bulmaro Vega León," *La Opinión*, August 24, 1977.

46. "Enviados a la Cárcel: Ellos son Rubén Sarabia 'El Simitrio' y José Luis Hernández Apodado 'El Polo,'" *La Opinión*, September 14, 1977.

47. "Información de Puebla," December 13, 1978, box 11511B, exp. 8, p. 225; December 15, 1978, p. 226; February 7, 1979, pp. 267–68, DGIPS, AGN.

48. "Información de Puebla," August 31, 1977, box 1511B, exp. 8, pp. 104–6, DGIPS, AGN.

49. "Información de Puebla," August 31, 1977, box 1511B, exp. 8, p. 105, DGIPS, AGN.

50. "Mercado Popular 28 de Octubre," November 19, 1979, exp. 100-19-1-79, leg. 71, hh. 18–22; September 20, 1977, exp. 100-19-1-77, leg. 59, h. 42; February 21, 1976, exp. 100-19-1-78, leg. 47, h. 346, DFS, AGN.

51. Teresa Rosales interview, March 8, 2007.

52. "Información de Puebla," September 16, 1977, box 1511B, exp. 8, p. 126; October 21, 1977, p. 137; September 19, 1977, pp. 113–15, DGIPS, AGN.

53. "Información de Puebla," December 28, 1977, box 1511B, exp. 8, pp. 152, 153; September 14, 1977, p. 111; January 16, 1979, p. 255, DGIPS, AGN.

54. Yolanda Bejarano interview, March 17, 2007.

55. "Imágen Manifestación," Colección Vida Universitaria, 25 AU-05/45, box 1, AHU, BUAP.

56. Teresa Rosales, interview by author, July 9, 2010, Puebla, México.

57. Teresa Rosales interview, March 8, 2007.

58. Isela Vega Rosales, interview by author, July 5, 2010, Puebla, México.

59. José Luis Díaz interview, January 16, 2007.

60. In 1977 Victoria Mendoza Salgado was kidnapped by the White Brigade in Jojutla, Morelos, when she was seventeen. She and her eighteen-year-old sister, Josefina, were tortured by the military in the infamous Military Camp No. 1. Victoria's sister Xóchitl, who was twenty-three, was raped a number of times by prison guards ("Tras la guerra sucia no hubo sicólogos para procesar la pesadilla: Mucho menos justicia," *La Jornada*, May 7, 2008).

61. Laura Castellanos, "La represión contra la familia de Genaro Vázquez Rojas: La historia se repite?," *La Jornada*, September 2, 2001. For a more thorough account of the kidnapping, see Castellanos, *México Armado*, 127–28. For a comprehensive analysis of the movements that Genaro Vázquez led, see Aviña, *Specters of Revolution*.

62. Castellanos, *México Armado*, 127–28. According to Alexander Aviña, the baby daughter of Lucio Cabañas ended up in captivity in a military prison in Mexico City with her mother and grandmother (*Specters of Revolution*, 160). Cabañas's partner and his daughter remained in the Campo Militar for twenty months. See "Piden ONG y abogados indemnización para la mujer e hija de Lucio Cabañas," *Proceso*, September 3, 2003.

63. Herrera Calderón and Cedillo, introduction to *Challenging Authoritarianism in Mexico*, 8.

64. "Testimonio de Bertha López de Zazueta," in Cilia Olmos and González Ruiz, *Testimonios de la guerra sucia*, 35–40; Informe de la CNDH sobre desaparecidos, "Heridas que nunca cierran," *La Jornada*, December 9, 2001, http://www.jornada.unam.mx/2001/12/09/mas-heridas.html; Herrera Calderón and Cedillo, introduction to *Challenging Authoritarianism in Mexico*, 17, n50; Castellanos, *México Armado*, 125, 305, 303.

65. Ulloa Bornemann and Camacho de Schimdt, *Surviving Mexico's Dirty War*, 21.

66. Castellanos, *Mexico Armado*, 129, 267.

67. In 1968, for example, the military took hundreds of students to the Military Camp No. 1, and this practice continued throughout the 1970s and 1980s. The military killed approximately 143 prisoners on these military bases. Ulloa Bornemann and Camacho de Schimdt, *Surviving Mexico's Dirty War*, 10.

68. "Investigación sobre Mercado '28 de Octubre,'" February 19, 1979, exp. 100-19-1-79, leg. 71, h. 19, DFS, AGN.

69. Castellanos, *México Armado*, 287.

70. "Informe, Sector Laboral, Puebla," February 2, 1982, box 1510-A, exp. 5, p. 34, DGIPS, AGN; "Mercado Popular 28 de Octubre," April 5, 1978, exp. 100-19-1-78, leg. 64, h. 125; July 28, 1978, exp. 100-9-1-78, leg. 65, h. 241, DFS, AGN.

71. "Informe, Sector Estudiantil, Puebla," August 28, 1981, box 1510-A, exp. 4, p. 273, DGIPS, AGN.

72. "Mercado Popular 28 de Octubre," June 6, 1978, exp. 100-19-1-78, leg. 64, h. 289, DFS, AGN.

73. Castellanos, *México Armado*, 284.

74. Linaloe R. Flores, "Desaparecidos e Impunidad, nueve sexenios," *Sin Embargo*, May 24, 2014, accessed June 21, 2016, http://www.sinembargo.mx/28-05-2014/1005889.

75. Teresa Rosales interview, July 9, 2010.

76. This organization was the Unidad de Fuerzas Democráticas de la Lucha contra la Represión por la Libertad de los Presos Políticos y la Presentación de los Desaparecidos. Newspaper clipping, *Excélsior*, August 28, 1981, box 1510-A-4, exp. 4, p. 263, DGIPS, AGN.

77. The Mexican authorities' report on the Dirty War created during the Vicente Fox administration counts over two thousand cases of torture from 1964 to 1982. See Special Prosecutor, *Informe Histórico a la Sociedad Mexicana 2006*.

78. Newspaper clipping, *Excélsior*, August 28, 1981, box 1510-A-4, exp. 4, p. 263, DGIPS, AGN.

79. Teresa Rosales interview, July 9, 2010.

80. Teresa Rosales interview, March 8, 2007.

81. Teresa Rosales interview, July 9, 2010.

82. "Mercado Popular 28 de Octubre," exp. 100-19-1-79, leg. 72, h. 196, DFS, AGN.

5. FROM LA VICTORIA TO WALMART

1. Here I am using Jones and Varley's definition of gentrification in cities of the developing world: "Gentrification involves the rehabilitation of deteriorated properties and a change in the social group *using* the property" ("The Reconquest of the Historic Centre," 1548).

2. The most dramatic case was the liquidation of Monterrey's Fundidora, a steel mill where four hundred thousand jobs were lost (Snodgrass, "New Rules for the Unions," 81–102, 100).

3. Kohn, *Radical Space*, 6.

4. Keally McBride quoted in Irazábal, *Ordinary Places, Extraordinary Events*, 15.

5. Leicht, *Las Calles de Puebla*, 74

6. "Documento por el cual el municipio de Puebla se adjudica la posesión del inmueble del Mercado de la Victoria," Gobierno de Mariano Piña Olaya, AHMP.

7. During the Porfiriato Puebla's municipal palace was also built. Across the country Porifirian authorities usually hired French, British, and Italian architects (Melé, *La producción del patrimonio*, 39).

8. "Documento por el cual el municipio de Puebla se adjudica la posesión del inmueble del Mercado de la Victoria," Gobierno de Mariano Piña Olaya, AHMP.

9. Santín Nieto, *El Mercado Guadalupe Victoria*, 15.

10. Barbosa Cano, *Plan de Ordenamiento*, 15.

11. EM, June 17, 1913, book 542, exp. 3, letter H; EM, book 532, file 10, p. 348; Comisión de Fomento, 1919, book 630, file 343, AHMP.

12. "Primer Informe de Gobierno del presidente Municipal Enrique Molina Johnson," January 2, 1949, vol. 1365, p. 154, Biblioteca, AHMP.

13. EM, 1948–49, vol. 1365, p. 154, AHMP.

14. "Tercer Informe de Gobierno," Rafael Artasánchez, 1960, Biblioteca, AHMP.

15. "Salón de clases, Mercado La Victoria," Administración del Presidente Municipal Carlos Vergara Soto, 1963–66, photograph 13, Fototeca, AHMP.

16. Twenty-five percent of the registered children at La Victoria's day care center were the sons and daughters of street vendors ("Registration Lists," Dirección General de Educación Pública and Report from Celia Quirós to Raúl González Medel, Regidor de Hacienda, February 23, 1963, box 57, file 28, AHMP).

17. Jones and Varley found the same phenomenon in the 1980s ("The Contest for the City Centre," 32).

18. In a 1913 document authorities fixed the fees for the vendors around the market and for the kinds of products they sold. ("Documento que explica las tarifas a pagar por los puestos en el nuevo edificio," March 12, 1913, book 544, exp. 8, h. 8, AHMP).

19. Letter form the Unión de Locatarios y Comerciantes en pequeño, La Victoria y anexos, to Puebla's Governor, November 17, 1969, box 42, exp. 5, AHMP.

20. In her work on Puebla's intangible heritage, namely the working-class carnival in the old barrios, Nancy Churchill uses the term *dignification* to refer to the "process in which carnival producers promoted their cultural practice as authentic and worthy of the respect of all Pueblans" ("Dignifying Carnival," 4).

21. Cordero y Torres, *Guía Turística de Puebla*, 76–84. In 1985 there were twenty-eight bus stations in the city, perhaps not all in downtown (Melé, *Puebla*, 102).

22. "Hay Comicionistas de Locatarios Entre Ambulantes," *La Opinión*, October 3, 1977.

23. "Se Buscará así la Descentralización del Primer Cuadro," *El Sol de Puebla*, September 25, 1973.

24. Paxman, "Espinosa Yglesias Becomes a Philanthropist," 9.

25. "Que ya es Antifuncional el Mercado de la Victoria," *El Sol de Puebla*, November 22, 1973.

26. "Acuerdo Conjunto de Organismos Oficiales y de Vendedores Para Resolver el Problema," *La Opinión*, February 28, 1977. Jones and Varley discuss the elite's

discourse on the "imagined loss" of downtown in "The Contest for the City Centre," 28.

27. "Decreto por el que se declara una zona de Monumentos Históricos en la ciudad de Puebla de Zaragoza, Estado de Puebla," *Periódico Oficial del Gobierno Constitucional del Estado de Puebla* 209, no. 41 (1977), AHMP.

28. Churchill, "Erasing Popular History," 1.

29. Before the 1970s the protection of historic heritage had been limited. In 1932 the state of Puebla passed the Law for the Protection and Conservation of Monuments and Natural Beauty (Ley sobre la Protección y Conservación de Monumentos y Bellezas Naturales del Estado de Puebla). Five years later officials produced a list of 255 monuments that needed protection. And in 1967 authorities began safeguarding certain colonial buildings (Melé, *La producción del patrimonio*, 301–2).

30. Shank, for instance, identifies these vendors as "descendents of indigenous people" ("A Return to Aztec and Mayan Roots," 67). Margarita Nolasco Armas also briefly describes the market as "indo-mestizo" (*Cuatro Ciudades*, 162).

31. Lourdes Arizpe analyzes "Las Marías," mostly Otomí and Mazahua female vendors of fruit and other products who are despised by the middle classes in Mexico City (*Indígenas en la ciudad de México*, 19–20, 132).

32. Jones and Varley, "The Reconquest of the Historic Centre," 1549.

33. Jones and Varley, "The Contest for the City Centre," 28.

34. Cordero y Torres, *Guía Turística de Puebla*, 15.

35. Scarpaci, *Plazas and Barrios*, 21.

36. Barbosa Cano, *Plan de Ordenamiento*, 55–57.

37. Melé, *La producción del patrimonio urbano*, 308, 313. Manjárrez states that the governor and the mayor were very good friends (*Puebla*, 17).

38. "Mercado Popular 28 de Octubre," November 5 and 13, 1984, exp. 021-056-002, DFS, AGN.

39. "Convenio entre Ayuntamiento y UPVA," August 1, 1986, box 42, file 9, AHMP.

40. "Los ambulantes amenazan," *Momento, en el vértice de Puebla*, February 19, 1987, 10–11.

41. EM, n.d., box 2590, exp. 1158, AHMP.

42. Rosa Martínez interview, February 6, 2006.

43. "Convenio entre Ayuntamiento y UPVA," August 1, 1986, box 42, file 9, AHMP.

44. Paxman, *Jenkins of Mexico*, chapter 10.

45. Manjárrez, *Puebla*, 168, 196–97, 253.

46. Vanderbush, "Assessing Democracy in Puebla," 14, 169, 253.

47. Paxman, *Jenkins of Mexico*, chapter 10.

48. "Murió esta Madrugada El Alcalde Jorge Murad," *El Sol de Puebla*, August 9, 1986.

49. "Operativo de Limpieza en Calles Ayer Tras la Salida de Ambulantes" and "500 Toneladas de Basura Dejaron los Ambulantes," *El Sol de Puebla*, August 4 and 6, 1986.

50. "Decomisan Armamento y 98 Bombas Molotov al Grupo 28 de Octubre," *El Sol de Puebla*, August 1, 1986.

51. "Histórica la Reubicación: Ciudadanía," *El Sol de Puebla*, August 1, 1986.

52. "Comercio Organizado," *Momento, en el vértice de Puebla*, February 19, 1987, 15.

53. "Se dignifica el Centro de la Ciudad con la Reubicación," *El Diario de Puebla*, August 1, 1986, HJN.

54. Manjárrez, *Puebla*, 196–97; "Histórica la Reubicación: Ciudadanía," *El Sol de Puebla*, August 1, 1986.

55. "El Retiro de Ambulantes es Avance en Protección a la Salud Pública," *El Sol de Puebla*, August 1, 1986.

56. Silvia Moreno, interview by author, summer 2010, Puebla, México.

57. Open letter from Unión de Locatarios to Jorge Murad Macluf, *El Sol de Puebla*, August 1, 1986.

58. Various documents written by Comité Pro-Defensa del Mercado La Victoria in 1986, box 15, file 3, AHMP.

59. "Acuerdo del Ayuntamiento," October 14, 1986, box 15, file 3, AHMP.

60. "Convenio para la reubicación de los comerciantes y locatarios del Mercado La Victoria," October 20, 1986, box 15, file 4, exp. 2167, AHMP.

61. Street vendors from PRI organizations had the same problems. In 1993 vendors were still complaining about how bad one of the "new" markets was: "Our market has no signs, no lights and there is no transportation to our market" (letter from Locatarios y Comerciantes Solidaridad del Mercado Héroes de Puebla to Mayor Rafael Cañedo, August 4, 1993, box 46, file 29, AHMP).

62. Zermeño, "Crisis, Neoliberalism, and Disorder," 170.

63. Babb, *Managing Mexico*, 176.

64. "Acuerdo del Ayuntamiento," October 14, 1986, box 15, file 3, AHMP. Authorities claimed that "La Victoria market evidently endangered public health."

65. In 1948, for example, the mayor stated that the campaign to kill rats was satisfactory; see "Primer Informe de Gobierno del Presidente Municipal Enrique Molina Johnson," January 2, 1949, vol. 1365, AHMP; "Esperan Matar 50,000 Ratas en el Mercado La Victoria," *El Sol de Puebla*, February 3, 1971.

66. "Otra limpieza en La Victoria," *El Sol de Puebla*, February 11, 1971.

67. Comercial Mexicana was the first supermarket in Puebla, followed in 1971 by Astor and in 1973 by Aurrera. In the inauguration advertisement Aurrera's owners called it the most modern supermarket in Mexico's provincial cities and invited people to participate in its happiness and great sales ("venga a participar en la alegría y en los grandes ahorros") ("Mañana se inaugura en Puebla," Aurrera advertisement, *El Sol de Puebla*, November 31, 1973).

68. Letter to Mayor Amado Camarillo from Colegio de Arquitectos de Puebla, October 27, 1986, box 15, file 4, pp. 1–6, AHMP.

69. Letter from Comité Pro-Defensa del Mercado La Victoria to President Miguel de la Madrid, March 20, 1986, AHMP.

70. Santín Nieto, *El Mercado Guadalupe Victoria*, 25.

71. Letter to Governor Guillermo Jiménez Morales from Unión de locatarios y comerciantes del Mercado de San Baltazar Campeche, March 28, 1986, box 45, file 302, p. 4, AHMP.

72. "Convenio para la Reubicación de los Comerciantes y Locatarios del Mercado La Victoria," October 20, 1986, box 15, file 4, AHMP.

73. Letter from Comité to President Miguel de la Madrid, March 20, 1986, AHMP.

74. The Municipal Archive houses dozens of photographs showing the marketers' removal and the destruction of stalls (Mercados, Fototeca, AHMP).

75. Most of La Victoria's marketers moved to Mercado Emiliano Zapata and Morelos (letter from Locatarios del Mercado La Victoria to Governor Mariano Piña Olaya, September 7, 1987, box 46, folder 13, AHMP).

76. González, *Dual Transitions from Authoritarian Rule*, chapter 4.

77. Letter to Governor Mariano Piña Olaya from locatarios del Mercado la Victoria, September 6, 1987, box 45, file 13, AHMP. See also "400 locatarios regresan a La Victoria," *Momento, en el vértice de Puebla*, February 19, 1987, 11.

78. "Mercado Emiliano Zapata," *Momento, en el vértice de Puebla*, February 19, 1987, 14.

79. In 1975 a group of vendors wrote a letter to the governor insisting that if he decided to build new markets, he had to consult with them to avoid old mistakes. Vendors claimed there were many old markets that were practically useless, the so-called *elefantes blancos* (letter from Federación de Locatarios y Comerciantes Ambulantes to Governor Alfredo Toxqui, February 22, 1975, box 42, file 218, AHMP).

80. Since 1977 UPVA members were aware that most of the commercial activities in the city were concentrated downtown and participated in negotiations and talks with authorities trying to provide their input to authorities ("Los de la 28 dicen que hay comicionistas entre ambulantes," *La Opinión*, October 3, 1977).

81. "Nomination of Properties for Inscription on the World Heritage List," Proposal, 1986, Patrimonio Mundial del Instituto Nacional de Antropología e Historia, INAH. The original nomination included the archaeological site of Cholula, but it was not named a World Heritage Site due to its contemporary man-made transformations.

82. "Report of the World Heritage Committee," Eleventh Session, UNESCO, Paris, January 20, 1988, accessed June 21, 2016, http://whc.unesco.org/archive/repcom87.htm#416.

83. Harvey, "The Right to the City," 38.

84. Scarpaci, *Plazas and Barrios*, 121.

85. Paxman, *Jenkins of Mexico*, chapter 10.

86. "Remozamiento de 62 Calles del Centro," *El Sol de Puebla*, August 5, 1986. Curiously, when Nicolás Vázquez was Puebla's mayor (1958–61), he received money (a considerable subsidy) from the Jenkins Foundation that allowed his administration to pay for the construction of covered public markets. See Paxman, *Jenkins of Mexico*, chapter 10.

87. Paxman, *Jenkins of Mexico*, chapter 10.

88. Paxman, *Jenkins of Mexico*, chapter 11.

89. Fundación Amparo, http://www.museoamparo.com/es/fundacion-amparo/.

90. Paxman, "Espinosa Yglesias Becomes a Philanthropist." For a comparison between Jenkins and Espinosa Yglesias, see Paxman, *Jenkins of Mexico*, chapter 10.

91. "Decreto del H. Congreso del Estado que autoriza al H. Ayuntamiento del Municipio de Puebla, a celebrar contrato de Comodato con la Fundación Amparo," *Periódico Oficial*, Puebla, July 3 1992, 5, AHMP.

92. "Contrato de Comodato, Cabildo Extraordinario," April 21, 1992, file 179, AHMP. The honorary witness of the signing of the contract was Puebla's governor, Mariano Piña Olaya. The Quinta Clausula of the commodatum stated that at the end of ninety-nine years the Fundación Amparo could extend the contract.

93. "Cabildo Extraordinario," April 21, 1992, file 179, pp. 038–039, AHMP. This *regidor's* statement could be a reflection of how these philanthropic organizations worked and how they were misunderstood in Mexico. As Paxman argues, these organizations were supposed to make money and reinvest the profits for charitable works (*Jenkins of Mexico*, chapter 10).

94. "Carta al Secretario General de Gobierno de Puebla, Héctor Jiménez Meneses, sobre el proyecto de la Fundación Amparo," March 23, 1992, II.A. 2.c/4, Centro de Estudios Espinosa Yglesias, Mexico City.

95. Paxman, "Espinosa Yglesias Becomes a Philanthropist," 10.

96. Melé, *La producción del patrimonio*, 307.

97. CIFRA's retailers included Aurrera, Superama, Suburbia, and Vips. See Tilly, "Walmart in Mexico," 195–96.
98. Tilly, "Wal-Mart Goes South," 357, 375. According to James Biles, in 1997 "Walmart de México acquired the majority stake in CIFRA, and in 2000 it changed its name to Wal-Mart de México" (Walmex). In 2005 the La Victoria Suburbia was one of the fifty department stores and Vips at La Victoria one of over 280 restaurants that Walmart operated in Mexico (Biles, "Globalization of Food Retailing and the Consequences of Wal-Martinization in Mexico," 345–47). In 2004 demonstrators protested the opening of the Walmart-owned Aurrera near Teotihuacán, a UNESCO World Heritage Site.

Walmart was not the first American retailer to occupy prime space in Puebla's downtown. In the late 1960s Sears opened its doors in what used to be one of the city's oldest buildings (Jones and Varley, "The Contest for the City Centre," 29, 42). For a history of Sears in Mexico, see Moreno, *Yankee Don't Go Home*. Woolworth occupied a two-story locale one block away from the zócalo and one away from La Victoria market. In Mexico City Woolworth opened its first store on Avenida Insurgentes in April 1956 (Pitrone, *F. W. Woolworth and the American Five and Dime*, 148, 165). Between 1940 and 1970, 140 old buildings (30 percent of which were built in the colonial period and in the nineteenth century) were demolished in order to make space for these stores, banks, apartment buildings, and hotels. Poblanos considered the opening of these businesses a "modern" feature of urban development (Melé, *La producción del patrimonio*, 302).
99. Biles, "Globalization of Food Retailing and the Consequences of Wal-Martinization in Mexico," 347; Tilly, "Wal-Mart Goes South," 375.
100. Letter from Markets Director, Lic. Valentín Meneses Rojas to Prof. José Alanis Morales, Presidente del Comité Ejecutivo Nacional de la Central Revolucionaria de Acción Social AC, July 6, 1994, exp. 1149, folio 80, AHMP.
101. In 1988 the UPVA recruited approximately one thousand former La Victoria marketers (Jones and Varley, "The Contest for the City Centre," 34).
102. "En Funciones Suburbía y Vip's" and "Se Inauguró el Centro Comercial La Victoria en Medio de Gran Polémica," *El Sol de Puebla*, November 12 and 13, 1994.
103. Nissen, "Urban Transformation," 1140.
104. Crawford, "The World in a Shopping Mall," 28.
105. Jones and Varley, "The Contest for the City Centre," 39.
106. In summer 2015 the *hemeroteca* was moved to the basement of a different location and dramatically reduced its collection and hours of operation.
107. Melé, *La producción del patrimonio urbano*, 309–10.

108. Melé, *La producción del patrimonio urbano*, 64.
109. Churchill, "El Paseo del Rio San Francisco," 26, 3, 156–57; Churchill, "Dignifying Carnival." For a comprehensive discussion of this area's gentrification up to the present, see Jones, "Gentrification, Neoliberalism and Loss in Puebla, Mexico."
110. In 2013 Walmart de México announced the sale of its 362 restaurants, Vips, El Portón, Ragazzi, and La Finca, to the group ALSEA, owner of Starbucks, Domino's Pizza, Italianni's, and The Cheesecake Factory ("Vende Walmart de México su división de restaurantes a Alsea," *La Jornada*, September 11, 2013).
111. Harvey, "The Right to the City," 32.
112. Jones and Varley, "The Contest for the City Centre," 35–36.

6. THE STRUGGLE CONTINUES

1. "Preso cantor" is a play on words that makes reference to the *grillo cantor*, the popular singing cricket Cri-Cri, a character created by the musician Gabilondo Soler.
2. Blanche Pietrich, "Moreno Valle, 'empeñado a destruir el movimiento popular urbano en Puebla,'" *La Jornada*, October 11, 2015.
3. He was imprisoned again in December 2014. See the conclusion.
4. Zermeño, "Crisis, Neoliberalism, and Disorder," 170; Babb, *Managing Mexico*, 176.
5. Bensusán and Middlebrook, *Organized Labour and Politics in Mexico*, 71–72.
6. Jones and Varley, "The Contest for the City Centre," 35–36.
7. "Los Ambulantes Amenzan," *Momento, en el vértice de Puebla*, February 19, 1987, 10.
8. Open letter from Departamento de Investigaciones Arquitéctonicas y Urbanísticas, UAP, *El Sol de Puebla*, December 19, 1988.
9. "Convenio celebrado entre el H. Ayuntamiento del Municipio de Puebla y el Consejo de Representantes de la Unión Popular de Vendedores Ambulantes 28 de Octubre ancabezada [*sic*] por el C. Rubén Sarabia Sánchez, para el traslado voluntario de los miembros de la organización que ocupaban las calles de la ciudad," August 1, 1986, box 42, file 9, AHMP.
10. As part of the decentralization of commercial activities from downtown, all bus stations relocated to the CAPU.
11. Kohn, *Radical Space*, 6, 43.
12. "Los Ambulantes Amenzan," *Momento, en el vértice de Puebla*, February 19, 1987, 10.
13. Jones and Varley, "The Contest for the City Centre," 34.
14. "28 de Octubre," *El Sol de Puebla*, November 15, 1988.
15. Rosa Martínez interview, February 6, 2006.

16. Castillo Palma, "El movimiento contra el alza del pasaje," 262–82.

17. "Inaugura," *El Sol de Puebla*, November 17, 1988.

18. Jones and Varley, "The Contest for the City," 36.

19. For the links between Mexico City's Alianza de Camioneros de la República Mexicana, their leadership, especially Rubén Figueroa, and the state, see Lettieri, "A Model Dinosaur."

20. "51 taxis y combis piratas de la 28 de Octubre, detenidas," *El Sol de Puebla*, December 11, 1988.

21. "Otro escándalo público de la '28 de Octubre,'" *El Sol de Puebla*, May 2, 1989.

22. "Contingentes de la 28," *El Sol de Puebla*, June 14, 1989. It is possible that the UPVA also made use of some *acarreo* among members or that the leadership pressured vendors to attend marches. For the quintessential *acarreado* practices, see Lettieri, "A Model Dinosaur."

23. "Hasta vehículos de dudoso origen," *El Sol de Puebla*, June 1, 1989.

24. Jones and Varley, "The Contest for the City Centre," 36.

25. "Hasta vehículos de dudoso origen," *El Sol de Puebla*, June 1, 1989.

26. Tirado Villegas, *Vientos de la Democracia*, 120.

27. José Luis Díaz, interview by author, July 19, 2014, Puebla, México.

28. "La Coordinadora de Colonias . . . ," *El Sol de Puebla*, January 10, 1989.

29. Harvey, "The Right to the City," 39.

30. "Mercado Popular 28 de Octubre," June 16, 1979, exp. 100-19-1-79, leg. 73, h. 176, DFS, AGN.

31. "Mercado Popular 28 de Octubre," May 26, 1979, exp. 100-19-1-79, leg. 72, h. 324, DFS, AGN.

32. On March 25, 1981, vendors decided to expel Lorenzo Hernández Becerra from the organization ("Rubén Sarabia Hernández," 021-056-002, November 29, 1979, and March 25, 1981, DGIPS, AGN).

33. Knight, "Caciquismo in Twentieth Century Mexico," 12, 17n69.

34. These are some of the characteristics that the historian Alan Knight refers to in his analysis of modern caciques ("Caciquismo in Twentieth Century Mexico").

35. "Expedientes de Mercados," n.d., box 2590, exp. 1158, AHMP.

36. Paula Maldonado interview, January 23, 2007; "Mercado Popular 28 de Octubre," October 25, 1983, exp. 021-056-002, DFS, AGN.

37. "Expedientes de Mercados," n.d., box 2590, exp. 1158, AHMP.

38. According to federal police files, Simitrio was in jail in 1975 for robbery and in 1977 for homicide ("Mercado 28 de Octubre," exp. 100-19-1-79, leg. 71, h. 21, DFS, AGN).

39. Castillo Palma and Patiño, "Puebla," 144, 145. Interestingly the Mexican authorities' report on the Dirty War created during the Vicente Fox administration

observed a similar pattern. See "Tema 10.-Desviaciones del poder por el régimen autoritario y corrupción de las instituciones de estado," National Security Archive, George Washington University, accessed August 2015, http://nsarchive.gwu .edu/NSAEBB/NSAEBB209/informe/tema10.pdf.

40. "Dictaron auto de formal prisión por el delito de privación ilegal de la libertad," *El Sol de Puebla*, May 20, 1989.

41. "Girarán Orden de Aprehensión contra Simitrio," *El Heraldo de México en Puebla*, May 17, 1989.

42. "Asesores de la 28 dan su versión del secuestro," *El Heraldo de México en Puebla*, May 18, 1989.

43. "Que no se archive una orden de aprehensión," *El Heraldo de México en Puebla*, May 18, 1989.

44. "No se puede crear un estado de derecho dentro de otro," *El Heraldo de México en Puebla*, May 18, 1989.

45. "Cateo a la bodega de la 28 de Octubre," *El Sol de Puebla*, June 17, 1989.

46. Letter to Chamber of Deputies from Consejo General de Representantes and Comisión Negociadora de la UPVA–28 de Octubre, March 23, 1995, box 58, AHMP; "Cateo a la bodega de la 28 de Octubre," *El Sol de Puebla*, June 17, 1989; "Catearon el edificio de la 28," *El Heraldo de México en Puebla*, June 17, 1989.

47. "Inquietud ciudadana," *El Heraldo de México en Puebla*, June 18, 1989.

48. "Cateo a la bodega de la 28 de Octubre," *El Sol de Puebla*, June 17, 1989; "Niegan todos y cada uno de los cargos 'los asesores' de la 28 de octubre detenidos," *El Heraldo de México en Puebla*, June 21, 1989.

49. "Niegan todos y cada uno de los cargos 'los asesores' de la 28 de octubre detenidos," *El Heraldo de México en Puebla*, June 21, 1989.

50. Letter from UPVA Consejo General de Representantes to President Carlos Salinas de Gortari and State Department Secretary Fernando Gutiérrez Barrios, December 14, 1989, box 42, file 9, AHMP; "Niegan todos y cada uno de los cargos 'los asesores' de la 28 de octubre detenidos," *El Heraldo de México en Puebla*, June 21, 1989.

51. Martínez de Murguía, *La policía en México*, 112.

52. "Niegan Todos y cada uno de los cargos 'los asesores' de la 28 de octubre detenidos," *El Heraldo de México en Puebla*, June 21 1989.

53. "La 5 norte entre 12 y 14 poniente quedó," *El Heraldo de México en Puebla*, June 17, 1989.

54. Silvestre Salazar Aguilar, "Poli-cortos," *El Heraldo de México en Puebla*, June 21, 1989.

55. "Niegan Todos y cada uno de los cargos 'los asesores' de la 28 de octubre detenidos." On June 17, 1989, the UPVA organized a massive march to protest that their

leaders had nothing to do with the Kiesslich kidnapping. Newspaper photographers were there to document the march that hot summer day. Having little idea that female vendors historically participated in these marches, one newspaper writer stated that many women were "dragged to [the] march." Undermining the women's autonomous political activism, the writer contemptuously labeled them "arrastradas" (the dragged ones). See photographs in *El Heraldo de México en Puebla*, May 19, 1989.

56. "Texto de la Conferencia de Prensa del Procurador Licenciado Humberto Fernández de Lara sobre la situación jurídica de Rubén Sarabia Sánchez, 'Simitrio,'" *El Sol de Puebla*, July 11, 1989; "Formal prisión a un líder de ambulantes poblano," *La Jornada*, July 11, 1989.

57. Letter from Rubén Sarabia Sánchez to Señores del Jurado de la Audiencia Transversal del Tribunal Permanente de los Pueblos, Capítulo México, November 23, 2013, SlideShare, accessed February 8, 2014, http://www.slideshare .net/simit-rita/seores-del-jurado; Amnesty International, *Out of Control*, 10; Amnesty International, *Mexico: Torture with Impunity*, 6, 9.

58. Letter from Rubén Sarabia Sánchez to Señores del Jurado de la Audiencia Transversal del Tribunal Permanente de los Pueblos, Capítulo México, November 23, 2013. Officials claimed that Simitrio had nine previous charges (letter from Deputy Maria Ynes Solis González to Puebla's governor Lic. Mariano Piña Olaya, January 18, 1990, box 42, file 9, AHMP). In a rather bureaucratic tone the deputy stated that the UPVA demanded that Puebla's authorities respect vendors' constitutional right to work and halt judicial and police harassment. Solis also suggested that there were some "irregularities" in Simitrio's case.

59. Letter to Chamber of Deputies from Consejo General de Representantes and Comisión Negociadora de la UPVA–28 de Octubre, March 23, 1995, box 58, AHMP.

60. Francisco Sánchez, "Libertad total demanda Simitrio," *Intolerancia Diario*, October 29, 2012, accessed February 8, 2014, http://intoleranciadiario.com /detalle_noticia.php?n=102201.

61. "El gobierno se niega al diálogo: 28 de Octubre," newspaper clipping, April 1997, box 46, file 36, AHMP; Senado de la República, "Proposiciones de Ciudadanos Legisladores," *Gaceta del Senado*, no. 17 (2005), accessed June 22, 2016, http:// www.senado.gob.mx/index.php?ver=sp&mn=2&sm=2&id=6124.

62. Caro Quintero was freed in August 2013.

63. For a fascinating yet disturbing description of the lavish life in prison of some of Mexico's most wanted criminals, see Scherer García, *Cárceles*. This award-winning journalist and founder of the political magazine *Proceso* also describes

the horrific experiences that common prisoners and their families witnessed in overcrowded prisons in Mexico City.

64. Teichman, *Privatization and Political Change in Mexico*, 124–25.

65. Castillo Palma and Patiño, "Ciudades provincianas de Puebla," 440, n30; Amnesty International, *Amnesty International Report 1987*, 186.

66. Manjárrez, *Puebla*, 203–4; Jiménez Huerta, *El vuelo del Fénix*, 67, 86, 87; Vázquez Rangel and Ramírez López, *Marginación y pobreza en México*, 257.

67. Sessions, "Cross-Border Blues," 61; Manjárrez, *Puebla*, 291.

68. Letter from UPVA Consejo General de Representantes to President Carlos Salinas de Gortari and State Department Secretary Fernando Gutiérrez Barrios, December 14, 1989, box 42, file 9, AHMP.

69. Senado de la República, "Proposiciones de Ciudadanos Legisladores." Indeed many prisoners in Almoloya suffer solitary confinement. Their cement cells are small, with no windows, and with artificial light all day long. Almoloya can hold 407 prisoners, who are classified by their alleged threat (*peligrosidad*). Scherer García, *Cárceles*, 108–10.

70. Fermín Alejandro García, "Simitrio no volverá a dirigir la UPVA; Busca recuperar sus derechos civiles: Amador," *La Jornada de Oriente*, April 4, 2002, accessed February 8, 2014, http://www.jornada.unam.mx/2002/04/04/oriente-g.htm.

71. Arturo Rodríguez, "La prisión como escarmiento," *Proceso*, October 21, 2015.

72. Yolanda Bejarano interview, July 27, 2010.

73. Rosa Martínez interview, February 6, 2006.

74. "Gente," *El Diario de Puebla*, August 7, 1986.

75. Newspaper clipping, *El Universal*, February 3, 1993. The following day the owners of the seafood restaurants sent a letter to the mayor, arguing that their businesses were not brothels and that they were honorable people (February 24 1993, box 46, file 30, AHMP).

76. "Mayor Roberto Cañedo Benítez's dictamen," February 1995, box 2590, file 1185, AHMP.

77. Circular No. 92 to Regidores y Síndico Municipal from Secretaría General del H. Ayuntamiento, María Laura Rojano Merino, February 27, 1995, no. 3, p. 2, box 58, AHMP.

78. "Convocatoria, Foro de Consulta Popular," *El Sol de Puebla*, February 22, 1995, box 2590, file 1156, p. 026, AHMP. In other parts of the country there were similar projects. For example, Mexico City had the Programa de Recuperación del Centro Histórico, and Morelia had the Patronato Pro-Rescate del Centro Histórico. See Cabrales Barajas, "The Historic Center of Morelia."

79. Circular No. 92 to Regidores y Síndico Municipal from Secretaria General del H. Ayuntamiento, María Laura Rojano Merino, February 27, 1995, no. 3, p. 2, box 58, AHMP.

80. Texto de carta from Armando Quiroz Alejandre to Director of magazine *Proceso*, "Represión en Puebla," *Proceso*, April 3, 1995.

81. Circular No. 92 to Regidores y Síndico Municipal from Secretaria General del H. Ayuntamiento, María Laura Rojano Merino, February 27, 1995, no. 3, p. 2, box 58, AHMP.

82. Letter to Chamber of Deputies from Consejo General de Representantes and Comisión Negociadora de la UPVA–28 de Octubre, March 23, 1995, box 58, AHMP.

83. Letter to President Ernesto Zedillo and Governor Manuel Bartlett from Comité Independiente por la Defensa de los Derechos Humanos del Estado de Puebla, March 8, 1995, box 58, file 11, AHMP.

84. Texto de carta from Armando Quiroz Alejandre to Director of magazine *Proceso*, "Represión en Puebla," *Proceso*, April 3, 1995; Martín Hernández Alcantara, "UPVA acusa al gobierno de sabotear las movilizaciones de apoyo a Simitrio," *La Jornada de Oriente*, August 27, 2002, accessed February 8, 2014, http://www.jornada.unam.mx/2002/08/27/oriente-e.htm.

85. Letter from Carlos Palafox Vázquez, Secretario de Gobernación to Teniente Coronel, Jorge Mauro Escudero Yerena, Director General de Seguridad Pública, March 3, 1995, box 58, AHMP.

86. Preston and Dillon, *Opening Mexico*, 127; Camp, *Mexican Political Biographies*, 88.

87. Camp, *Mexico's Mandarins*, 69.

88. Hamnett, *A Concise History of Mexico*, 304.

89. Cook, *Organizing Dissent*, 270.

90. "Reconocimiento de militantes de la UPVA que participaron en los actos violentos del pasado 22 de marzo en el zócalo," April 21, 1995, box 2590, file 1156, AHMP. The document includes the names of the UPVA's militants. It states that the *presidencia*, *cabildo*, *sindicatura*, and *contraloria*, all municipal offices, were damaged by the protestors when they threw Molotov cocktails into the municipal building.

91. Texto de carta from Armando Quiroz Alejandre to Director of magazine *Proceso*, "Represión en Puebla," *Proceso*, April 3, 1995.

92. Letter to Governor Manuel Bartlett Díaz from UPVA members, August 1, 1995, box 58, file 11, AHMP.

93. La Tía, interview by author, August 2010, Puebla, México.

94. Letter to Governor Manuel Bartlett Díaz from UPVA members, August 1, 1995, box 58, file 11, AHMP.

95. Letter to Governor Manuel Bartlett Díaz from UPVA's Comisión Negociadora, March 24, 1994, box 58, file 11, AHMP.

96. Letter to Chamber of Deputies from Consejo General de Representantes and Comisión Negociadora de la UPVA–28 de Octubre, March 23, 1995, box 58, AHMP.

97. Letter to Governor Manuel Bartlett Díaz from UPVA members, August 1, 1995, box 58, file 11, AHMP.

98. The Mexican political magazine *Proceso* published the document, which is very similar to the documents the secret police wrote in the 1970s and 1980s. See "En un documento recibido por el Centro de Derechos Humanos 'Miguel Pro,' se mencionan nombres y se asignan responsabilidades," *Proceso*, February 10, 1996.

99. Bensusán and Middlebrook, *Organized Labour and Politics in Mexico*, 72.

CONCLUSION

1. UPVA photographs uploaded to Facebook by the union's leadership.

2. For a discussion of the UAP as a neoliberal institution, see Pansters, "Building a *Cacicazgo*" and "El rector tiene la palabra."

3. Javier Puga Martínez, "Con RMV no ha terminado la represión contra el comercio popular: Simitrio," *La Jornada de Oriente*, October 30, 2013, accessed June 28, 2016, http://www.lajornadadeoriente.com.mx/2013/10/30 /con-rmv-no-ha-terminado-la-represion-contra-el-comercio-popular-simitrio/.

4. "Discurso de Simitrio," Conferencia en el Auditorio de la Facultad de Economía, Benemérita Universidad Autónoma de Puebla, personal tape recording, October 29, 2013. Subsequent references are to this recording.

5. Francisco Toledo refers to changes occurring in Oaxaca. I am using his phrase because these dramatic changes also apply in Puebla. See Reed Johnson, "McDonald's Loses a Round to Oaxacan Cultural Pride," *Los Angeles Times*, January 5, 2003, accessed December 31, 2013, http://articles.latimes.com/2003/jan/05 /entertainment/ca-johnson5/2.

6. Lefebvre argues that "only the working class can become the agent" of an urban transformation which should encompass the interests of all inhabitants (*Writings on Cities*, 158).

7. Arturo Rodríguez, "La prisión como escarmiento," *Proceso*, October 21, 2015.

8. The formal name of this law is Ley Para Proteger los Derechos Humanos y Que Regula el Uso Legítimo de la Fuerza por Parte de los Elementos de las

Instituciones Policiales del Estado de Puebla, which briefly translates as Law for the Protection of Human Rights and Police Force Regulation.

9. His authoritarian policies have resulted in the incarceration of twenty-three activists in two months. See Alvaro Delgado, "Moreno Valle, el góber mafioso y represor," *Proceso*, July 14, 2014, accessed July 20, 2014, http://www.proceso.com.mx/?p=377204.

10. Delgado, "Moreno Valle, el góber mafioso y represor."

11. Blanche Pietrich, "Moreno Valle, 'empeñado a destruir el movimiento popular urbano en Puebla,'" *La Jornada*, October 11, 2015.

12. Gerardo Peláez Ramos, "Libertad a Rubén Sarabia, 'Simitrio,'" *La Haine*, December 29, 2014, accessed August 27, 2015, http://www.lahaine.org/mundo.php/libertad-a-ruben-sarabia-sanchez.

13. Simitrio quoted in Pietrich, "Moreno Valle, 'empeñado a destruir el movimiento popular urbano en Puebla.'"

14. Jorge Castillo, "Detienen a Xihuel, hijo de Simitrio," *Intolerancia*, December 9, 2015, http://intoleranciadiario.com/detalle_noticia/139536/politica/detienen-a-xihuel-hijo-de-simitrio (includes the short video).

15. David Shanik, "Mercado Hidalgo busca reubicarse cerca de vw," *Puebla Online*, August 15, 2011, http://pueblaonline.com.mx/index.php?option=com_k2&view=item&id=16323:mercado-hidalgo-busca-reubicarse-cerca-de-vw&Itemid=125.

16. Javier Puga Martínez, "Con más de 9 mil personas, la 28 de Octubre repudiará falta de empleo," *La Jornada de Oriente*, April 19, 2013.

GLOSSARY

abuelita grandmother

acarreados people paid, bribed, or coerced
("hauled" or "dragged") to attend political events

acto brief sketch or skit with a political message

amparo(s) legal instrument(s) similar to writs of habeas corpus

avilacamachista(s) Puebla's political machine (1937–73)
created by Maximino Ávila Camacho

cacicazgo political machine

camotes sweet potatoes

caudillo(s) military or political leader(s)

charro(s) leader(s) of official unions

combis Kombinationskraftwagen van made by Volkswagen

commodatum gratuitous bailment; a free concession
of something for a specific time

compañero(s) comrade(s)

El Corralón literally, the Yard; refers to the UPVA
makeshift market and main office

dignificación the process of dignifying something

fayuca contraband

fayuqueros sellers of contraband

huaraches sandals

inquilino(s) tenant(s)

lechero(s) seller(s) of milk

mamecas sympathizers of the Movimiento Marxista
Leninista de México (MMLM)

manta cheap cotton cloth

Ministerio Público Office of the State Prosecutor

mítines relámpago brief political rallies or meetings

mujeres de la calle women of the street; prostitutes

"Nota Roja" crime section of newspaper

novatada(s) hazing ritual(s)

pan de muerto sweet bread flavored with anise seeds and
orange flower water and decorated with sesame seeds

Pax Priísta supposed peace and stability brought by the
PRI from approximately the 1940s to 1968

pinta(s) painting(s) of slogans on walls of buildings or sides of buses

priísta belonging to the PRI

pueblo, el pueblo the people; the working class

rebozo(s) shawl(s)

separo(s) detention cell(s)

tiangui(s) open-air market(s)

vecindade(s) tenement(s)

vendedores ambulantes street vendors

BIBLIOGRAPHY

ARCHIVAL SOURCES

Archiv der Internationalen Kurzfilmtage Oberhausen, Germany

Archivo General de la Nación (AGN), Mexico City

    Departamento Federal de Seguridad (DFS)

    Dirección General de Investigaciones Políticas y Sociales (DGIPS)

Archivo General del Poder Judicial (AGPJ) de Puebla

Archivo Histórico Municipal de Puebla (AHMP), renamed Archivo General Municipal de Puebla (AGMP)

    Biblioteca

    Expedientes de Mercados

    Fototeca

Archivo Histórico Universitario, Benemérita Universidad Autónoma de Puebla (AHU)

    Vida Universitaria Files

    Vida Universitaria Photographs

Centro de Estudios Espinosa Yglesias (CEEY), Mexico City

Hemeroteca Juan Nepomuceno (HJN), Puebla

Universidad Nacional Autónoma de México (UNAM), Mexico City

    Filmoteca

PUBLISHED SOURCES

Aguayo Quezada, Sergio. *La Charola: Una historia de los servicios de inteligencia en México*. México DF: Grijalbo, 2001.

——. *1968 Los Archivos de la Violencia*. México DF: Grijalbo, 1998.

Aguiar, José Carlos G. "Policing New Illegalities: Piracy, Raids, and Madrinas." In *Violence, Coercion, and State Making in Twentieth-Century Mexico: The Other Half of the Centaur*, edited by Wil Pansters, 159–81. Stanford: Stanford University Press, 2012.

——. "'They Come from China': Pirate CDs in Mexico in Transnational Perspective." In *Globalization from Below: The World's Other Economy*, edited by Gordon Mathews, Gustavo Lins Ribeiro, and Carlos Alba Vega, 36–53. New York: Routledge, 2012.

Aguilar-Rodríguez, Sandra. "Cooking Modernity: Nutrition Policies, Class, and Gender in the 1940s and 1950s Mexico City." *Americas* 64, no. 2 (2007): 177–205.

Alba, Carlos. "Local Politics and Globalization from Below: The Peddler Leaders of Mexico City's Historic Center Streets." In *Globalization from Below: The World's Other Economy*, edited by Gordon Mathews, Gustavo Lins Ribeiro, and Carlos Alba Vega, 203–21. New York: Routledge, 2012.

Alegre, Robert. "Las Rieleras: Gender, Politics, and Power in the Mexican Railway Movement 1958–1959." *Journal of Women's History* 23, no. 2 (2011): 162–86.

———. *Railroad Radicals in Cold War Mexico: Gender, Class, and Memory*. Lincoln: University of Nebraska Press, 2013.

Alexander, Robert Jackson. *International Maoism in the Developing World*. Westport CT: Praeger, 1999.

Alfaro-Velcamp, Theresa. *So Far from Allah, So Close to Mexico: Middle Eastern Immigrants in Modern Mexico*. Austin: University of Texas Press, 2007.

Amnesty International. *Amnesty International Report 1987*. London: Amnesty International, 1987.

———. *Mexico: Torture with Impunity*. New York: Amnesty International, 1991.

———. *Out of Control: Torture and Other Ill-Treatment in Mexico*. London: Amnesty International, 2014.

Arizpe, Lourdes. *Indígenas en la ciudad de México: El caso de las "Marías."* México DF: SEP Diana, 1979.

———. "Women in the Informal Sector: The Case of Mexico City." *Signs* 3, no. 1 (1977): 25–77.

Arrom, Silvia. *The Women of Mexico City, 1790–1830*. Stanford: Stanford University Press, 1985.

Aviña, Alexander. *Specters of Revolution: Peasant Guerrillas in the Cold War Mexican Countryside*. Oxford: Oxford University Press, 2014.

Avritzer, Leonardo. *Democracy and the Public Space in Latin America*. Princeton NJ: Princeton University Press, 2002.

Babb, Florence E. *Between the Field and the Cooking Pot: The Political Economy of Marketwomen in Peru*. Austin: University of Texas Press, 1998.

———. "Producers and Reproducers: Andean Market Women in the Economy." In *Women and Change in Latin America*, edited by June Nash and Helen I. Safa, 53–64. South Hadley MA: Bergin and Garvey, 1985.

Babb, Sarah. *Managing Mexico: Economists from Nationalism to Neoliberalism*. Princeton NJ: Princeton University Press, 2001.

Barbosa Cano, Manlio. *Plan de Ordenamiento Espacial de la Actividad Comercial para la ciudad de Puebla*. Puebla: Centro Regional Puebla, Instituto Nacional de Antropología e Historia, Secretaría de Educación Pública, 1981.

Barbosa Cruz, Mario. *El trabajo en las calles: Subsistencia y negociación política en la ciudad de México a comienzos del siglo XX.* México DF: El Colegio de México, 2008.

———. "Trabajadores en las calles de la ciudad de México: Subsistencia, negociación y pobreza urbana en tiempos de la Revolución." *Historia Mexicana* 60, no. 2 (2010): 1077–118.

Behar, Ruth. "Rage and Redemption: Reading the Life Story of a Mexican Marketing Woman." *Feminist Studies* 16, no. 2 (1990): 223–58.

Benemérita Universidad Autónoma de Puebla. *Sucesos Universitarios (1970–1980) en la revista Siempre!* Puebla: BUAP-Cuadernos del Archivo Histórico Universitario, 2000.

Bennett, Vivienne. "The Evolution of Urban Popular Movements in Mexico between 1968 and 1988." In *The Making of Social Movements: Identity, Strategy, and Democracy*, edited by Arturo Escobar and Sonia E. Alvarez, 240–59. Boulder CO: Westview Press, 1992.

———. "Orígenes del movimiento urbano popular mexicano: Pensamiento político y organizaciones políticas clandestinas, 1960–1980." *Revista Mexicana de Sociología* 55, no. 3 (1993): 89–102.

Bensusán, Graciela, and Kevin J. Middlebrook. *Organized Labour and Politics in Mexico: Changes, Continuities and Contradictions.* London: Institute for the Study of the Americas, 2012.

Bhowmik, Sharit, ed. *Street Vendors in the Global Urban Economy.* New Delhi: Routledge, 2010.

Biles, James. "Globalization of Food Retailing and the Consequences of Wal-Martinization in Mexico." In *Wal-Mart World: The World's Biggest Corporation in the Global Economy*, edited by Stanley D. Brunn, 343–55. New York: Routledge, 2006.

Blacker, O'Neill. "Cold War in the Countryside: Conflict in Guerrero Mexico." *Americas* 66, no. 2 (2009): 181–210.

Blacker-Hanson, O'Neill. "La lucha sigue! (The Struggle Continues!): Teacher Activism and the Continuum of Democratic Struggle in Mexico." PhD diss., University of Washington, 2005.

Bleynat, Ingrid. "Trading with Power: Mexico City's Markets, 1867–1958." PhD diss., Harvard University, 2013.

Blum, Ann S. *Domestic Economies: Family, Work, and Welfare in Mexico City, 1884–1943.* Lincoln: University of Nebraska Press. 2009.

———. "Speaking of Work and Family: Reciprocity, Child Labor, and Social Reproduction, Mexico City, 1920–1940." *Hispanic American Historical Review* 91, no. 1 (2011): 63–95.

Boris, Eileen, and S. J. Kleinberg. "Mothers and Other Workers: (Re)Conceiving Labor, Maternalism, and the State." *Journal of Women's History* 15, no. 3 (2003): 90–117.

Bortz, Jeffrey. "Authority Reseated: Control Struggles in the Textile Industry during the Mexican Revolution." *Labor History* 44, no. 2 (2003): 171–88.

———. *Revolution within the Revolution: Cotton Textile Workers and the Mexican Labor Regime, 1910–1923*. Stanford: Stanford University Press, 2008.

Breña Valle, Gabriel. *Las mil caras de la moneda: Comercio en México*. Mexico City: BANPECO, 1991.

Brewster, Claire. "The Student Movement of 1968 and the Mexican Press: The Case of *Excélsior* and *Siempre!*" *Bulletin of Latin American Research* 21, no. 2 (2002): 171–90.

Bromley, Ray. "A New Path to Development? The Significance of Hernando de Soto's Ideas on Underdevelopment, Production, and Reproduction." *Economic Geography* 66, no. 4 (1990): 328–48.

Buechler, Hans, and Judith-Maria Buechler. *The World of Sofía Velasquez: The Autobiography of a Bolivian Market Vendor*. New York: Columbia University Press, 1996.

Buechler, Judith-Maria. "The Visible and Vocal Politics of Female Traders and Small-Scale Producers in La Paz, Bolivia." In *Women and Economic Change: Andean Perspectives*, edited by Ann Miles and Hans Buechler, 75–88. Washington DC: Society for Latin American Anthropology Publication Series, 1997.

Bunster, Ximena. "Taking Pictures: Field Method and Visual Mode." *Signs* 3, no. 1 (1977): 279–93.

Bunster, Ximena, and Elsa M. Chaney. *Sellers and Servants: Working Women in Lima, Peru*. New York: Praeger, 1985.

Bustamante, Celeste. *Muy Buenas Noches: Mexico, Television, and the Cold War*. Lincoln: University of Nebraska Press, 2013.

Cabrales Barajas, Luis Felipe. "The Historic Center of Morelia: A Case of Successful Negotiation." *Journal of Latin American Geography* 4, no. 2 (2005): 35–56.

Camp, Roderic Ai. *Mexican Political Biographies, 1935–2009*. Austin: University of Texas Press, 2011.

———. *Mexico's Mandarins: Crafting a Power Elite for the Twenty First Century*. Berkeley: University of California Press, 2002.

Carey, Elaine. *Plaza of Sacrifices: Gender, Power, and Terror in 1968 Mexico*. Albuquerque: University of New Mexico Press, 2005.

———. *Women Drug Traffickers: Mules, Bosses, and Organized Crime*. Albuquerque: University of New Mexico Press, 2014.

Carpenter, Victoria. "The Echo of Tlatelolco in Contemporary Mexican Protest Poetry." *Bulletin of Latin American Research* 24, no. 4 (2005): 496–512.

Carr, Barry. *Marxism and Communism in Twentieth-Century Mexico*. Lincoln: University of Nebraska Press, 1992.

——. *Mexican Communism, 1968–1983: Eurocommunism in the Americas?* San Diego: Center for U.S.-Mexican Studies, University of California, 1985.

Carrillo, Teresa. "Women and Independent Unionism in the Garment Industry." In *Popular Movements and Political Change in Mexico*, edited by Ann Craig and Joe Foweraker, 213–33. Boulder CO: Lynne Rienner, 1990.

Castellanos, Laura. *México Armado: 1943–1981*. México DF: Ediciones Era, 2007.

Castillo Palma, Jaime. "El movimiento contra el alza del pasaje y por la municipalización del servicio de transportación colectiva urbana." In *Los movimientos sociales en Puebla*, vol. 2, edited by Jaime Castillo, 262–82. Puebla: Departamento de Investigaciones Arquitectónicas y Urbanísticas, Instituto de Ciencias, UAP, 1986.

——. "El movimiento urbano popular en Puebla." In *Los movimientos sociales en Puebla*, vol. 2, edited by Jaime Castillo, 201–360. Puebla: Departamento de Investigaciones Arquitectónicas y Urbanísticas, Instituto de Ciencias, UAP, 1986.

Castillo Palma, Jaime, and Elsa Patiño. "Ciudades provincianas de Puebla: Crisoles de cambio o enclaves de resistencia?" In *Ciudades Provincianas de México: Historia, modernización y cambio cultural*, edited by Victor Gabriel Muro, 423–52. Zamora: El Colegio de Michoacán, 1998.

——. "Puebla: Sociedad y creación de alternativas." In *Creación de alternativas en México*, edited by Daniel Cazés Menache, 133–55. México DF: CEIIH-UNAM, 1999.

Castillo Palma, Jaime, Elsa Patiño, and Severino Cortés, eds. *Los movimientos sociales en Puebla*. 2 vols. Puebla: Departamento de Investigaciones Arquitectónicas y Urbanísticas, Instituto de Ciencias, UAP, 1986.

Churchill, Nancy. "Dignifying Carnival: The Politics of Heritage Recognition in Puebla, Mexico." *International Journal of Cultural Property* 13, no. 1 (2006): 1–24.

Churchill, Nancy Conner. "El (re) Desarrollo urbano neoliberal: El Paseo del Río San Francisco." In *Sujetos Neoliberales en México*, edited by Ricardo F. Macip Ríos, 123–54. Puebla: BUAP, 2009.

Churchill, Nancy E. "El Paseo del Rio San Francisco: Urban Development and Social Justice in Puebla, Mexico." *Social Justice* 26, no. 3 (1999): 156–73.

——. "Erasing Popular History: State Discourse of Cultural Patrimony in Puebla, Mexico." Paper presented at the 22nd International Congress of the Latin American Studies Association, Miami FL, March 16–18, 2000.

Cilia Olmos, David, and Enrique González Ruiz, eds. *Testimonios de la guerra sucia*. México DF: Editorial Tierra Roja, 2006.

Cohen, Barbara. *Braceros: Migrant Citizens and Transnational Subjects in the Postwar United States and Mexico*. Chapel Hill: University of North Carolina Press, 2011.

Condés Lara, Enrique. *Represión y rebelión en México (1959–1985)*. Vol. 3. México DF: Editorial Miguel Ángel Porrúa, 2009.

Cook, Maria Lorena. *Organizing Dissent: Unions, the State, and the Democratic Teachers' Movement in Mexico*. University Park: Pennsylvania State University Press, 2004.

Cordero y Torres, Enrique. *Guía Turística de Puebla*. Puebla: Centro de Estudios Históricos de Puebla, 1968.

Córdova, Arnaldo. *La política de masas y el futuro de la izquierda en México*. México DF: Editorial Era, 1979.

Craig, Ann L., and Joe Foweraker, eds. *Popular Movements and Political Change in Mexico*. Boulder CO: L. Rienner, 1990.

Crawford, Margaret. "The World in a Shopping Mall." In *Variations on a Theme Park: The New American City and the End of Public Space*, edited by Michael Sorkin, 3–30. New York: Hill and Wang, 1992.

Cross, John C. "Co-optation, Competition and Resistance: State and Street Vendors in Mexico City." *Latin American Perspectives* 25, no. 2 (1998): 41–61.

———. *Informal Politics: Street Vendors and the State in Mexico City*. Stanford: Stanford University Press, 1998.

———. "Pirates in the High Streets: The Street as Sites of Local Resistance to Globalization." In *Street Entrepreneurs: People, Place, and Politics in Local and Global Perspectives*, edited by John C. Cross and Alfonso Morales, 125–43. New York: Routledge, 2007.

Cross, John C., and Alfonso Morales, eds. *Street Entrepreneurs: People, Place, and Politics in Local and Global Perspectives*. New York: Routledge, 2007.

Cruz-Torres, María Luz. *Lives of Dust and Water: An Anthropology of Change and Resistance in Northwestern Mexico*. Tucson: University of Arizona Press, 2008.

De la Garza Toledo, Enrique. "Independent Trade Unionism in Mexico: Past Developments and Future Perspectives." In *Unions, Workers and the State in Mexico*, edited by Kevin J. Middlebrook, 153–83. San Diego: Center for U.S.-Mexican Studies, University of California, 1991.

Denning, Michael. "Wageless Life." *New Left Review* 66 (November–December 2010): 79–97.

De Soto, Hernando. *The Other Path: The Invisible Revolution in the Third World*. New York: Harper and Row, 1989.

Dias, Maria Odila da Silva. *Power and Everyday Life: The Lives of Working Women in Nineteenth-Century Brazil*. New Brunswick NJ: Rutgers University Press, 1995.

Dirlik, Arif, ed. *Critical Perspectives on Mao Zedong's Thought*. Atlantic Highlands NJ: Humanities Press International, 1997.

Doyle, Kate. "'Forgetting Is Not Justice': Mexico Bares Its Secret Past." *World Policy Journal* 20, no. 2 (2003): 61–72.

Dubinsky, Karen, et al., eds. *New World Coming: The Sixties and the Shaping of Global Consciousness.* Toronto: Between the Lines, 2009.

Elbaum, Max. *Revolution in the Air: Sixties Radicals Turn to Lenin, Mao, and Che.* New York: Verso, 2006.

Escobar Latapí, Arturo, and Mercedes González de la Rocha. Introduction to *Social Responses to Mexico's Economic Crisis of the 1980s*, edited by Mercedes González de la Rocha and Arturo Escobar Latapí, 1–18. La Jolla: Center for U.S.-Mexican Studies, University of California, San Diego, 1991.

Estrada Urroz, Rosalina. *Del telar a la cadena de montaje: La condición obrera en Puebla, 1940–1976.* Puebla: BUAP, 1997.

Fernández-Kelly, Patricia, and Jon Shefner, eds. *Out of the Shadows: Political Action and Informal Economy in Latin America.* University Park: Pennsylvania State University Press, 2006.

Ferrer Mac-Gregor, Eduardo. "El amparo iberoamericano." *Pensamiento Constitucional* 12, no. 12 (2006): 191–220.

Fink, Carol, Philipp Gassert, and Detlef Junker, eds. *1968: The World Transformed.* New York: Cambridge University Press, 1998.

Foweraker, Joe. "Popular Organization and Institutional Change." In *Popular Movements and Political Change in Mexico*, edited by Joe Foweraker and Ann L. Craig, 43–58. Boulder CO: Lynne Rienner, 1990.

Francois, Marie Eileen. *A Culture of Everyday Credit: Housekeeping, Pawnbroking, and Governance in Mexico City, 1750–1920.* Lincoln: University of Nebraska Press, 2006.

Frazier, Lessie Jo, and Deborah Cohen. "Defining the Space of Mexico '68: Heroic Masculinity in the Prison and 'Women' in the Streets." *Hispanic American Historical Review* 83, no. 4 (2003): 617–60.

Gamboa Ojeda, Leticia. *Los empresarios de ayer: El grupo dominante en la industria textil en Puebla.* Puebla: Universidad Autónoma de Puebla, 1985.

Garmendia, Arturo. *Los sucesos del 10. de mayo en Puebla.* Puebla: Imprenta Universitaria Genaro Vázquez, 1974.

Garza Villarreal, Gustavo. *La urbanización de México en el siglo XX.* México DF: El Colegio de México, Centro de Estudios Demográficos y de Desarrollo Urbano, 2003.

Gauss, Susan. *Made in Mexico: Regions, Nation, and the State in the Rise of Mexican Industrialism, 1920s-1940s.* University Park: Pennsylvania State University Press, 2010.

———. "Masculine Bonds and Modern Mothers: The Rationalization of Gender in the Textile Industry in Puebla, 1940–1952." *International Labor and Working Class History* 63, no. 1 (2003): 63–80.

———. "Working-Class Masculinity and the Rationalized Sex: Gender and Industrial Modernization in the Textile Industry in Postrevolutionary Puebla." In *Sex and Revolution: Gender, Politics, and Power in Modern Mexico*, edited by Jocelyn Olcott, Mary Kay Vaughn, and Gabriela Cano, 181–96. Durham NC: Duke University Press, 2006.

Gilbert, Alan, ed. *The Mega-City in Latin America*. Tokyo: United Nations University Press, 1996.

Gilbert, Alan G. "Self-Help Housing during Recession: The Mexican Experience." In *Social Responses to Mexico's Economic Crisis of the 1980s*, edited by Mercedes González de la Rocha and Agustín Escobar Latapí, 221–42. San Diego: Center for U.S.-Mexican Studies, University of California, 1991.

Gilbert, Alan, and Ann Varley. *Landlord and Tenant: Housing the Poor in Mexico*. London: Routledge, 1991.

Gillingham, Paul. "Maximino's Bulls: Popular Protest after the Mexican Revolution, 1940–1952." *Past and Present*, no. 206 (February 2010): 175–211.

Gillingham, Paul, and Benjamin Smith, eds. *Dictablanda: Politics, Work, and Culture in Mexico, 1938–1968*. Durham NC: Duke University Press, 2014.

Gómez Tagle, Silvia, and Marcelo Miquet. "Integración o democracia sindical: El caso de los electricistas." In *Tres Estudios sobre el Movimiento Obrero en Mexico*, edited by José Luis Reyna et al., 151–202. México DF: El Colegio de México, 1976.

González, Francisco E. *Dual Transitions from Authoritarian Rule: Institutionalized Regimes in Chile and Mexico, 1970–2000*. Baltimore: Johns Hopkins University Press, 2008.

González de la Rocha, and Agustín Latapí, eds. *Social Responses to Mexico's Economic Crisis of the 1980s*. San Diego: Center for U.S.-Mexican Studies, University of California, 1991.

González Ruiz, Édgar. *Muro: Memorias y Testimonios, 1961–2002*. Puebla: Benemérita Universidad Autónoma de Puebla, 2004.

Gordon, Gary. "Peddlers, Pesos, and Power: The Political Economy of Street Vending in Mexico City." PhD diss., University of Chicago, 1997.

Gould, Jeffrey. "Solidarity under Siege: The Latin American Left, 1968." *American Historical Review* 114, no. 2 (2009): 348–75.

Guerra, François-Xavier, and Annick Lempérière, eds. *Los espacios públicos en Iberoamérica: Ambigüedades y problemas*. México DF: Fondo de Cultura Económica, 1998.

Haber, Paul Lawrence. *Power from Experience: Urban Popular Movements in Late Twentieth-Century Mexico*. University Park: Pennsylvania State University Press, 2005.

Habermas, Jürgen. *The Structural Transformation of the Public Sphere: An Inquiry into a Category of Bourgeois Society*. Boston: MIT Press, 1991.

Hamnett, Brian R. *A Concise History of Mexico*. New York: Cambridge University Press, 2006.

Hansen, Karen Tranber, Walter E. Little, and Lynne Milgram, eds. *Street Economies in the Urban Global South*. Santa Fe NM: School for Advanced Research Press, 2013.

Hart, Keith. "Informal Income Opportunities and Urban Employment in Ghana." *Journal of Modern African Studies* 11, no. 1 (1973): 61–89.

Harvey, David. *Rebel Cities: From the Right to the City to the Urban Revolution*. London: Verso, 2013.

———. "The Right to the City." *New Left Review* 53 (September–October 2008): 23–40.

Hathaway, Dale. *Allies across the Border: Mexico's Authentic Labor Front and Global Solidarity*. Boston: South End Press, 2000.

Hellman, Judith Adler. *Mexican Lives*. New York: New Press, 1994.

———. *Mexico in Crisis*. New York: Holmes and Meier, 1983.

Henderson, Timothy, and David LaFrance. "Maximino Avila Camacho of Puebla." In *State Governors in the Mexican Revolution*, edited by Jürgen Buchenau and William H. Beezley, 157–76. Lanham MD: Rowman and Littlefield, 2009.

Henderson, Timothy J. "Rural Unrest and Political Control: The Destruction of the Central Campesina Independiente, 1962–1967." *Latin Americanist* 58, no. 1 (2014): 3–12.

Hernández Rodríguez, Rogelio. *El centro dividido: La nueva autonomía de los gobernadores*. México DF: El Colegio de México, 2008.

Herrera Calderón, Fernando. "From Books to Bullets: Youth Radicalism and Urban Guerrillas in Guadalajara." In *Challenging Authoritarianism in Mexico: Revolutionary Struggles and the Dirty War, 1964–1982*, edited by Fernando Herrera Calderón and Adela Cedillo, 105–28. New York: Routledge, 2012.

Herrera Calderón, Fernando, and Adela Cedillo, eds. *Challenging Authoritarianism in Mexico: Revolutionary Struggles and the Dirty War, 1964–1982*. New York: Routledge, 2012.

Huerta, Jorge. *Chicano Drama: Performance, Society, and Myth*. Cambridge, UK: Cambridge University Press, 2000.

———. *Chicano Theater: Themes and Forms*. Ypsilanti MI: Bilingual Press, 1982.

Iber, Patrick. "Managing Mexico's Cold War: Vicente Lombardo Toledano and the Uses of Political Intelligence." *Journal of Iberian and Latin American Research* 19, no. 1 (2013): 11–19.

Iragorri, Raúl Victoria. *Diagnóstico del ambulantismo en la ciudad de Puebla y sus posibles soluciones.* Puebla: H. Ayuntamiento, 1980.

Irazábal, Clara. "Citizenship, Democracy, and Public Space in Latin America." In *Ordinary Places, Extraordinary Events: Citizenship, Democracy, and Public Space in Latin America,* edited by Clara Irazábal, 11–34. New York: Routledge, 2008.

———, ed. *Ordinary Places, Extraordinary Events: Citizenship, Democracy, and Public Space in Latin America.* New York: Routledge, 2008.

Jiménez, Christina. "From the Lettered City to the Sellers' City: Vendor Politics and Public Space in Urban Mexico: 1880–1926." In *The Spaces of the Modern City: Imaginaries, Politics, and Everyday Life,* edited by Gyan Prakash and Kevin M. Kruse, 214–46. Princeton NJ: Princeton University Press, 2008.

———. "Making the City Their Own: Popular Groups and Political Culture in More-lia, Mexico, 1880 to 1930." PhD diss., University of California, San Diego, 2001.

Jiménez, Christina M. "Performing Their Right to the City: Political Uses of Public Space in a Mexican City, 1880–1910s." *Urban History* 33, no. 3 (2006): 435–56.

———. "Popular Organizing for Public Services: Residents Modernize Morelia, Mexico, 1880–1920." *Journal of Urban History* 30, no. 4 (2004): 495–518.

Jiménez Huerta, Fernando. *El vuelo del Fénix? Antorcha Campesina en Puebla.* Puebla: BUAP, 1992.

Jones, Gareth. "Gentrification, Neoliberalism and Loss in Puebla, Mexico." In *Global Gentrifications: Uneven Development and Displacement,* edited by Loretta Lees, Hyun Bang Shin, and Ernesto López-Morales, 265–84. Bristol, UK: Policy Press, 2015.

Jones, Gareth, and Ann Varley. "The Contest for the City Centre: Street Traders versus Buildings." *Bulletin of Latin American Research* 13, no. 1 (1994): 27–44.

Jones, Gareth A., and Ann Varley. "The Reconquest of the Historic Centre: Urban Conservation and Gentrification in Puebla." *Environment and Planning A* 31, no. 9 (1999): 1547–66.

Kaplan, Temma. *Red City, Blue Period: Social Movements in Picasso's Barcelona.* Berkeley: University of California Press, 1993.

———. *Taking Back the Streets: Women, Youth, and Direct Democracy.* Berkeley: University of California Press, 2004.

Kearny, Michael. "La Llorona as a Social Symbol." *Western Folklore* 28 no. 3 (1969): 199–206.

Kiddle, Amelia, and María L. O. Muñoz, eds. *Populism in Twentieth Century Mexico: The Presidencies of Lázaro Cárdenas and Luis Echeverría.* Tucson: University of Arizona Press, 2010.

Knight, Alan. "Caciquismo in Twentieth Century Mexico." In *Caciquismo in Twentieth-Century Mexico*, edited by Alan Knight and Wil Pansters, 1–48. London: Institute for the Study of the Americas, 2005.

Knight, Alan, and Wil Pansters, eds. *Caciquismo in Twentieth-Century Mexico.* London: Institute for the Study of the Americas, 2005.

Kohn, Margaret. *Radical Space: Building the House of the People.* Ithaca NY: Cornell University Press, 2003.

La Botz, Dan. *Mask of Democracy: Labor Suppression in Mexico Today.* Boston: South End Press, 1992.

LaFrance, David G. *Revolution in Mexico's Heartland: Politics, War, and State Building in Puebla, 1913–1920.* Wilmington DE: SR Books, 2003.

Lara y Parra, Manuel. *La lucha universitaria en Puebla: 1923–1965.* Puebla: Benemérita Universidad Autónoma de Puebla, 2000.

Larson, Brooke, Olivia Harriss, and Enrique Tandeter, eds. *Ethnicity, Markets, and Migration in the Andes: At the Crossroads of History and Anthropology.* Durham NC: Duke University Press, 1995.

Lear, John. *Workers, Neighbors, and Citizens: The Revolution in Mexico City.* Lincoln: University of Nebraska Press, 2001.

Lefebvre, Henri. *Writings on Cities.* Translated and edited by Eleonore Kofman and Elizabeth Hebas. Oxford: Blackwell, 1996.

Leicht, Hugo. *Las Calles de Puebla.* Puebla: Compañía Editorial Continental, 1967.

Lessinger, Johanna. "'Nobody Here to Yell at Me': Political Activism among Petty Retail Traders in an Indian City." In *Markets and Marketing*, edited by Stuart Plattner, 309–31. Lanham MD: University Press of America, 1985.

Lettieri, Michael. "A Model Dinosaur: Power, Personal Networks, and the Career of Rubén Figueroa." *Mexican Studies/Estudios Mexicanos* 31, no. 2 (2015): 305–42.

Lira González, Andrés. *El amparo colonial y el juicio de amparo mexicano.* México DF: Fondo de Cultura Económica, 1972.

Little, Walter E. "Getting Organized: Political and Economic Dilemmas for Maya Vendors." *Latin American Perspectives* 32, no. 5 (2005): 80–100.

——. *Mayas in the Marketplace: Tourism, Globalization, and Cultural Identity.* Austin: University of Texas Press, 2010.

Lomnitz, Claudio. *The Return of Comrade Ricardo Flores Magón.* Brooklyn NY: Zone Books 2014.

Loukaitou-Sideris, Anastasia, Evelyn Blumberg, and Renia Ehrenfeucht. "Sidewalk Democracy: Municipalities and the Regulation of Public Space." In *Regulating Place: Standards and the Shaping of Urban America*, edited by Eran Ben-Joseph and Terry S. Szold, 141–61. New York: Routledge, 2005.

Mabry, Donald J. *The Mexican University and the State: Student Conflicts, 1910–1971*. College Station: Texas A&M University Press, 1982.

Mackin, Robert Sean. "Becoming the Red Bishop of Cuernavaca: Rethinking Gill's Religious Competition Model." *Sociology of Religion* 64, no. 4 (2003): 499–514.

Manjárrez, Alejandro C. *Puebla: El rostro olvidado*. Puebla: Benemérita Universidad Autónoma de Puebla, 1999.

Márquez Carrillo, Jesús, and Paz Diéguez Delgadillo. "Política, universidad y sociedad en Puebla, el ascenso del Partido Comunista Mexicano en la UAP, 1970–1972." *Revista Historia de la Educación Latinoamericana* 11, no. 11 (2008): 111–30.

Marti, Judith E. "Breadwinners and Decision Makers: Nineteenth-Century Mexican Women Vendors." In *The Other Fifty Percent: Multicultural Perspectives on Gender Relations*, edited by Mari Womack and Judith Marti, 218–24. Long Grove IL: Waveland Press, 1993.

———. "Nineteenth-Century Views of Women's Participation in Mexico's Markets." In *Women Traders in Cross-Cultural Perspective*, edited by Linda Seligmann, 27–44. Stanford: Stanford University Press, 2001.

———. "Subsistence and the State: The Case of Porfirian Mexico." In *The Economic Anthropology of the State*, edited by Elizabeth M. Brumfiel, 316–23. Lanham MD: University Press of America, 1994.

Marti, Judith Ettinger. "Subsistence and the State: Municipal Government Policies and Urban Markets in Developing Nations. The Case of Mexico City and Guadalajara, 1877–1910." PhD diss., University of California, Los Angeles, 1990.

Martínez de Murguía, Beatriz. *La policía en México: ¿Orden social o criminalidad?* México DF: Editorial Planeta Mexicana, 1999.

Martínez Novo, Carmen. "The 'Culture' of Exclusion: Representations of Indigenous Women Street Vendors in Tijuana, Mexico." *Bulletin of Latin American Research* 22, no. 3 (2003): 249–68.

Mathews, Gordon, Gustavo Lins Ribeiro, and Carlos Alba, eds. *Globalization from Below: The World's Other Economy*. New York: Routledge, 2012.

McCormick, Gladys I. *The Logic of Compromise in Mexico: How the Countryside Was Key to the Emergence of Authoritarianism*. Chapel Hill: University of North Carolina Press, 2016.

Melé, Patrice. *La producción del patrimonio urbano*. México DF: Centro de Investigaciones y Estudios Superiores en Antropología Social, CIESAS, 2006.

———. *Puebla: Urbanización y Políticas Urbanas*. Puebla: BUAP and UAM Azcapotzalco, 1994.

Mendiola García, Sandra C. "Food Gentrification in Downtown Puebla, UNESCO World Heritage Site." In *Latin@s' Presence in the Food Industry: Changing How*

We Think about Food, edited by Meredith Abarca and Consuelo Salas, 59–76. Fayetteville: University of Arkansas Press, 2016.

———. "Vendors, Mothers, and Revolutionaries: Street Vendors and Union Activism in 1970s Puebla, Mexico." *Oral History Forum/d'histoire orale* 33 (2013). Online.

Middlebrook, Kevin J. *The Paradox of Revolution: Labor, the State, and Authoritarianism in Mexico.* Baltimore: Johns Hopkins University Press, 1996.

———, ed. *Unions, Workers and the State in Mexico.* San Diego: Center for U.S.-Mexican Studies, University of California, 1991.

Monnet, Jérôme. *Usos e imágenes del centro histórico de la ciudad de México.* México DF: Centro de Estudios Mexicanos y Centroamericanos, 1995.

Montes de Oca, Rosa Elena. "The State and the Peasants." In *Authoritarianism in Mexico*, edited by José Luis Reyna and Richard S. Weinert, 47–63. Philadelphia: Institute for the Study of Human Issues, 1977.

Moreno, Julio. *Yankee Don't Go Home: Mexican Nationalism, American Business Culture, and the Shaping of Modern Mexico, 1920–1950.* Chapel Hill: University of North Carolina Press, 2007.

Muñoz, María L. O. "State Spying on the State: Consejo Nacional de Pueblos Indígenas Meetings in 1980." *Journal of Iberian and Latin American Research* 19, no. 1 (2013): 62–70.

Muro, Victor Gabriel, ed. *Ciudades Provincianas de México: Historia, modernización y cambio cultural.* Zamora: El Colegio de Michoacán, 1993.

Navarro, Aaron W. *Political Intelligence and the Creation of Modern Mexico, 1938–1954.* University Park: Pennsylvania State University Press, 2010.

Niblo, Stephen R. *Mexico in the 1940s: Modernity, Politics, and Corruption.* Wilmington DE: Scholarly Resources, 1999.

Nissen, Sylke. "Urban Transformation: From Public and Private Space to Spaces of Hybrid Character." *Czech Sociological Review* 44, no. 6 (2008): 1129–49.

Nolasco Armas, Margarita. *Cuatro Ciudades: El Proceso de Urbanización Dependiente.* México DF: Instituto Nacional de Antropología e Historia, 1981.

Ochoa, Enrique. *Feeding Mexico: The Political Uses of Food since 1910.* Wilmington DE: Scholarly Resources, 2000.

Olcott, Jocelyn. "Miracle Workers and State Mediation among Textile and Garment Workers in Mexico's Transition to Industrial Development." *International Labor and Working Class History* 63, no. 1 (2003): 45–62.

Owensby, Brian. *Empire of Law: Justice in Colonial Mexico.* Stanford: Stanford University Press, 2011.

Padilla, Tanalís. *Rural Resistance in the Land of Zapata: The Jaramillista Movement and the Myth of the Pax Priísta, 1940–1962.* Durham NC: Duke University Press, 2008.

Padilla, Tanalís, and Louise E. Walker. "In the Archives: History and Politics." *Journal of Iberian and Latin American Research* 19, no. 1 (2013): 1–10.

Palacios Alonso, Angelina. *Los libaneses y la industria textil en Puebla*. México DF: SEP, 1983.

Pansters, Wil. "Building a *Cacicazgo* in a Neoliberal University." In *Caciquismo in Twentieth-Century Mexico*, edited by Alan Knight and Wil Pansters, 296–326. London: Institute for the Study of the Americas, 2005.

———. *Historia regional de Puebla: Perfil socioeconómico*. México DF: Editorial Limusa, 2000.

———. *Política y poder en Puebla: Formación y ocaso del cacicazgo avilacamachista, 1937–1987*. Puebla: BUAP, 1998.

———. *Politics and Power in Puebla: The Political History of a Mexican State, 1937–1987*. Amsterdam: CEDLA, 1990.

Pansters, Wil G. "El rector tiene la palabra: Ritual, narrativa e identidad en la educación superior en México." *Relaciones: Estudios de historia y sociedad* 27, no. 106 (2006): 81–131.

———, ed. *Violence, Coercion, and State Making in Twentieth-Century Mexico: The Other Half of the Centaur*. Stanford: Stanford University Press. 2012.

Paxman, Andrew. "Espinosa Yglesias Becomes a Philanthropist: A Private-Sector Response to Mexico's Political Turns, 1963–1982." Paper presented at the 13th Reunión de Historiadores MEXEUACAN, Querétaro, October 29, 2010.

———. *Jenkins of Mexico: Money, Power, Gringophobia, and the Mexican Revolution*. New York: Oxford University Press, forthcoming.

———. "William Jenkins, Business Elites, and the Evolution of the Mexican State: 1910–1960." PhD diss., University of Texas at Austin, 2008.

Pearson, Chad. "From the Labour Question to the Labour History Question." *Labour/Le Travail* 66, no. 1 (2010): 195–230.

Pensado, Jaime. "Student Politics in Mexico in the Wake of the Cuban Revolution." In *New World Coming: The Sixties and the Shaping of Global Consciousness*, edited by Karen Dubinsky et al., 330–38. Toronto: Between the Lines, 2009.

Pensado, Jaime M. *Rebel Mexico: Student Unrest and Authoritarian Political Culture During the Long Sixties*. Stanford: Stanford University Press, 2013.

———. "'To Assault with the Truth': The Revitalization of Conservative Militancy in Mexico During the Global Sixties." *Americas* 70, no. 3 (2014): 489–521.

Pérez, Domino Renee. *There Was a Woman: La Llorona from Folklore to Popular Culture*. Austin: University of Texas Press, 2008.

Piccato, Pablo. *City of Suspects: Crime in Mexico City 1900–1931*. Durham NC: Duke University Press, 2001.

———. "Urbanistas, Ambulantes and Mendigos: The Dispute for Urban Space in Mexico City, 1890–1930." In *Reconstructing Criminality in Latin America*, edited by Carlos A. Aguirre and Robert Buffington, 113–48. Wilmington DE: Scholarly Resources, 2000.

Pilcher, Jeffrey. "Was the Taco Invented in Southern California?" *Gastronomica* 8, no. 1 (2008): 26–38.

Pitrone, Jean Maddern. *F. W. Woolworth and the American Five and Dime: A Social History*. Jefferson NC: McFarland, 2003.

Poniatowska, Elena. *Massacre in Mexico*. Columbia: University of Missouri Press, 1992.

Porter, Susie S. *Working Women of Mexico City: Public Discourses and Material Conditions, 1879–1931*. Tucson: University of Arizona Press, 2003.

Portes, Alejandro. "The Informal Economy: Perspectives from Latin America." In *Exploring the Underground Economy: Studies of Illegal and Unreported Activity*, edited by Susan Pozo, 147–65. Kalamazoo MI: W. E. Upjohn Institute for Employment Research, 1996.

Portes, Alejandro, Manuel Castells, and Lauren A. Benton, eds. *The Informal Economy: Studies in Advanced and Less Developed Countries*. Baltimore: Johns Hopkins University Press, 1989.

Preston, Julia, and Samuel Dillon. *Opening Mexico: The Making of a Democracy*. New York: Farrar, Straus and Giroux, 2004.

Quintana, Alejandro. *Maximino Ávila Camacho and the One-Party State: The Taming of Caudillismo and Caciquismo in Post-Revolutionary Mexico*. Lanham MD: Lexington Books, 2010.

Rath, Thomas. *Myths of Demilitarization in Post-Revolutionary Mexico, 1920–1960*. Chapel Hill: University of North Carolina Press, 2013.

Reyna, José Luis. "Redefining the Authoritarian Regime." In *Authoritarianism in Mexico*, edited by José Luis Reyna and Richard S. Weinert, 155–71. Philadelphia: Institute for the Study of Human Issues, 1977.

Rodiles, Saúl. "El Mercado La Victoria." *Puebla Mágica* 1, no. 16 (1993): 6–13.

Rothwell, Mathew. *Transpacific Revolutionaries: The Chinese Revolution in Latin America*. New York: Routledge, 2013.

———. "Transpacific Revolutionaries: The Creation of Latin American Maoism." In *New World Coming: The Sixties and the Shaping of Global Consciousness*, edited by Karen Dubinsky et al., 106–14. Toronto: Between the Lines, 2009.

Roxborough, Ian. *Unions and Politics in Mexico: The Case of the Automobile Industry*. Cambridge, UK: Cambridge University Press, 1984.

Rubin, Jeffrey W. *Decentering the Regime: Ethnicity, Radicalism, and Democracy in Juchitán, Mexico*. Durham NC: Duke University Press, 1997.

Santín Nieto, Socorro. *El Mercado Guadalupe Victoria*. Puebla: Benemérita Universidad Autonóma de Puebla, Colección Tercer Milenio, Serie Casas de Puebla, 1999.

Sausi Garavito, María José Rhi. "Las primeras tres décadas del juicio de amparo: Notas entorno a la percepción pública de un nuevo instrumento jurídico." In *Actores, espacios y debates en la esfera pública de la Cd. de México*, edited by Cristina Sacristán and Pablo Piccato, 121–44. México DF: Instituto Mora, 2005.

Scarpaci, Joseph L. *Plazas and Barrios: Heritage Tourism and Globalization in the Latin American Centro Histórico*. Tucson: University of Arizona Press, 2005.

Scherer García, Julio. *Cárceles*. México DF: Aguilar, Altea, Taurus Alfaguara, 1998.

Seligmann, Linda. "To Be in Between: The *Cholas* as Market Women in Peru." *Comparative Studies in Society and History* 31, no. 4 (1989): 694–721.

———, ed. *Women Traders in Cross-Cultural Perspective*. Stanford: Stanford University Press, 2001.

Sessions, Jim. "Cross-Border Blues." *Forum for Applied Research and Public Policy* 14, no. 1 (1999): 58–64.

Shank, Theodore. "A Return to Aztec and Mayan Roots: At the Chicano and Latin American Festival." Indigenous Theater Issue. *Drama Review: TDR* 18, no. 4 (1974): 56–70.

Snodgrass, Michael. *Deference and Defiance in Monterrey: Workers, Paternalism and Revolution in Mexico: 1890–1950*. Cambridge, UK: Cambridge University Press, 2003.

———. "The Golden Age of Charrismo: Workers, Braceros, and the Political Machinery of Postrevolutionary Mexico." In *Dictablanda: Politics, Work, and Culture in Mexico, 1938–1968*, edited by Paul Gillingham and Benjamin Smith, 175–95. Durham NC: Duke University Press, 2014.

———. "How Can We Speak of Democracy in Mexico? Workers and Organized Labor in the Cárdenas and Echeverría Years." In *Populism in Twentieth Century Mexico: The Presidencies of Lázaro Cárdenas and Luis Echeverría*, edited by Amelia M. Kiddle and María L. O. Muñoz, 159–73. Tucson: University of Arizona Press, 2010.

———. "'New Rules for the Unions': Mexico's Steelworkers Confront Privatization." *Labor: Studies in Working-Class History of the Americas* 4, no. 3 (2007): 81–103.

Sotelo, Humberto. "La reforma universitaria y el movimiento popular de 1973." In *Los movimientos sociales en Puebla*, edited by Jaime Castillo, Elsa Patiño, and Severino Cortés, 125–258. Puebla: Departamento de Investigaciones Arquitectónicas y Urbanísticas, Instituto de Ciencias, UAP, 1986.

Soto Laveaga, Gabriela. *Jungle Laboratories: Mexican Peasants, National Projects, and the Making of the Pill*. Durham NC: Duke University Press, 2009.

——— . "Shadowing the Professional Class: Reporting Fictions in Doctors' Strikes." *Journal of Iberian and Latin American Research* 19, no. 1 (2013): 30–40.

Staudt, Kathleen A. *Free Trade: Informal Economies at the U.S.-Mexico Border*. Philadelphia: Temple University Press, 1998.

Tamayo, Sergio, and Xóchitl Cruz-Guzmán. "Political Appropriation of Public Space: Extraordinary Events in the Zócalo of México City." In *Ordinary Places, Extraordinary Events: Citizenship, Democracy and Public Space in Latin America*, edited by Clara Irazábal, 35–58. New York: Routledge, 2008.

Teichman, Judith A. *Privatization and Political Change in Mexico*. Pittsburgh PA: University of Pittsburgh Press, 1996.

Tilly, Chris. "Wal-Mart Goes South: Sizing Up the Chain's Mexican Success Story." In *Wal-Mart World: The World's Biggest Corporation in the Global Economy*, edited by Stanley D. Brunn, 357–68. New York, Routledge, 2006.

——— . "Walmart in Mexico: The Limits of Growth." In *Wal-Mart: The Face of Twenty First-Century Capitalism*, edited by Nelson Lichtenstein, 189–209. New York: New Press, 2006.

Tinker, Irene. *Street Foods: Urban Food and Employment in Developing Countries*. New York: Oxford University Press, 1997.

Tirado Villegas, Gloria. *La otra historia: Voces de mujeres del 68*. Puebla: Benemérita Universidad Autónoma de Puebla, 2004.

——— . *Vientos de la Democracia: Puebla, 1968*. Puebla: Benemérita Universidad Autónoma de Puebla, 2001.

Ulloa Bornemann, Alberto, and Aurora Camacho de Schimdt. *Surviving Mexico's Dirty War: A Political Prisoner's Memoir*. Philadelphia: Temple University Press, 2007.

Valdez, Luis. *Actos*. San Juan Bautista: Cucaracha Press, 1971.

Vallejo Romero, Walter, and Enedelia Ramírez Ramírez. "Escuela Preparatoria Popular Emiliano Zapata." In *Preparatorias de la BUAP*, 113–27. Puebla: BUAP, 2004.

Vanderbush, Walt. "Assessing Democracy in Puebla: The Opposition Takes Charge of Municipal Government." *Journal of Interamerican Studies and World Affairs* 41, no. 2 (1999): 1–27.

Vanderbush, Walter Kinloch. "Independent Organizing in Puebla, Mexico, 1961–1992: Social Movements, the Struggle for Autonomy, and Democratization." PhD diss., Northwestern University, 1993.

Vázquez Rangel, Gloria, and Jesús Ramírez López, eds. *Marginación y pobreza en México*. México DF: Ariel Divulgación, 1995.

Velikanova, Olga. *Popular Perceptions of Soviet Politics in the 1920s: Disenchantment of the Dreamers*. Basingstoke, UK: Palgrave Macmillan, 2013.

Véliz, Rodrigo J., and Kevin Lewis O'Neill. "Privatization of Public Space: The Displacement of Street Vendors in Guatemala City." In *Securing the City: Neoliberalism, Space, and Insecurity in Postwar Guatemala*, edited by Kevin Lewis O'Neill, 83–102. Durham NC: Duke University Press, 2011.

Venkatesh, Sudhir Alladi. *Off the Books: The Underground Economy of the Urban Poor*. Cambridge MA: Harvard University Press, 2006.

Viya, Miko. *Puebla Ayer*. Puebla: Ed. Cajica, 1989.

Vrana, Heather. "Revolutionary Transubstantiation in 'The Republic of Students': Death Commemoration in Urban Guatemala from 1977 to the Present." *Radical History Review*, no. 114 (Fall 2012): 66–90.

Walker, Louise. *Waking from the Dream: Mexico's Middle Classes after 1968*. Stanford: Stanford University Press, 2013.

Weismantel, Mary. *Cholas and Pishtacos: Stories of Race and Sex in the Andes*. Chicago: University of Chicago Press, 2001.

Zermeño, Sergio. "Crisis, Neoliberalism, and Disorder." In *Popular Movements and Political Change in Mexico*, edited by Joe Foweraker and Ann L. Craig, 160–80. Boulder CO: Lynne Rienner, 1990.

Zlolniski, Christian. *Janitors, Street Vendors, and Activists: The Lives of Mexican Immigrants in Silicon Valley*. Berkeley: University of California Press, 2006.

Zolov, Eric. "Expanding Our Conceptual Horizons: The Shift from an Old to a New Left in Latin America." *A Contracorriente* 5, no. 2 (2008): 47–73.

———. *Refried Elvis: The Rise of the Mexican Counterculture*. Berkeley: University of California Press, 1999.

INDEX

Page numbers in italics refer to illustrations.

Confederación Regional Obrera Mexicana (CROM), 6, 51, 113

Confederación Revolucionaria de Obreros y Campesinos (CROC), 51, 52, 113

Consejo General Campesino (CGC), 85–86

conservative groups (UAP), 59–60, 63

Constitution (Mexican), 44, 48

Contreras, Jaime, 175

Corona, Adolfo, 1–2, 17, 22, 92, 101

Corona, Olga, 101, 216n26

Corona family, 95, 98, 99

Cortés, Margarita, 205n60

Crawford, Margaret, 161

CROC (Revolutionary Confederation of Workers and Peasants), 51, 52, 113

CROM (Regional Confederation of Mexican Workers), 6, 51, 113, 207n98

Cross, John C., 196n7, 196n15

CTM (Confederation of Mexican Workers), 4, 6–7, 57, 113

Cuban Revolution, 68–69

Cué Merlo, Eduardo, 88

Daniel, Micaela, 130

daycare (La Victoria market), 142, 224n16

democracy: in independent unions, 5–6, 92–93, 197n20; limits on, 140, 164; in official unions, 197n20; in public spaces, 106–7, 140, 190; through the UPVA, 3, 115–16, 190, 219n74

democratic opening (Echeverría's), 7, 56–57, 64, 65, 135, 210n31

Denning, Michael, 13

detentions, 10, 124–31, 133–36, 177–78, 182, 183–85, 190–91, 222n62

DFS (Federal Security Directorate), 24–25, 122–24, 138, 208n1, 220n18

DGIPS (General Directorate of Political and Social Investigations), 24, 122–24, 138

Díaz, José Luis, 58–59, 93–94, 98

Díaz de León, Jesús, 196n17, 208n101

Díaz Ordaz, Gustavo, 52

Díaz Rubín, Angel, 36, 203n30

Dirección Federal de Seguridad (DFS), 24–25, 122–24, 138, 208n1, 220n18

Dirección General de Investigaciones Políticas y Sociales (DGIPS), 24, 122–24, 138

disappearances. See kidnappings

documentaries, 100–102, 216n31

downtown (Puebla): *dignificación* process for, 11–12, 142–47, 151–55, 163–64; economic activities in, 33–35, 227n80; gentrification of, 146, 161–62, 193, 223n1, 223n7; impact of vendors on, 139–40, 151; importance of La Victoria to, 140–42; number of vendors in, 21; political activism in, 106–7; private renovation of, 156–62; as World Heritage Site, 155–56

Drama Review: TDR, 92

drug trafficking, 199n74

Echeverría Álvarez, Luis, 10, 65–66, 67–68, 105, 210n40, 211n41, 212n64; democratic opening of, 7, 56–57, 64, 65, 135, 210n31

economy, 2, 20–21, 152, 155, 200n90

El Corralón market, 88–89, 90, 125

El Heraldo de México en Puebla, 176–77

elites (social class): antipathy of, toward street vendors, 29–30, 35–37, 53, 146; and the *dignificación* project, 153–54; during the *avilacamachista* years, 30–32; ethnic identity of, 31–32; locations of, 202n16; social monopolies of, 15–16

Elivar, Javier, 78

El Sol de Puebla, 17, 24, 105, 150, 177, 180

Emiliano Zapata market, 182, 184

Espinosa Rugarcía, Angeles, 160

Espinosa Yglesias, Ernesto, 29

Espinosa Yglesias, Manuel, 144, 149, 157–60

Excélsior, 112

fayuca (pirated goods), *18*, 19, 169

FBI (Federal Bureau of Investigation), 122

Federación Regional de Obreros y Campesinos (FROC), 6, 51, 52, 207n98

federal government. *See* government (federal)

fee collectors, 38–40, *39*, 46, 203n36

fees: in city markets, 38–40, 44, 46, 203n35, 224n18; in the UPVA, 82, 87–88, 129

Fernández Dávalos, David, 184–85

Fernández de Lara, Humberto, 177, 179

festivals (theater), 91–92

films, 100–102, 216n31

Flores Narro, Felipe, 126

Flores Suárez, Sergio, 63

food commissions, 109–10, 218n55

Foro de Consulta Popular, 181–82

Francisco I. Madero market, 169

Frente Universitario Anti-comunista (FUA), 32

FROC (Regional Federation of Workers and Peasants), 6, 51, 52, 207n98

FUA (Anticommunist University Front), 32

Fundidora, 223n2

Galindo, Carlos, 151

García, Gregorio, 43

García Paniagua, Javier, 123

Garmendia, Arturo, 100–102, 216n26

Gauss, Susan, 200n83

General Assembly (UPVA), 81–82

General Confederation of Workers and Peasants of Mexico (CGOCM), 6

General Peasant Council (CGC), 85–86

Gilbert, Alan G., 201n98

Goethe Institute, 102

González Morfín, Efraín, 105

González Román, Ignacio, 64

government (federal): and *amparo* suits, 48–50; challenge of UPVA to, 8–9; infiltration of UPVA by, 24–25, 121–24; kidnappings by, 133; and Labor Day parades, 113–15; neoliberal reforms of, 10–12; portrayal of, through song, 103–4; relationship of, with unions, 165–66; and resistance movements, 3–4; and Simitrio, 174–80; torture used by, 127–28, 133–34; violent repression by, 10, 120–21, 185–86, 191–92. *See also* PRI (Institutional Revolutionary Party)

government (Puebla): *amparo* suits against, 48–50; archival material of, 22–24, 199n72; and challenges for vendors, 15; complaints received by, against vendors, 29, 181–82; and *dignificación* process, 151–55; during protests, 107–8; and El Corralón market, 88–89; relationship of, with vendors, 46–47, 53–54; removals of vendors by, 49–50, 139–40, 146–49; response of, to vendor petitions, 45–46; and Simitrio, 174–80; torture used by, 127–28; violent repression by, 10, 40–41, 120–21, 186, 191–92

Guevara, Ernesto (Che), 68

Guzmán, Cristina, 199n73

Guzmán, Marcela, 199n73

Habermas, Jürgen, 92

Hanan, Elías David, 31

Harvey, David, 10, 11, 13, 15, 156, 198n47

hazing rituals (*novatadas*), 60–61

Hernández, Alberto, 194

Hernández Becerra, Lorenzo, 173, 231n32

Hernández Galicia, Joaquín, 179

Hernández López, José Luis (El Polo), 125–29

Herrera, Guillermo, 176–77

Herrera, Ramón, 183

Hidalgo market. *See* Miguel Hidalgo market

hijackings, 110–11, 130

Huerta, Jorge, 94

Huerta, Victoriano, 113

Ibarra de la Piedra, Rosario, 135–36

INAH (National Institute of Anthropology and History), 145, 152–53, 198n45

incarcerations, 124–31, 133–36, 222n62, 222n67; marches against, 119–20;

and prison conditions, 234n69; of Simitrio, 125–29, 165, 175–80, 185, 190–91, 231n38

independent organizations, 174–75, 197n20, 207n97

Independent Peasant Organization (CCI), 7, 85, 172, 213n79

independent unions: challenges to state posed by, 8–9; democracy in, 5–6, 197n20; and the democratic opening, 7; impact of neoliberalism on, 11–12, 165, 186; in Labor Day parades, 113–15; relationship of, with PRI, 4–7, 9–10, 53; state infiltration of, 121–22; state repression of, 125, 128, 179, 185; and the university reform movement, 62–63; women's roles in, 25. *See also* UPVA (Popular Union of Street Vendors)

Independent Workers Union (UOI), 7, 114

industrialization, 19–20

infiltration (state repression), 24–25, 121–24, 220n18

informal economy, 13, 20–21, 138

inquilinos (tenants), 171–72

Institutional Revolutionary Party (PRI). *See* PRI (Institutional Revolutionary Party)

Instituto Nacional de Antropología e Historia (INAH), 145, 152–53, 198n45

Instituto Politécnico Nacional (IPN), 69, 99, 109, 212n55

intelligence agencies, 24–25, 122–24, 138, 208n1, 220n18

International Short Film Festival (Germany), 102, 216n31

interrogations, 126–28, 177–78

official unions: democracy in, 197n20; impact of neoliberalism on, 12, 152, 165, 186; in Labor Day parades, 113–14; and La Victoria's closure, 154; political coercion in, 51–55; relationship of, with PRI, 4–7, 10, 50–53, 57, 196n16; representing street vendors, 50–53

Olympic Games, 112

One Continent, One Culture, 91–92

PAN (National Action Party), 9, 149

Pansters, Wil, 56

parades, 113–15

Pardiñas, Felipe, 66–67

Partido Revolucionario Institucional (PRI). *See* PRI (Institutional Revolutionary Party)

Pastrana, Blanca, 40

Patiño, Elsa, 174–75

Paxman, Andrew, 228n93

Pax Priísta, 3, 69, 134

Paz, Octavio, 218n63

PCM (Mexican Communist Party), 59, 63–64, 72–73

Peking Review, 2, 72

PEMEX union, 179

Peña Nieto, Ernesto, 187

Pensado, Jaime, 69, 196n9

Pérez, Elías, 175

Piedra Ibarra, Jesús, 135–36

Piña Olaya, Mariano, 152, 165, 166, 171, 172, 228n92

pintas, 104–6, 217n38

pirated products (*fayuca*), 18, 19, 169

plays, 93–100, 216n23

police: and Bullet Law, 190; detention of UPVA leaders by, 125–31, 174–80, 190–91; during the *lechero* conflict, 74; infiltration of UPVA by, 24–25,

121–24; kidnappings by, 133, 184; and October 1973 raid, 77–78, 111; and Oscar Vega Rosales's disappearance, 119–20, 132–33; planting of evidence by, 150, 191; portrayal of, in theater, 95–97; sexual harassment by, 41; torture used by, 127–28, 133–34, 183; violent repression of street vendors by, 10, 40–41, 77–78, 182, 183–85; violent repression of students by, 64–66. *See also* government (federal)

political activism: attempts to decentralize, 144; financial impact of, 180; in Hidalgo market, 168; impact of neoliberalism on, 164; impact of state repression on, 138; impact of university reform on, 66–71; protesting illegal detentions, 129–31; retaliation for, 119–21, 133–36; role of women in, 232n55; of Simitrio, 173–74; strategies of, 69–70; of students, 69–70, 212n55; through bus hijackings, 110–11; through commemorations, 111–13; through film, 100–102; through marches, 106–9; through parades, 113–15; through *pintas*, 104–6; through song, 102–4; through theater, 93–100, 116; of UPVA members, 8–9, 115–17, 124–25, 189, 190, 192

Popular Union of Street Vendors (UPVA). *See* UPVA (Popular Union of Street Vendors)

Porter, Susie, 201n102, 216n17

Portes, Alejandro, 20

PRD (Party of the Democratic Revolution), 9

Preparatoria Benito Juárez, 60

preparatory schools, 58–62

Prepa Zapata, 58–62, 68, 72–73, 209n14

PRI (Institutional Revolutionary Party): buses used by, 111; challenge of UPVA to, 8–9; compartmentalizing society, 57; co-opting unions, 4–7, 9–10, 50–53, 196nn15–16; and Labor Day parades, 113–15; in Morelos, 196n10; neoliberal reforms of, 2, 10–12, 152, 165–66; and Puebla's elite, 149; repressive campaigns of, 56–57, 137–38; and resistance movements, 3–4; street vendors' activism against, 86–87; UPVA's independence from, 1, 82–83; use of commemorations by, 111. *See also* government (federal)

professors, 58, 71–73, 209n14

progressive groups: impact of, on political activism, 66–68; and the Prepa Zapata, 58, 59–60; role of, in university reform, 59–60, 62–63; state repression of, 63–66

protests, *76*; against Bullet Law, 190; against Centro Comercial La Victoria, 160; against illegal detentions, 129–31, 180; against kidnappings, *132*; against La Victoria's closure, 154; against state violence, 61–62, 65, 183; alternative methods of, 104–5; attempts to decentralize, 144; food commissions during, 109–10; objectives of, 106, 217n50; public complaints against, 181; state's criminalizing of, 174–75; strategies for, 69–70; street vendor participation in, 76–77; by students, 61–62, 69–70; vehicles used

in, 111, 170–71. *See also* marches; political activism

public scribes, 42

public spaces: activities performed in, 33–35, 98; differing views on use of, 29, 35–36, 146; hybridization of, 14–16, 161; neoliberal limitations on, 11–12, 139–40, 163–64; political activism in, 8–9, 92–93, 104–7

public transportation, 167–68, 169–71, 170–71. *See also* buses

Puebla: *avilacamachista* politics in, 30–33; commercial spaces of, 33–35; demographics of, 20, 199n66, 200n86; employment statistics of, 200n90; industrialization of, 19–20; informal economy in, 20–21; monumental zone of, 145, 152–53, 225n29; social class conflict in, 16. *See also* downtown (Puebla); government (Puebla)

Ramírez Alvarado, Guillermo, 77

reform movements, 33, 58–66

Reyes, Gabina, 38

Reyes, José Maldonado, 176–77

Rodoreda, José, 151

Rodríguez, Gabina, 21

Rodríguez Verdín, José Ventura, 176–77, 179

Rojas Flores, Marco Antonio, 157

Romero, Oscar, 86

Ronquillo Hernández, Raúl, 177

Rosales, Teresa: detention of husband of, 126; kidnapping of son of, 119–20, 124, 131–33; and police violence, 40, 71, 130; political activism of, 134–36; reunion of, with son, 136–37; as a street vendor, 18–19, 55; in the UPVA, 81, 124

Rothwell, Mathew, 73
Roxborough, Ian, 197n20
Ruíz Massieu, José Francisco, 178

Salinas de Gortari, Carlos, 12, 165, 183
Salinas de Gortari, Raúl, 178
Sánchez, Juana, 75
Sarabia Reyna, Atl Rubén, 191
Sarabia Reyna, Xihuel, 191
Sarabia Sánchez, Rubén (Simitrio). *See*
    Simitrio (Rubén Sarabia Sánchez)
Sastre, Alfonsa, 49
self-help housing, 22, 201n98
sexual harassment, 41, 97–98
Shank, Theodore, 92, 97, 225n30
shopping malls, 159–62
Siempre!, 112
Simitrio (Rubén Sarabia Sánchez):
    commemoration speech of, 187–89;
    and family political background, 69;
    on government infiltration, 122; incar-
    ceration of (1977), 125–29, 231n38;
    incarceration of (1989), 165, 175–80,
    185; incarceration of (2014), 190–91;
    leadership role of, 84, 148, 149, 173–
    74, 214n102; and union fees, 82, 87
Snodgrass, Michael, 7
social classes: discrimination based
    on, 225nn30–31; and downtown
    gentrification, 145–46, 153–54, 193;
    impact of neoliberalism on, 11; power
    hierarchies based on, 15–16; tensions
    between, 29–30, 35–36; and the uni-
    versity reform movement, 59–60
social media, 192
social reproductive labor, 13–14, 21, 24
songs, 102–4
state repression, 137–38, 185–86; and
    crime fabrication, 174–75; during

the *lechero* conflict, 74; during the
    university reform movement, 63–66;
    objectives of, 138; and October 1973
    raid, 77–78; by political parties,
    196n9; portrayal of, in film, 101; por-
    trayal of, in theater, 95–97; protests
    against, 119–20; through beatings,
    10, 40–41, 177–78, 182, 183–85;
    through defamation campaigns,
    180–82; through detentions, 10,
    124–31, 177–78, 182, 183–85, 190–91,
    222n62; through incarcerations,
    124–31, 191–92, 222n62, 222n67,
    234n69; through infiltration, 121–
    24; through interrogations, 126–28,
    177–78; through intimidation, 40–
    41, 183–85; through kidnappings,
    119–20, 124, 131–37, 175–76, 184,
    191–92, 222n60; through merchan-
    dise seizure, 10, 40; through torture,
    120–21, 124, 127–28, 133–34, 177–78,
    183–85, 191–92, 222n60, 223n77;
    through transportation monopolies,
    171; UPVA's commemoration of,
    111–13
state university. *See* UAP (Autonomous
    University of Puebla)
street vendors, *18, 23, 37, 39, 96*; alliance
    between students and, 55–56, 57,
    73–77, 78–79, 89–90; alliances
    of, with independent groups, 108,
    124–25; archival material on, 22–
    25; challenges faced by, 22, 29–30,
    35–42, 155, 193–94; city responses to
    petitions of, 45–46; commonalities
    between students and, 57–62;
    complaints against, 29–30, 142–43,
    150, 181–82; complaints of, against
    fees, 203n35; constitutional rights

of, 44, 48–50; defense strategies of, 41–45, 183–84; democracy exercised by, 92–93, 115–17; demographics of, 16–17; employers of, 201n96; grassroots education of, 82–85; hybrid spaces of, 14–16; impacts of, on economy, 20–22, 53–54, 151; impacts of relocation on, 139–40, 164, 166–67; as market vendors, 199n64; numbers of, 201nn94–95; in official unions, 50–53; petitions written by, 23, 42–45, 205n62, 205n64, 216n17; products sold by, 18–19; protesting Centro Comercial La Victoria, 160; relationships of, with government, 46–47; removals of, 49–50, 77–78, 145–49; self-identification of, as workers, 12–14; social reproductive labor of, 13–14, 21, 24. *See also* political activism; state repression; UPVA (Popular Union of Street Vendors)
"Street Vendors' Anthem," 102–4
students (university): alliance between vendors and, 2–3, 55–56, 57, 73–77, 78–79, 89–90; attempts to under-cut activism of, 144; commonalities between vendors and, 57–62; during the *avilacamachista* years, 32, 33; education of street vendors by, 82–85; impact of, 85; impact of liberation theology on, 67–68, 73; isolation of, 213n78; massacres of, 210n34, 210n36, 211n41, 222n67; organizing the UPVA, 8, 79–82; political activism of, 2–3, 105–6, 212n55; politicization of, 66–73; state repression of, 56–57, 63–66, 210n34, 210n36, 211n41, 222n67

study groups, 83–85
Suárez Lara, José Norberto, 64
supermarkets, 153, 193, 227n67, 229n98
Supreme Court (Mexican), 48–50

Tapia, Juan, 184
taxis, 170–71
teachers, 58, 71–73, 209n14
Teatro Campesino, 91, 94–95
Tehuatlie Tamayo, José Alberto, 190
TENAZ (National Theater of Aztlán), 91–92
textile industry, 19, 200n79, 200n83
Teyssier, María, 29
theater, 91–92, 93–100, 116
Tlatelolco massacre (1968), 70–71, 112–13, 218n63
Toledo, Francisco, 189
Torres, Anselmo, 129
Torres, Juana, 49
Torres Ordóñez, Luis, 72
torture, 120–21, 124, 127–28, 133–34, 177–78, 183–85, 191–92, 222n60, 223n77
tourism, 159
Tovar Cano, Felipe Jesús, 177
Toxqui Fernández de Lara, Alfredo, 123, 131
Treviño, Ericka, 93–94

UAP (Autonomous University of Puebla): and downtown restoration, 159; during the *avilacamachista* years, 32–33; hazing rituals at, 60–61; and *Los Vendedores Ambu-lantes*, 100; marches at, 144; and Oscar Vega Rosales's disappearance, 132–33; politicization of students at, 66–71; preparatory schools for, 58–62; professors at, 71–73; reform movements at, 58–63; relationship

173; kidnapping of son of, 120, 124, 131–33; political activism of, 71–72, 131, 134–35; reunion of, with son, 136–37; state monitoring of, 208n1; as a teacher, 71–72; violent repression experienced by, 124, 126–28

Vega Rosales, Oscar, 119–20, 124, 131–33, 136–37

Vendedores Ambulantes, 2, 92, 93, 95–100, 116

vending permits, 46

vendors. *See* market stall owners; street vendors

Vera y Zuria, Pedro, 31

Vidal Pérez, Antonio, 183

Villa Escalera, Ricardo, 149

violence. *See* state repression

Viya, Miko, 94

Walmart, 160–61, 163–64, 193, 229n98, 230n110

White Brigade, 133–34, 222n60

women: discrimination faced by, 41, 123, 188; and drug trafficking, 199n74; economic role of, 198n54; employment options for, 20; empowerment of, 84; increased political activism of, 71; in Labor Day parades, 113; at La Victoria market, 141–42; letter writing of, 42–43, 205n60, 216n17; portrayal of, in film, 101; portrayal of, in theater, 95–98; role of, in protests, 107, 109–10, 218n55, 232n55; role of, in the UPVA, 25, 188; sexual harassment experienced by, 41, 97–98; social reproductive labor of, 13–14, 21, 24, 201n102; as street vendors, 17; in the textile industry, 200n83; violence faced by, 40–41, 134

working classes: elites' antipathy toward, 29–30, 153–54; impact of downtown gentrification on, 193; and student reform, 57–61; tensions between elites and, 35–36; vendors' identification with, 12–14. *See also* social classes

World Heritage Sites (UNESCO), 11, 155–56, 228n81

Zarate, Rita, 43

Zedillo Ponce de León, Ernesto, 184

Zolov, Eric, 94

To order or obtain more information on these or other University of
Nebraska Press titles, visit nebraskapress.unl.edu.